Simon Geissbühler (ed.)

Romania and the Holocaust

Events – Contexts – Aftermath

Simon Geissbühler (ed.)

ROMANIA AND THE HOLOCAUST

Events – Contexts – Aftermath

ibidem-Verlag
Stuttgart

Bibliographic information published by the Deutsche Nationalbibliothek
Die Deutsche Nationalbibliothek lists this publication in the Deutsche Nationalbibliografie; detailed bibliographic data are available in the Internet at http://dnb.d-nb.de.

Bibliografische Information der Deutschen Nationalbibliothek
Die Deutsche Nationalbibliothek verzeichnet diese Publikation in der Deutschen Nationalbibliografie; detaillierte bibliografische Daten sind im Internet über http://dnb.d-nb.de abrufbar.

Cover picture: Holocaust monument in Zhabokrych. © Simon Geissbühler.

ISBN-13 Paperback edition: 978-3-8382-0954-8

ISBN-13 Hardcover edition: 978-3-8382-0984-5

Printed in the United States of America

Table of Contents

Simon Geissbühler

Introduction

Seventy-five years ago, on July 2, 1941, Romanian troops and the allied German Eleventh Army launched offensive combat operations on the southern front against the USSR (Operation München), crossing from Romania into Northern Bukovina and Bessarabia.[1] On July 3, 1941, Romanian troops reached the village of Ciudei close to the Romanian-Soviet border. Moses Eisig, a young Jewish man from Ciudei, ran away in time. He first hid with a local peasant who told him—invoking the propaganda stereotype of Judeo-Bolshevism—that the Romanians were "mad at the Jews" because the Jews were all Communists and had blown up a bridge—when in fact the Soviets had destroyed it during their retreat a few days earlier. Moses then fled into the woods. There he "heard such a tremendously loud echo that the whole woods trembled. That's when they shot all our people. ... We thought they were shooting men, but not women and children like that."[2] Sneaking back into the village a few days later, he found it deserted and destroyed, and Jewish property looted by villagers.[3] As he recounted, "The windows were gone! The doors were gone! The bricks were missing. And you couldn't see a dog, or a cat. No people! Nothing!" Survivors later detailed what had happened. The Romanian troops, with the help of locals,[4] had herded some of the village's Jews together and summarily shot them all: "[Not] everyone had the luck to get a bullet in the heart or in the head. My father and my brothers and sister had to watch their own children dying. And the children had to watch how their parents died." Other Jews were slain by villagers and

1 Operation München did not start on June 22, 1941, as it is sometimes assumed, but on July 2. See: Hans-Jacobsen, Adolf (ed.) (1965). *Kriegstagebuch des Oberkommandos der Wehrmacht*. Frankfurt am Main, p. 504; Bundesarchiv Freiburg/Breisgau, RH/19/I (71).

2 Eisig, Moses (1998). *Yizkor Book for the Martyrs of Ciudin*: www.jewishgen.org/yizkor/Chudyn/chu001.html (accessed on March 15, 2016).

3 Oral history interview with Constantin Padure (2011), in United States Holocaust Memorial Museum (USHMM), RG-50.575*0103.

4 Oral history interview with Constantin Burla (2011), in USHMM, RG-50.575*0104.

peasants who joined in the massacre. Around 500 Jews were killed in Ciudei in early July 1941.[5]

Seventy-five years ago, at the end of July 1941, in the small town of Zhabokrych in Romanian-controlled Transnistria in today's southwestern Ukraine, German and Romanian military units drove approximately 600 Jews, among them many women and children, into cellars and shot them.[6] A little girl, Manya, survived the mass shooting:

> In July 1941, the German army entered the town, followed by the Romanian army. The Jews were ordered to gather in five cellars where the Romanian soldiers proceeded to shoot them. Manya lost consciousness. When she awoke, she saw that her mother had been killed. Her father had survived. Manya and her father hid in the cellar until nightfall. They then escaped to the forest but after a week, starving and cold, they returned. A few days later, they were herded into the town ghetto, where they lived under grueling conditions in one apartment with several other families. One day, the police ordered both adults and children back to the cellars to remove the bodies of those killed in the massacre. The bodies were in a terrible state of decomposition, and the horrified prisoners were forced to bury them in a mass grave. Manya identified her mother's body by the red boots she had been wearing. She and her father managed to bury her in a grave near their house.[7]

Today, Zhabokrych is a nondescript, rundown village on the Ukrainian periphery. The brick synagogue still exists, but it was closed long ago and is used for other purposes. The modest Holocaust memorial in Zhabokrych is pictured on the cover of this volume.[8]

These are the stories of two survivors of the Holocaust perpetrated by Romanians or in Romanian-controlled territories during the Second World War. From the summer of 1941 onward, Romania pursued at its own initiative the mass killing of Jews in the territories it controlled. By the end of June 1941, approximately 13,000 Jews were killed in the Romanian city of Iași and in the death trains from that city. When the Ro-

---

5 Ioanid, Radu (2000). *The Holocaust in Romania*. Chicago, p. 96f.; Ancel, Jean (2011). *The History of the Holocaust in Romania*. Lincoln/Jerusalem, p. 223.

6 Vinokurova, Faina A. (not dated). *The Holocaust in Vinnitsa Oblast*: www.rtrfoundation.org/webart/UK-arch-d2.pdf (accessed on May 22, 2016).

7 Yad Vashem (ed.) (2007). *Bearing Witness. Holocaust Martyrs' and Heroes' Remembrance Day 2007*: www.yadvashem.org/yv/en/remembrance/2007/brodeski-titelman.asp#!prettyPhoto (accessed on May 23, 2016).

8 Geissbühler, Simon (2014). *Once Upon a Time Never Comes Again. The Traces of the Shtetl in Southern Podolia (Ukraine)*. Bern, pp. 106–110.

manian army invaded the Soviet Union on the southern front at the beginning of July 1941, thousands of Jews were exterminated in Northern Bukovina and Bessarabia by Romanian troops and local people.[9] This first wave of violence with up to 43,500 victims was followed in autumn 1941 by large-scale deportations of Jews from Southern and Northern Bukovina as well as Bessarabia to camps and ghettos in Transnistria. Many perished on the deportation marches, many more in the following years in the camps and ghettos. Tens of thousands of Jews were massacred by Romanian units in and around Odessa. Overall, more than 300,000 Jews of Romanian and of Soviet or Ukrainian origin were murdered in Romanian-controlled territories during the Second World War.

This volume sheds light on the events, the contexts, and the aftermath of this under-researched and lesser-known chapter of the Holocaust. The fact that Romania was "Germany's major ally on the eastern front after 1941 [and] the only other state to generate an autonomous policy of the direct mass murder of Jews" is little known.[10] Seventy-five years after these events, this book gives much-needed impetus to research on the Holocaust perpetrated by Romanians and in Romanian-controlled territories.

The idea to publish this volume about Romania and the Holocaust was born at the one-day symposium "The Holocaust in Romania—Revisiting Research and Public Discourse" on October 29, 2015, at Yad Vashem in Jerusalem. The symposium showed that considerable progress has been made in recent years in researching the Holocaust perpetrated by Romania. It has been positively noted that young historians, also Romanians, are now doing research on Romania and the Holocaust. Different organizations, research groups, and individuals are working on specific aspects of Romania and the Holocaust. Also, Romania is currently (2016–17) holding the presidency of the International Holocaust Remembrance Alliance (IHRA), which is another positive step.

At the same time, however, the event in Jerusalem once more revealed that much work is still to be done. Under the Communist regimes, recognition of the Holocaust was all but impossible. The Shoah indeed

---

9 Geissbühler, Simon (2013). *Blutiger Juli. Rumäniens Vernichtungskrieg und der vergessene Massenmord an den Juden 1941*. Paderborn.

10 Snyder, Timothy (2015). *Black Earth. The Holocaust as History and Warning*. London, p. 229.

was a taboo for almost 50 years, and Romania was no exception. In fact, having been a close ally of Nazi Germany and having implemented the mass murder of Jews autonomously, Romania felt an even more acute urge to draw a veil of silence over its inglorious past. The breakup of the Soviet bloc and the end of the Ceaușescu regime did not lead to a comprehensive reassessment of Romanian history or a broad evidence- and research-based critical reevaluation of Romania's role in the Second World War and the Holocaust. The fascist ghosts of the past, and especially questions concerning collaboration with Nazi Germany and the Holocaust perpetrated by Romania, remained untouched. Fascism was presented as an alien, German concept and Romania as a victim, innocent of any wrongdoing or crime.[11] The so-called revisionist school is still relatively influential in Romania. It minimizes and trivializes Romanian crimes during the Second World War in general and Romania's responsibility for the Holocaust in Northern Bukovina, Bessarabia, and Transnistria in particular.[12]

But there is also a vast gap between scholarly research and public knowledge about the Holocaust in Romania. Not even a third of the respondents in a poll commissioned by the Elie Wiesel Institute in Bucharest in 2015 believe that the Holocaust also happened in Romania.[13] Among the meager 28 percent who admit that the Holocaust also took place in Romania, 69 percent see Germany as the main culprit of the Holocaust in their country. Only a tiny minority among Romanians is therefore prepared to acknowledge the historical fact of who the main perpetrators were in the killing of more than 300,000 Jews of Romanian and of Soviet or Ukrainian origin in Romanian-controlled territories during the Second World War: the Romanians themselves.

---

11 Cioflâncă, Adrian (2004). A "Grammar of Exculpation" in Communist Historiography: Distortion of the History of the Holocaust under Ceausescu, *Romanian Journal of Political Sciences* 2: 29–46.

12 Shafir, Michael (2014). Unacademic Academics: Holocaust Deniers and Trivializers in Post-Communist Romania, *Nationalities Papers* 42(6): 942–964; Geissbühler, Simon (2012). Staring at the Past with Eyes Wide Shut: Holocaust Revisionism and Negationism in Romania, *Israel Journal of Foreign Affairs* VI(3): 127–135.

13 Institutul Naţional pentru Studierea Holocaustului din România "Elie Wiesel" (INSHR-EW) (ed.) (2015). *Sondaj de opinie privind Holocaustul din România și percepția relațiilor interetnice*. Bucharest.

The German historian Armin Heinen claimed in 2007 that the Romanian historiography of the Holocaust had reached approximately the state of research in Germany in the mid-1960s.[14] Methodologically, many Romanian studies on the Holocaust have indeed been and remain descriptive and positivistic.[15] They do not take into account the state of international research on the Holocaust in general and do not work with specific research questions and theses. The research controversies about the nature of the Nazi dictatorship in general and the Holocaust in particular that Ian Kershaw so aptly summarized already in 1985, or later debates, for example, between Daniel Jonah Goldhagen and Christopher Browning, or the discussion surrounding the publications of Timothy Snyder seem to have had only a marginal, if any, impact on Romanian researchers and on research about Romania and the Holocaust.[16] International research on the Holocaust in Romanian-controlled territories remains relatively scarce to this day too. Little is published on the topic in English-language scholarly journals. There is also a lack of coordination between different groups and scholars dealing with the topic; and new findings and research results should be better and more rapidly communicated within the scholarly community and to a broader public, as well as be made available in Romania, Ukraine, and the Republic of Moldova.

But there has been some progress. Radu Ioanid's *The Holocaust in Romania*, published in 2000, and the Final Report of the International Commission on the Holocaust in Romania, published in English in 2005, are crucial synoptic works and important starting points for further research.[17] These publications have helped to break the "recurring cycle of official denial."[18] They have been complemented in the last few years by

---

14 Heinen, Armin (2007). *Rumänien, der Holocaust und die Logik der Gewalt*. München, p. 34.

15 Ursprung, Daniel (2010/2011). Geschichtsschreibung und Vergangenheitsbewältigung in Rumänien. Von den Mühen des Umgangs mit zeitgeschichtlichen Themen, *Südost-Forschungen* 69/70: 358–388.

16 Kershaw, Ian (1985). *The Nazi Dictatorship: Problems and Perspectives of Interpretation*. London; Browning, Christopher (1993). *Ordinary Men: Reserve Police Battalion 101 and the Final Solution in Poland*. New York; Goldhagen, Daniel Jonah (1996). *Hitler's Willing Executioners: Ordinary Germans and the Holocaust*. New York.

17 Ioanid 2000; International Commission on the Holocaust in Romania (ed.) (2005). *Final Report*. Iași.

18 Shapiro, Paul A. (2015). *The Kishinev Ghetto 1941–1942. A Documentary History of the Holocaust in Romania's Contested Borderlands*. Tuscaloosa, p. 91.

new studies, for example, by Jean Ancel and Vladimir Solonari.[19] Certain topics such as the Iași massacres, with over 13,000 victims at the end of June 1941, as well as the camps and ghettos in Transnistria have at last received the scholarly attention they deserve.[20]

This volume presents new research on Romania and the Holocaust. All the contributions assembled here are original texts that have not been published before. *Mariana Hausleitner* exposes the myth that the Jews were responsible for the "national disgrace" in the summer of 1940 when Romania had to retreat from Northern Bukovina and Bessarabia due to the Soviet ultimatum. There were some abuses of fleeing Romanians also by young Jews, but they are neither quantitatively nor qualitatively

19 See, for example: Solonari, Vladimir (2007). Patterns of Violence: Local Population and the Mass Murder of Jews in Bessarabia and Northern Bukovina, July–August 1941, *Kritika: Explorations in Russian and Eurasian History* 8(4): 749–787; Solonari, Vladimir (2009). *Purifying the Nation: Population Exchange and Ethnic Cleansing in Nazi-Allied Romania*. Baltimore; Solonari, Vladimir (2010). The Treatment of the Jews of Bukovina by the Soviet and Romanian Administrations in 1940–1944, *Holocaust and Modernity* 2(8): 149–180; Ancel, Jean (2005). The German-Romanian Relationship and the Final Solution, *Holocaust and Genocide Studies* 19: 252–275; Ancel 2011; Chioveanu, Mihai (2008). Death Delivered, Death Postponed: Romania and the Continent-Wide Holocaust, *Studia Hebraica* 8: 136–69; Chioveanu, Mihai (2012). The Dynamics of Mass Murder. Grasping the Twisted Decision-Making Process behind the Romanian Holocaust, *Sfera Politicii* 2(168): 25–36; Deletant, Dennis (2012). Ion Antonescu and the Holocaust in Romania, *East Central Europe* 39: 61–100; Geissbühler, Simon (2014). "He spoke Yiddish like a Jew": Neighbors' Contribution to the Mass Killing of Jews in Northern Bukovina and Bessarabia, July 1941, *Holocaust and Genocide Studies* 28(3): 430–449.

20 Voicu, George (ed.) (2006). *Pogromul de la Iași (28–30 iunie 1941)—prologul Holocaustului din România*. Iași; Eaton, Henry (2013). *The Origins and Onset of the Romanian Holocaust*. Detroit; Ofer, Dalia (1993). The Holocaust in Transnistria. A Special Case of Genocide, in Dobroszycki, Lucjan and Jeffrey S. Gurock (eds.). *The Holocaust in the Soviet Union*. New York, pp. 133–154; Deletant, Dennis (2003). Transnistria: soluţia românească la "problema evreiască", in *Despre Holocaust şi Comunism. Anuarul IRIR, vol. 1, 2002*. Iaşi, pp. 79–101; Golbert, Rebecca L. (2004). Holocaust Sites in Ukraine: Pechora and the Politics of Memorialization, *Holocaust and Genocide Studies* 18: 205–233; Mihok, Brigitte (2009). Orte der Verfolgung und Deportation, in Benz, Wolfgang und Brigitte Mihok (Hrsg.). *Holocaust an der Peripherie. Judenpolitik und Judenmord in Rumänien und Transnistrien 1940–1944*. Berlin, pp. 71–80; Vynokurova, Faina (2010). The Fate of Bukovinian Jews in the Ghettos and Camps of Transnistria, 1941–1944: A Review of the Source Documents at the Vinnytsa Oblast State Archive, *Holocaust and Memory* 2(8): 18–26; Baum, Herwig (2011). *Varianten des Terrors. Ein Vergleich zwischen der deutschen und der rumänischen Besatzungsverwaltung in der Sowjetunion 1941–1944*. Berlin.

comparable to the murder of Jews by the Romanian military and the bloody pogroms in Dorohoi and Galaţi in the summer of 1940. In fact, the alleged Jewish-Communist gangs in Czernowitz and elsewhere, which neatly fitted the "thesis" of Judeo-Bolshevism, were an invention of the Romanian propaganda machine to create a scapegoat and justify violence against the Jewish population.

In his contribution, *Henry Eaton* meticulously analyzes the Iași pogrom at the end of June 1941. More than 13,000 Jews were killed in this pogrom and in the death trains. Eaton disentangles the web of lies, falsified statements, and half-truths that were "created" to cement the idea that Romania was not responsible for the Holocaust in Romanian-controlled territories during the Second World War in general and the Iași pogrom in particular.

Alti Rodal's article is an outstanding example of a micro-study of localized eliminationist violence.[21] She looks at the massacre of Jews in the village of Borivtsi in Northern Bukovina that was planned and organized by the Organization of Ukrainian Nationalists (OUN). It is micro-studies like these that are needed to better understand the contexts, the dynamics, and the perpetrators of the mass murders of Jews in many villages and small towns throughout Northern Bukovina and Bessarabia.

What happened in the summer of 1941 in Northern Bukovina and Bessarabia were by no means isolated and unique events, as *Kai Struve* shows in his reconstruction of the anti-Jewish violence in about thirty cities and small towns as well as in a number of villages during July 1941 in eastern Galicia. He makes the distinction between three main contexts of the violence: the retrieval of murdered prison inmates, punishments and executions by OUN-B (group led by Stepan Bandera) insurgents, and the violent excesses of units of the *Waffen-SS*. Struve compares eastern Galicia with other Eastern European regions and argues that deadly violence against Jews from the side of the local population emanated mostly from insurgent groups whose aim was to remove or punish alleged supporters of Soviet rule and to establish their own nation-states. *Witold Mędykowski* complements Struve's contribution by looking at the

21 Kallis, Aristotle (2007). "Licence" and Genocide in the East: Reflections on Localised Eliminationist Violence during the First Stages of "Operation Barbarossa" (1941), *Studies in Ethnicity and Nationalism* 7(3): 6–23.

same events in the summer of 1941 from another point of view and against a different theoretical background.

Sarah Rosen and *Gali Tibon* take a closer look at the ghettos in Transnistria. They are interested in the complex relations between different Jewish groups within the ghettos, on the one hand, and between the Jewish ghetto population and the Romanian authorities and the local Ukrainian population, on the other. Rosen concentrates on the Djurin ghetto and bases her research mainly on the diary of Lipman Kunstadt. Tibon discusses the Jewish opposition to the established Jewish leadership in the ghettos of the Mogilev district in Transnistria. *Diana Dumitru* looks at how Holocaust crimes in Romanian-controlled territories were reviewed after Stalin's death in 1953. Even if some of the reviews showed that there were inconsistencies and even legal faults in the previous investigations, in the overwhelming majority of cases, the Soviet prosecutors had little or no reason at all to assume that convicted criminals were in fact innocent. *Tuvia Friling* was one of the co-vice chairs of the International Commission on the Holocaust in Romania and one of the editors of its Final Report. He gives, for the first time, a personal insight into the inner workings of and the conflicts within the Commission and discusses its main conclusions and recommendations.

Michael Shafir dissects the public discourse in Romania. He distinguishes between the official versus unofficial memory of the Holocaust and its remembrance, and shows that there is indeed an official and an unofficial narrative. The unofficial narrative is still surprisingly widespread and influential in Romania and extends deep into the political mainstream. To conclude, I give a short overview of ten insights to be gained from research into the Holocaust perpetrated by Romanians and in Romanian-occupied areas. What we can learn from the history of Romania and the Holocaust matters because it complements, sharpens, and broadens our understanding of the origins and the background, the contexts, the perpetrators, collaborators and bystanders, the victims, and the aftermath of the Holocaust.

While Romania remains a laggard with regard to dealing with the past, there have been—as I underlined earlier—some positive developments, also in comparison with other Eastern European countries, some of which have regressed in recent years when it comes to confronting their role as allies or collaborators of Nazi Germany in the Second World

War and in the Holocaust. International research and pressure, increased and broader education in schools and universities, the educational efforts of civil society and state institutions, as well as Romania's presidency of the IHRA are factors that can, in the medium and long term, undermine the widespread attitude of wanting-not-to-know.

Pierre Nora has rightly emphasized that "there must be a will to remember."[22] Remembrance and the will to deal with one's past should not be imposed primarily from the outside and from above. But researchers, Romanian and international, can and should more forcefully contribute to change by exposing again and again the historical facts, as we reconstruct them on the basis of the available sources, even though—or especially because—they are everything but pleasant. This volume is a small contribution to that effort seventy-five years after the Holocaust in the east was unleashed.

---

22 Nora, Pierre (1989). Between Memory and History: Les Lieux de Memoire, *Representations* 26: 7–24.

Mariana Hausleitner

Jewish-Communist Gangs in Czernowitz? The Origin and Impact of a Constructed Enemy Stereotype[1]

On the dissemination of the enemy stereotype of "Jewish gangs"

The image of Jewish-Communist gangs was omnipresent in northeastern Romania in the summer of 1940 and was time and again revived even decades later. When Romania was forced to retreat from Northern Bukovina and Bessarabia following the Soviet ultimatum, the Romanian press was full of reports of attacks. The high-circulation Bucharest newspaper *Universul*, for example, repeatedly published articles about armed Jewish gangs allegedly attacking soldiers and officers.[2] The Jewish writer Emil Dorian immediately understood that a scapegoat was wanted to be blamed for the chaotic retreat of the Romanian army and administration. On June 30, 1940, he noted in his diary that he doubted if the Jews had attacked the retreating armed Romanian soldiers by throwing stones at them.[3] The president of the Bucharest Jewish community, Wilhelm Filderman, cast doubts on reports that the mostly Jewish-owned shops in the center of Czernowitz were plundered by Jews. He assumed that the plunderers were rather Ukrainians or Communists.[4]

The eyewitness Fritz Schellhorn who was the German consul in Czernowitz confidentially reported to the legation in Bucharest that the tense situation was mainly due to the catastrophic organization and implementation of the withdrawal. The withdrawing units were overrun by the quick arrival of the first Soviet forces. But Schellhorn also sent reports

1 Translated from German by Simon Geissbühler.

2 Cum s-a făcut transportul refugiaţilor, *Universul* 57(179) (July 2, 1940).

3 Dorian, Emil (1996). *Jurnal din vremuri de prigoană 1937–1944*. Bucharest, p. 110.

4 Iancu, Carol (2013). *Alexandru Şafran şi Şoahul neterminat în România, Culegere de documente 1940–1944*. Bucharest, p. 215 (document 38).

about "Jewish gangs" making trouble in the towns of the Bukovina. According to the German consul, they plundered shops and attacked men and women. Some Romanian units shot on Jews, for example, in Ciudei where they were said to be waiting along the road with red flags to greet the Soviets only to have realized too late that the troops were in fact retreating Romanians.[5]

Due to censorship, the Romanian press reported little about the chaos of the retreat. Only insiders got to know that a great many soldiers had deserted in these days.[6] Nothing at all was published about the attacks of Soviet advance troops on Romanian units in order not to complicate the negotiating position of the Romanian general in Odessa. Until October 1940, a Soviet-Romanian commission held meetings in Odessa. While the Soviet negotiators were mainly concerned about the return of locomotives the Romanians had confiscated, the Romanians wanted to ensure the departure of as many compatriots as possible.

Even though the Soviet Union was barely criticized publicly, the Romanian leader Ion Antonescu claimed that the Romanian people were thinking day and night of fighting the Soviets and were yearning for revenge. That is how he justified vis-à-vis Hitler on June 12, 1941, the readiness of his army to join the German attack against the Soviet Union.[7] Immediately after the beginning of the war, Romanian military units often reported about the defense of so-called Communist spies who were allegedly supported by the Jewish population. The massacre in Iaşi at the end of June 1941, with 14,850 victims, was presented as an attempt of insurrection by Communist Jews.[8] In October 1941, Antonescu justified the deportation of all Jews from Bessarabia and Northern Bukovina on account of their allegedly disloyal behavior in 1940. When Wilhelm Filderman protested, Antonescu, his former school colleague, answered as follows: "What did you do last year when you heard how the Jews in Bessarabia and in the Bukovina behaved who pulled of the badges of rank of our officers, who teared apart the soldiers' uniforms, who killed

5 Cited in: Politisches Archiv des Auswärtigen Amtes (PAAA) Berlin, Deutsches Konsulat Czernowitz, Paket 6/8 Russenbesetzung ("Sammlung nicht nummerierter Seiten"): reports dated July 13, 1940, and July 15, 1940.

6 Some 48,629 deserted soldiers are mentioned in: International Commission on the Holocaust in Romania (ed.) (2005). *Final Report*. Iaşi, p. 80.

7 Calafeteanu, Ion (1999). *Români la Hitler*. Bucharest, p. 92.

8 Final Report 2005, p. 126.

soldiers by beating them up?"[9] This letter was published in several newspapers.

In the following, I analyze the role of Jewish Communists in the Bukovina during the days of the Soviet ultimatum. The enemy stereotype of Judeo-Communists appeared much later in Romania than in Germany where the Communists were already an important political factor in 1933. In Romania, the Communist Party was banned in 1924. Very few people supported the Communists in view of the drastic punishment for doing so. Furthermore, the population consisted overwhelmingly of peasants for whom the Soviet model with collective ownership of land was not attractive.

In Romania, the disenfranchisement of the Jews was mainly justified because of the high percentage of Jews in leading economic and social positions in the country. Only when the propaganda began to declare that the separation of the two eastern provinces was the wish of the Jews did the stereotype of Judeo-Communism become more important. Because of the Soviet occupation in 1940, tens of thousands of Romanians had to flee the eastern provinces. They linked their distress with the Jews. The despair of having lost their homes was expressed in feelings of revenge against the Jews.

This enemy stereotype of the Communist Jews was revived in 1990 when politicians from different parties wanted to rehabilitate Ion Antonescu. In the 1990s many pamphlets and booklets were published in which the stereotype of Jewish gangs was mentioned.

I will also analyze this kind of information about the activities of Communist Jews in 1940 in Northern Bukovina. As Northern Bukovina is a much smaller territory than Bessarabia with only a handful of towns, the analysis of existing information is easier. Furthermore, the most important activities were concentrated in the provincial capital Czernowitz. Most persons branded in contemporary documents as masterminds can therefore be identified easily on the basis of other documents. Finally, there are other useful contemporary witness accounts in Northern Bukovina.[10]

---

9 Carp, Matatias (1996). *Cartea Neagră. Suferinţele evreilor din România (vol. 3)*. Bucharest, p. 191f.

10 For a reconstruction of events in Bessarabia in 1940 see: Hausleitner, Mariana (2005). *Deutsche und Juden in Bessarabien*. München, pp. 175–182.

The most important sources for this contribution are those of the Romanian historian Vitalie Văratic who intensively researched the events in Northern Bukovina in the summer of 1940 and published a 555-page volume with 160 documents in 2001. Most of these documents were published by members of the Romanian army and security forces,[11] many containing the stereotype of "terror gangs." The author presents these documents as realistic appraisals of the events during the retreat of the Romanian army. For me, these documents were useful to gain an overview of the enemy stereotype of Jewish Communists.

Further evidence can be found in the reports of the aforementioned German consul in Czernowitz, which have not been analyzed so far and which can be checked in the Political Archive of the *Auswärtige Amt* (Foreign Offcie) in Berlin. I also consulted the memoirs of Jewish and German contemporaries. Furthermore, the Romanian side often refers to a pamphlet written in March 1941 by Pepe Georgescu, a Romanian actor who had fled Czernowitz.[12]

The transition from one regime to another is difficult to examine because of the lack of independent and neutral sources. Representatives of the losing side create their own myths, while winners create their legitimizing stories. In an open society, one can gain important insights through analysis of the media of that time. The Bukovina indeed had a very diverse press landscape until 1938. But the authoritarian governments in Romania since December 1937 established harsh censorship of the press. No hints at the preparation of a possible Soviet aggression could be published, as the government wanted to prevent a mass flight. Even on the day of the invasion of the Red Army, the last edition of the *Czernowitzer Morgenblatt* contained not a single article on the impending regime change.[13]

By piecing together the different contemporary testimonies, I first reconstructed the events in the Bukovina after the Soviet ultimatum. I then

11 Văratic, Vitalie (2001). *Şase zile din istoria Bucovinei 28 iunie–3 iulie 1940. Invazia şi anexarea nordului Bucovinei de către U.R.S.S.* Rădauţi.

12 This pamphlet was republished in 1991, again without a critical annotation: Georgescu, Pepe (1991). 265 de zile la Cernăuţi sub ocupaţia bolşevică 28 iunie 1940–20 martie 1941, *Patrimoniu* 2: 84–124.

13 Rostoş, Ioana (2008). *Czernowitzer Morgenblatt. Eine Monografie*. Suceava, p. 47.

discuss the direct impact of the anti-Semitic agitation on the Jews in Romania after the evacuation of the two eastern provinces. At the same time, I sketch the reasons why some young Jews in Romania saw a bright future in the Soviet system and emigrated to the east. Finally, I analyze who in Romania revived the stereotype of Jewish gangs after 1990 and how historians dealt with it.

Events in Czernowitz immediately before and during the Red Army invasion

After the conclusion of the German-Soviet Non-Aggression Pact on August 23, 1939, Romanian politicians reckoned that the Soviet Union might again lay claim to Bessarabia.[14] The occupation of eastern Poland and the breakup of the Baltic states proved the expansionist nature of the Soviet Union. But in contrast to Finland, the Romanian army was not prepared for a defensive war.[15] The foreign minister noted in his diary on November 12, 1939, that the defense of the borders contested by Russia, Hungary, and Bulgaria was simply impossible.[16] In May 1940, the minister of defense ordered his staff to prepare plans for the army to retreat from Bessarabia. With regard to the Bukovina for which the Soviet Union voiced no claims until 1940, no plans for a worst-case scenario were drawn up.

But this worst-case scenario materialized the day after the capitulation of the French army when most German troops were still engaged in the west. On June 23, 1940, Soviet foreign minister Molotov told the German ambassador in Moscow that the Soviet government would ask Romania to retreat from Bessarabia and the Bukovina. As only Bessarabia was mentioned in the secret Additional Protocol, Ribbentrop answered that the Soviet claim on the Bukovina was something new. The Bukovina was, Ribbentrop remarked, a former Austrian Crown Land and densely

14 The secret Additional Protocol had not been made public in Romania. See: Müller, Dietmar (2011). Von Moskau über Jalta nach Malta, in Kaminsky, Anna et al. (eds.). *Der Hitler-Stalin-Pakt 1939 in den Erinnerungskulturen der Europäer*. Göttingen, pp. 361–376.

15 Hovi, Kalervo (1989). Der Hitler-Stalin-Pakt und Finnland, in Oberländer, Erwin (ed.). *Der Hitler-Stalin-Pakt. Das Ende Ostmitteleuropas*. Frankfurt am Main, pp. 61–74.

16 Gafencu, Grigore (1991). *Insemnări politice 1929–1939*. Bucharest, p. 342.

populated by Germans.[17] The density of German population was exaggerated because the Romanian census had established the following nationalities' percentages in 1930: 44.5 percent Romanians, 29.1 percent Ukrainians, 10.8 percent Jews, and only 8.9 percent Germans; the rest being made up of smaller groups.[18] Molotov claimed that the Ukrainians were the biggest ethnic group in the Bukovina, which was only true for the part north of Czernowitz. In the afternoon of June 26, he reduced the Soviet claim to this part and Bessarabia.

The Romanian envoy to Moscow, Gheorghe Davidescu, received the ultimatum on June 26 at 22:00. Due to technical problems, he was able to transmit it to Bucharest only the next morning. However, he did not send the map showing the territories the Soviet Union demanded from Romania.[19] The German envoy recommended to the Romanian foreign minister to accept the Soviet ultimatum. The Romanian chief of staff saw no possibility of defending three borders at the same time as Hungary and Bulgaria had also amassed troops. The Crown Council held two sessions on June 27, in which only a minority voted for a confrontational approach. On June 27, the Romanian government accepted evacuation. Its request for a prolongation of the deadline was ignored by Molotov.[20]

In the morning of June 27, defensive lines were reinforced in the Bukovina. Based on the decision of the Crown Council, Radio Bucharest announced at 20:45 that Romania had accepted the Soviet ultimatum according to which Bessarabia and Northern Bukovina had to be evacuated within four days. The line of demarcation between the northern and southern parts of the Bukovina was not mentioned. Only early in the

---

17 Brügel, J. W. (1975). *Stalin und Hitler. Pakt gegen Europa*. Wien, p. 225 ("Der Anspruch der Sowjetregierung auf die Bukowina ist ein Novum. Die Bukowina war früher österreichisches Kronland und ist stark von Deutschen besiedelt"); Romanian version: Neagoe, Stelian (ed.) (1992). *Bătălia pentru Bucovina*. Bucharest, p. 138.

18 A much higher percentage indicated Ukrainian as their main language. Cf. Trebici, Vladimir (1996). *Demografia. Exerpta et selecta*. Bucharest, p. 130.

19 That is why the Soviet claim on the region Herţa was not known in Romania. See: Final Report 2015, p. 75.

20 Hausleitner, Mariana (2013). Romania in the Second World War, in Cattaruzza, Maria et al. (eds). *Territorial Revisionism and the Allies of Germany in the Second World War*. New York/Oxford, pp. 173–192; Heinen, Armin (1989). Der Hitler-Stalin-Pakt und Rumänien, in Oberländer, Erwin (ed.). *Der Hitler-Stalin-Pakt 1939*. Frankfurt am Main, pp. 98–113.

morning of June 28 did the military commanders learn that the strategically important cities of Czernowitz, Chişinău, and Cetatea Albă had to be surrendered to the Soviets by 20:00 the same day.[21]

In Czernowitz, members of the army, the gendarmerie, and the security police hectically started to pack weapons and ammunition. State employees learned the same morning (June 28) from the Royal Resident that they had to immediately evacuate the most important documents to the south of the Bukovina. Many senior staff were mainly concerned with getting themselves and their families out as quickly as possible. A teacher, Bohdan Fedorovych, for example, tried to get his salary from the school inspectorate, but the inspectors had already left.[22]

At that time, only few people owned a radio, and there was no public notification in Czernowitz. One reason for this was probably the fact that there was an explicit order not to let members of national minorities over the new border into Romania.[23] This order particularly affected the Jews who in 1940 represented 37.9 percent of the population of Czernowitz (42,592 individuals).[24] In Czernowitz, the struggle for seats in cars, horse carts, and extra trains started in the morning of June 28. The streets toward the south were soon jammed because many military units also evacuated animals from peasants in order to supply the troops.[25]

As the first Soviet units moved into the northern parts of the Bukovina from Galicia, the retreat took place amid great panic. Some officers simply fled their units, while some Romanian troops marching toward the border were overtaken by Soviet units. The Soviets summoned those who were from the Bukovina or from Bessarabia to return to their families. Many soldiers from peasant families indeed did so. Large quantities of

21 Neagoe 1992, p. 152; Văratic 2001, p. 353, pp. 381–385.

22 Fedorowytsch, Bohdan (1990). Von den grauen Tagen–September 1939–1940, in Bornemann, Irma and Rudolf Wagner (eds.). *Mit Fluchtgepäck die Heimat verlassen*. Stuttgart/München, pp. 57–62.

23 Stanciu, Sergiu (ed.). (1997). *Evreii din România între anii 1940–1944 (vol. 3/1)*. Bucharest, p. 16.

24 "Spovedania fostului primar al Municipiului Cernăuţi Dr. Traian Popovici," in Carp 1996, p. 188.

25 Gerber, Martin (1990). Erinnerungen an die Zeit nach der Besetzung der Bukowina durch die Sowjets im Juni 1940, in Bornemann/Wagner 1990, p. 54.

weapons and official documents as well as much ammunition were left on the roadside.[26]

The connections with many gendarmerie posts in the north were broken off due to the rapid advance of the Soviet troops. The gendarmes tried to flee together with their families. Telephone connections of many more gendarmerie and military units were taken down as Soviet troops took over gendarmerie posts and barracks. These Red Army advance units also prevented the Romanians from blowing up bridges during their retreat. The first motorized units arrived at 17:00 in Czernowitz and overtook many fleeing Romanians on their way to the city.[27]

The terror of the "Communist gangs" in Czernowitz is usually said to have taken place on June 28 between 9:00 and 17:00. There are two hotspots in these reports, namely the aggressive behavior of demonstrators around the military prison in the morning and close to the train station in the afternoon.

When the surrender of Northern Bukovina was made public on the radio in the morning, many inhabitants of Czernowitz flocked to the city center. A big crowd assembled after 9:00 in front of the military prison next to the barracks of the 8th Division. It is possible that the information had spread that prisoners had been evacuated. Indeed, the gendarmerie had already evacuated some prisoners in the morning. The bodies of forty-eight prisoners shot dead were found later, some 15 kilometers from Czernowitz.[28] Among the approximately 400 prisoners were many Communists and their supporters. The appeal proceedings against these persons had taken place shortly before the surrender of Northern Bukovina. As the Communist Party was banned, activities of organizations in its environment were severely punished. In September 1939, for example, nineteen women were sentenced for their part in providing "Red Aid," for having supported prisoners. In April 1940, 250 individuals were preventively arrested because of an order from Bucharest demanding that

26 Stanciu 1997, p. 23.

27 Văratic 2001, p. 262.

28 The discovery of these dead bodies is mentioned by the German consul Schellhorn. Cf. PAAA, 6/8, report dated July 1, 1940.

all "subversive elements" be detained.[29] The speaker for the political prisoners vis-à-vis the prison administration was the Ukrainian Vasyl' Rusnak.[30]

The crowd in front of the prison demanded the release of the political prisoners. As nothing happened, the crowd started to threaten the guards (*gardeini publici*). When the latter started to shoot into the air, the demonstrators attacked them. Not all guards were able to flee, and three were arrested. The demonstrators also apprehended the prison director Alexandru Racoce and later handed him over to Soviet units. He disappeared in the Gulag.[31]

The descriptions of the liberation of the prisoners given to a committee of inquiry in Bucharest in July 1940 by guards and policemen who had fled the scene differed widely. Roman Ardeleanu reported that around 200–300 persons had assembled in front of the prison on June 28. After the attack by the demonstrators, the guards had been forced to withdraw. According to Ardeleanu, five guards were shot and one defected to the crowd. Police Commissioner Stefan Nedelcu, on the other hand, claimed that at around 13:00, 2,000–3,000 youths aged 15–20 had besieged the prison.[32]

During the siege of the prison, the situation escalated because of the shots fired by the guards. Colonel Gheorghe Barozzi, the inspector of the gendarmerie, had given the order to shoot, and one guard targeted and shot dead a youth, Mosche Schayer, trying to mount a red flag on the building.[33] The reason for the shooting order can only be explained by

29 Because of these mass arrests, the Royal Resident, Gheorghe Flondor, was charged in 1953 and sentenced to 10 years in prison. Cf. Pânzaru, Mihai (2000). *Gheorghe Flondor, ultimul rezident regal al Bucovinei.* Radăuţi, pp. 128–132.

30 He was active in the Social Democratic movement in the 1920s and was a candidate on the workers' and peasants' block ticket in 1931. Hausleitner, Mariana (2001). *Die Rumänisierung der Bukowina. Die Durchsetzung des nationalstaatlichen Anspruchs 1918–1944.* München, p. 202f, p. 241.

31 The Communist inmate Voloch allegedly had them arrested because of their brutal treatment of prisoners. See the interrogation protocol of Vasile Luca dated August 6, 1953, in Văratic 2001, p. 468.

32 Văratic 2001, p. 510f.

33 Levin, Dov (1976). The Jews and the Inception of Soviet Rule in Bukovina, *Soviet Jewish Affairs* 6(2): 52–70, here p. 53.

the hatred Colonel Barozzi felt against the demonstrators.[34] Major Constantin Cichindel, the commander of the gendarmerie in Czernowitz, legitimized the firing order on the alleged attacks of Jews against his units. Some youths had blocked the passage of these units that tried to support the guards. Cichindel also reported various attacks by "Communists" in other quarters, for example in the suburb of Sadagura.[35]

To legitimize the use of armed force, some gendarmes later claimed that there had been an uprising of Communist Jews in Czernowitz. In order to shore up this construct, the security forces looked for the organizers of the unrest. In the police reports, the same five or six names of the alleged leaders of the "Red Guards" are mentioned again and again. These persons were not prisoners who were liberated but individuals who allegedly called for the storming of the prison. In the documents published by Vitalie Văratic, four names are most often mentioned, which can be, even though their spelling varies, assigned to specific individuals: Siegfried Hitzig, Adolf Glaubach, Josef Brüll, and Max Weissmann.

According to the security forces, the lawyer Dr. Siegfried Hitzig was the mastermind behind the unrest. They had had an eye on him for many years as he and his wife Ida Hitzig had together with other lawyers defended left-wing activities in court already in 1932. The newspaper *Der Tag*, then, reported in great detail that several defendants, severely beaten by police guards, had been forced into wrong confessions. The guards were described as torturers by the newspaper. They protected neither the defendants nor their defense attorneys when they were attacked by Romanian right-wing extremists during the trial.[36] The security policy claimed that the Hitzigs had had connections with Communists, but a house search in November 1936 brought no incriminating material to light.[37] In late 1937, the police in Czernowitz arrested thirty-seven schoolgirls for distributing left-wing flyers. Siegfried Hitzig was once more one of the defense attorneys in this case. Promptly, the security forces

34 He was among the masterminds behind the massacre of Jews in Iași at the end of June 1941. Ancel, Jean (2005). *Preludiu la asasinat. Pogromul de la Iaşi, 29 iunie 1941*. Iaşi, p. 39, p. 68.

35 Văratic 2001, p. 403.

36 For the persecution of Communists and their supporters cf. Hausleitner 2001, pp. 241–245.

37 Arhiva Naţionala Istorică Centrală (ANIC), Bucureşti, Ministerul Justiţiei, 9/1936. Cf. Derzhavhyi Arkhiv Chernovits'koj Oblasti (DAChO), f. 38, 1, 9724, p. 95, pp. 110–141.

again searched Hitzig's house.[38] It is unlikely that Hitzig played a main role in the storming of the prison, as he traveled to Bucharest in the summer of 1940. If he had been the mastermind of the storming, he would have faced very harsh punishment in Romania and would have therefore not traveled there.[39]

Most policemen were already on the run by mid-day on June 28 and could therefore not know who the many young people in front of the prison were. Only the head of the security police *Siguranţa*, Ioan Pihal, wanted to leave later by an extra train but protesters at the train station recognized him and handed him over to Soviet troops.[40] This fact was reported by the head of the information department, together with the false report of the plunder of the Orthodox cathedral in Czernowitz.[41] In the summer of 1940, the Bucharest inquiry committee submitted a list of names and pictures of suspects to the guards and policemen who had fled Czernowitz. Three guards went on record saying that they did not see Hitzig in front of the prison. Neither did they name any other mastermind of the protests. This is rather surprising as the security police put them under considerable pressure, also with regard to substantial amounts of money they had brought with them from Czernowitz.[42]

It is remarkable how much energy the military authorities spent trying to identify the offenders even though it was in any case no longer possible to punish them. Did Bureau II of the General Staff have nothing better to do at a time when Romanian soldiers indeed threw Jews out of trains and when plundering raids took place all over Southern Bukovina? The bureau with the cover name "Statistics" put together a report on "Jewish action" in the "lost" provinces on July 2, 1940. The report was supposed to explain the chaos during the retreat. With regard to Czernowitz, the

38 ANIC, Ministerul Justiţiei, 63, 1937; DAChO, f. 38, 1, 10213, pp. 10–20; 10762, p. 10.

39 E-mail from Emil Hitzig (nephew of Siegfried Hitzig) to the author on November 19, 2015.

40 A Soviet court sentenced him because of his role in the persecution of Communists, but he was liberated in March 1941. He had to appear in a Romanian court in 1953 and died in prison in 1960. Văratic 2001, pp. 467–477.

41 Văratic 2001, p. 475f.

42 The guard Ioan Popescu was interrogated in September 1940 because he wanted to open a fruit shop in Bucharest with the stolen money. Iosif Romaniuc, who was also interrogated, kept the origin of his money secret. Văratic 2001, pp. 513–520.

report mentions Hitzig as well as another lawyer by the name of Glaubach as the leaders of a so-called people's committee.[43] Glaubach is most probably Dr. Adolf Glaubach, who had a law firm in Czernowitz and sometimes defended left-wing activists. On June 28, he was indeed, together with his son, among the protesters in the city center, but he did not hold a speech there.[44] Most probably, the security police had put him and Hitzig on a list of "dangerous elements" well before June 28. Interestingly, neither of them was among the 250 other "subversive elements" the Romanian security police had arrested as a preventive measure.

The same report by Bureau II mentioned one "Sale" Brüll as another mastermind of the unrest. The report alleged that Josef (Salo) Brüll was appointed people's commissar by the crowd in front of the prison.[45] He was a famous photographer with his own studio in Czernowitz. From time to time he had published photographs in *Vorwärts*, and, after it was banned, in the bourgeois *Czernowitzer Morgenpost*. He was never able to state his point of view as he was deported to Transnistria where he died. In police reports Brüll's friend Max Weissmann is also mentioned as one of the key persons behind the unrest. It is claimed that Weissmann was elected mayor by the crowd. Weissmann owned a printing house, and he had represented his guild—labor unions had been banned since 1938—in the Employees Chamber (*Arbeiterkammer*). The police documents state that he was a "covert informant."[46] Weissmann was probably not the only one who would have had to fear negative consequences if the People's Commissariat for Internal Affairs (NKVD) had got hold of the Romanian court documents.

It is clear that none of the persons mentioned in the security forces' documents as masterminds of the unrest in front of the prison were prom-

---

43 See the respective documents in Stoenescu, Alex Mihai (1998). *Armata, Mareşalul şi Evreii.* Bucharest, pp. 83–90. The Bureau II was headed by Colonel Ion Palade who played a key role in the 1941 Iaşi pogrom. See: Ancel 2005, p. 25.

44 At the beginning of the 1930s, he supported the workers' and peasants' block, but he then distanced himself from the Communists because of the Stalinist show trials. This information is from his son Berti Glaubach who had accompanied him to the city center on June 28 as a 17-year old (e-mail to the author dated December 8, 2015).

45 Văratic 2001, p. 467, p. 496.

46 Văratic (2001, p. 496) mentions that Weissmann illegally fled to Romania on September 7, 1940, to then emigrate to Palestine.

inent Communist leaders as they were never mentioned again in contemporary documents. According to Ukrainian documents from the Communist period, the main leaders of the illegal Communist Party before 1940 were Rusnak, Karl Terletzki, and Bernhard Katz, who all played an important role in the Communist administration.[47]

The attacks against Romanians after the storming of the prison is well documented. Some individuals in the crowd in the city center used the moment and the sudden powerlessness of the main decision-makers to attack. This becomes evident in the memoirs of Franz Kopecki who has been the deputy mayor of Czernowitz since October 1938. On June 27, in the afternoon, Kopecki together with the Romanian mayor of the city, Nicu von Flondor, was on his way to the bridge over the Prut in order to hand over Czernowitz to the Soviet commander. But in the town hall square, a few Jewish youth with red cockades in their buttonholes blocked them. Kopecki later wrote,

> Those closest to us shouted at us and threatened us. Somewhere on the margins of the crowd gun shots were heard, but probably only alarm shots. The mayor turned to me, white with rage and fear, and crunched: "And I nurtured this brood on my breast for years." Indeed, he had always been well-disposed and friendly towards the Jewish population.[48]

In all the police reports, it is indicated that after the burning of the court records close to the prison, the demonstrators moved from the city center to the train station. Many Romanians were taking the same way to try to get on an extra train to the south. Many of these people were civil servants originally from the Romanian Old Kingdom fleeing with their families. Some better-off individuals of all ethnic backgrounds were also on their way out of the city. Some affluent Jews had been advised by their informants in the administration already on June 27 that Czernowitz would be evacuated.[49]

---

47 Gusar, J. S. (1991). *Chernivci*. Czernowitz, p. 83. Information on Karl Teletzki from his wife Jewgenija Finkel, in: Finkel, Jewgenija and Markus Winkler (2004). *Juden aus Czernowitz*. Konstanz, p. 123.

48 Cited in: Kopecki, Franz (1990). Meine Erinnerungen an den Einmarsch der Truppen der UDSSR in Czernowitz im Juni 1940, in Bornemann, Irma and Rudolf Wagner (eds.). *Mit Fluchtgepäck die Heimat verlassen*. Stuttgart/München, pp. 45–49.

49 Contemporary witness Käthe Krauthammer, in Coldewey, Gaby et al. (2003). *Zwischen Pruth und Jordan*. Köln, p. 27f.

The second venue of attacks was this route to the train station. In the afternoon, many young men blocked cars and carriages that were on their way to the train station, and some persons had their luggage stolen. According to the police documents, the perpetrators were Jews and Ukrainians, some of them just freed from prisons. A lot of luggage was simply left at the train station as the trains were massively overcrowded. Some of the boxes left at the train station contained official documents.[50] When the last train left Czernowitz at 17:00, the passengers could already see the first Soviet tanks close to the train station.[51]

The commander of the advance units of the Red Army immediately ordered all crowds to be dispersed. He also decreed a curfew from 21:00. The official handover of the city dragged on into the night until the Soviet commander responsible for the handover finally arrived in Czernowitz. After the invasion by Soviet troops, there were only a few plunders. The "Red Guards," who had been spontaneously created to protect the main factories from being dismantled by the Romanian army, were dissolved on June 29. All weapons had to be handed over within 24 hours.[52]

Jews seldom received posts in the new administration. Most of the posts went to Ukrainians, many of them from the Soviet Republic of Ukraine.[53] At least two former inmates of the Czernowitz military prison received important posts, namely Vasyl' Rusnak (new leader of the Komsomol), and Szekler Vasile Luca/Laszlo Lukacz (deputy mayor on the side of the Ukrainian mayor Mihailov), who was originally from Transylvania. Later on, Luca was appointed delegate to the Supreme Soviet of Ukraine.[54]

---

50 The most important documents from the state archive were found in twelve boxes. See: Căruntu, Mihai-Aurel (2004). *Bucovina în al doilea război mondial*. Iaşi, p. 120.

51 There are many eyewitness accounts of the siege on the street to the train station. See, e.g.: Flondor, Sergiu Mircea (2011), Când a început războiul, in Vultur, Smaranda and Adrian Onică (eds.), *Basarabeni şi bucovineni în Banat*. Timişoara, p. 271.

52 Văratic 2001, p. 487f.

53 Levin, Dov (1995). *The Lesser of Two Evils. Eastern European Jewry Under Soviet Rule 1939–1941*. Philadelphia, p. 17.

54 Kurylo, V. et al. (1969). *Pivnichna Bukovyna ii' mynule i suchastne*. Uzhhorod, p. 135. Since 1991, very little research has been done in Ukraine on the Communist movement, as the Ukrainian nationalists are now the new heroes. In a history of the city, the role of the worker guards in 1940 is mentioned in one single line. Botushanskiy, V. M. (2009). *Chernivci*. Chernivci , p. 225.

How and why did the enemy stereotype of Jewish gangs develop in 1940?

Summarizing the situation in Czernowitz on June 28, one can state that a crowd of up to 3,000 mostly young men assembled. It is probable that some Communist agitators were in the crowd. Some men took weapons off the guards and liberated the prisoners. Then, unarmed men molested fleeing Romanians. Some shops were plundered.

Why did the Bureau II of the General Staff put so much energy into identifying the masterminds of the unrest when it was clear they could not be punished in the territorially reduced Romania? This happened at the same time that the General Staff would have had to determine how much the Romanian units had been reduced by desertion. But already on June 30, First Lieutenant Ion Palade, the head of the Statistical Bureau of the General Staff in Iași, submitted a secret report to the King of Romania that claimed that the entire Jewish population in Bessarabia was involved in attacking the Romanian military and in taking away its weapons.[55]

The same Bureau II wrote a second, extended report, dated July 22, 1940, with the title "Attitude of the Jews in regard to the evacuation of the lost territories." The report summarizes the alleged attacks by Jews from Bessarabia and the Bukovina. With regard to Czernowitz, the report talks about Communist youths aged 15–16 committing barbaric acts. They supposedly disarmed Romanian soldiers, officers, and policemen and used the bayonets of the rifles. The report claimed that Jews and Ukrainians were responsible for the unrest in the town of Vyzhnytsia/Vijniţa to the west of Czernowitz.[56] With the expression "Jewish gangs," the Bureau II implied that the unrest was well organized and steered by Communists. The fact that many units of the military as well as the gendarmerie received no order at all on June 28 to retreat was not analyzed.[57] These units, especially in the north of the Bukovina, were overrun by the Red Army and had to hand over their weapons. Many did not make it to the demarcation line by July 3 and were interned.

---

55 Reprinted in Stoenescu 1998, p. 90f.

56 Stanciu 1997, p. 30.

57 Report of Constantin Hrehorciuc, ANIC, Inspectoratul General al Gendarmeriei, 99/1940, p. 9f.

The chaotic retreat made it possible for many soldiers, especially from the "lost" territories, to desert. In July 1940, about 12,800 men were missing from the units that had retreated from Northern Bukovina and Bessarabia. For quite some time, it was unclear whether they were dead, interned, or had deserted. Only when the number of POWs was clarified did the Romanian military authorities estimate that approximately 11,000 soldiers had deserted.[58] The General Staff mentioned in July 1940 that five officers had been killed.[59] A Soviet advance unit took a Romanian unit that was in the act of blowing up a bridge during the ultimatum by surprise. The Soviet unit is said to have executed forty Romanian soldiers.[60]

The Soviet representatives to the mixed commission holding its meetings in Odessa promised the repatriation of 21,000 Romanians in November 1940 if Romania restituted the locomotives that had pulled the many extra trains from the Bukovina and Bessarabia.[61] Many Romanians were indeed freed in March 1941, among them the already-sentenced police inspector Ioan Pihal, others not.

Even though the high concentration of Soviet troops on the borders was known to the General Staff, the planning for an evacuation was inadequate. A mass flight of the population should have been prevented. The king was given a distorted picture of the realities on the ground, as he wrote in his diary on June 29: "Desertions of Bessarabian soldiers, excesses of all kinds from the minority populations, especially the Jews who attacked and mocked our people, ridiculed officers."[62]

The General Staff justified the encroachments of its own soldiers, which continued throughout July, citing the alleged attacks by Jews in the "lost" territories.[63] Upset by the spreading anarchy, General Antonescu asked the king to completely reorganize the army. He was not given an

---

58 Hausleitner 2001, p. 340.

59 Solonari, Vladimir (2010). The Treatment of the Jews of Bukovina by the Soviet and Romanian Administrations in 1940–1944, *Holocaust and Modernity* 2(8): 149–180, here p. 153.

60 PAAA, Deutsches Konsulat Czernowitz, Paket 6/8, report dated July 1, 1940.

61 Şişcanu, Ion (1995). *Uniunea Sovietică—România 1940. Tratativele în cadrul comisiilor mixte*. Chişinău, p. 59.

62 Cited in: Neagoe 1992, p. 174.

63 A corporal relieved the factory owner Kinnsbrunner, who was fleeing Czernowitz from the Red Army, of a considerable sum of money. Cf. Stanciu 1997, p. 55.

audience. Instead, on July 9, 1940, Carol II ordered the isolation of the general in a monastery.[64] The Bureau II of the General Staff tried to cover up the general chaos with its reports about alleged attacks of Jews against the retreating army.

At the same time, the report was intended to "legitimize" two massacres of Jews by retreating Romanian soldiers. In Dorohoi, a small town in northern Moldavia, scattered retreating units opened fire on mourners in the Jewish cemetery on June 28, 1940, killing fifty people, among them women and children.[65] The commanding officer, Valeriu Carp, justified the murders by claiming that the honorary shots fired at the cemetery for the buried Jewish (Romanian) soldier were interpreted as an attack. After the massacre at the Dorohoi cemetery, the Romanian soldiers involved in the attack then plundered Jewish property in Dorohoi and close-by towns and villages.[66] The investigator sent to Dorohoi informed the Prime Minister on July 11 that many Romanian officers backed anti-Semitic unrest thereby possibly creating a pretext for the neighboring countries to occupy more Romanian territory.[67] Major Carp was never brought to justice.[68]

On June 29, there was yet another, much bloodier crime in Galaţi about which very different accounts exist. The Romanian military authorities gave the following version of the mass killing of people trying to emigrate to now-Soviet Bessarabia:

> A group of 2,000 Bessarabians, 90% of them Jews, were waiting at the train station, accompanied by Romanian soldiers, to take the ferry boat to Bessarabia. Some of them rioted because the transports were not organized quickly enough, and some tried to escape. After warnings, those fleeing [*sic*] started to shoot. Then the soldiers shot back. They killed 10 to 12 people and injured about 40. 80 more were arrested by the Galaţi police.[69]

64 Letter of Ion Antonescu to the king, in Kareţki, Aurel and Adrian Pricop (eds.) (1993). *Lacrima Basarabie*. Chişinău, p. 235f.

65 Stanciu 1997, pp. 33–35.

66 See for such reports: Stanciu 1997, pp. 39–43.

67 Stanciu 1997, p. 50f.

68 He was again active in the region killing Jews in the summer of 1941. Cf. Carp 1996, p. 31f.

69 Stanciu 1997, p. 30.

The number of those killed is today estimated at over 300.[70] Even though this had been the first big massacre of Jews in Romania since 1907, it was never properly investigated. Those who survived the massacre made it to Bessarabia where most of them probably perished in the Holocaust in 1941.

Another version of the Galaţi events was provided by the German consul, Alfred Lörner, who certainly did not have any sympathies for the Jews. He described the incidents on July 4, 1940, because he went to the prisoners' camp to search for Bessarabian Germans there. A German eyewitness described the events to Lörner as follows: As some civilians insulted retreating Romanian troops in Reni, there were some arrests. The arrested individuals were held outdoors in the hot July sun by 20 to 30 Romanian soldiers. At 16:00, five Russian-speaking Jews urged the arrested individuals to escape. When some tried to do so, the soldiers shot on them with machine guns and killed approximately 300. Lörner reported that there was a nightly search for the individuals who had escaped, and many more persons were shot.[71]

By inventing rioting Jewish agents, the Romanian authorities tried to cover up the breakdown of the command structures. The fear of attacks by the three neighboring countries paralyzed many officers. Some let their subordinates plunder because supply channels were broken off. Members of the gendarmerie and the army killed Jews everywhere in Romania in July 1940. Very often, Jews were thrown off trains. Fritz Schellhorn, the German consul in Czernowitz, referred to the plunder of Jewish shops and houses throughout Romanian Southern Bukovina. He wrote on July 13 that the authorities themselves had given the figure of 2,000 Jews killed who were traveling by train.[72] Nobody even tried to stop the killers. The general prosecutor, Constantin Maroxim, who had fled Czernowitz said laconically that when he traveled to Bucharest on July 2, 1940, twenty Jews had been thrown out of the windows of his train.

70 Final Report 2005, p. 86.

71 Deletant, Dennis and Ottmar Traşcă (eds.) (2007). *Al III-lea Reich şi Holocaustul din România 1940–1944. Documente din arhivele germane*. Bucharest, p. 133f.

72 PAAA, Deutsches Konsulat Czernowitz, Paket 6/8, Bericht vom 13.7.1940, p. 3.

The perpetrators, Maroxim explained, were students of the military academy in Czernowitz who justified their action citing the "disloyal" behavior of the Jews of Czernowitz.[73]

The speaker of the Jewish Communities in Romania tried to counter the general accusations. On July 10, a newspaper of the Bucharest Jewish community, the *Curierul Israelit*, published the following statement:

> Whatever the truth is, why are we made responsible for these acts of crazy violence by human beings who were born under a different regime and who did not have time to connect their souls to the Romanian people and land? We cannot be made responsible for acts which have nothing to do with our perceptions and our historical tradition.[74]

The Romanian press reported that tens of thousands of Jews were about to emigrate to "lost" Northern Bukovina and Bessarabia thereby corroborating the myth of Communist sympathies of the Jews. The press obviously did not report the fact that most emigrating Jews were originally from Northern Bukovina and Bessarabia and had lost their Romanian citizenship with the enactment of a new law. Until November 1939, approximately 225,000 Jews had lost their citizenship (36.5 percent of all Romanian Jews).[75] They were excluded from all educational institutions and many professional associations. That is why many Jews hoped for a better future in the northeast after the change of regime there in 1940. A document produced by Bureau II of the General Staff accordingly predicted that all intellectuals and individuals with liberal professions would emigrate to the Soviet Union.[76]

The distancing of the Bucharest Jewish leadership from their brethren in Bessarabia and Northern Bukovina has to be understood against the backdrop of menacing developments. On July 2, 1940, King Carol II asked Hitler to send a military mission to Romania with a view to protecting Romania's borders in anticipation of the Soviet annexation. Ion Gigurtu, who had particularly good relations with Germany, was named prime minister on July 4. In addition to several generals, some members

---

73 Văratic 2001, p. 469f.

74 Cited in: Comisia Internaţionala pentru studierea Holocaustului în România (2005). *Documente*. Iaşi, p. 80.

75 Florian, Alexandru (2010). The Fate of Jews from Northern Bukovina under the Antonescu Regime, *Holocaust and Modernity* 2(8): 207–218, here p. 209.

76 Document dated July 2, 1940, in Stoenescu 1998, p. 88.

of the Legionary movement were appointed as ministers for the first time. The new government signaled that Romania would join the German-Italian alliance.[77] It introduced key measures to further marginalize the Jews. These measures were pooled on August 8, 1940, in a law that gave precedence to ethnic Romanians. The Jews were dismissed from all positions in the army. They were no longer allowed to work either as civil servants or notaries. They were pushed off the boards of all major companies. At the same time, marriages between Jews and non-Jews were banned.[78] Foreign Minister Mihail Manoilescu declared the ethnic homogenization to be the most important goal of the government.[79]

Finally, it should be mentioned that many Jews in Czernowitz had a very difficult "Russian year." Many lost their jobs due to the nationalization of factories, shops, banks, craft businesses, hospitals, and pharmacies. As work was compulsory, many intellectuals and civil servants had to accept hard physical work.[80] Many who had been active politically were deported by the NKVD, especially former members of the Social Democratic Bundists and of Zionist organizations.[81] The number of Jews deported from Northern Bukovina in 1940–41 is estimated at approximately 10,000.[82]

The anti-Semitic enemy stereotype in the Romanian public after 1990

In the Communist period, little was published in Romania about Northern Bukovina and Bessarabia because these territories again became part of the Soviet Union in April 1944.[83] After the breakup of the Soviet Union,

77 Hausleitner 2001, p. 340f.

78 Benyamin, Lya (1993). *Evreii (vol. 2)*. Bucharest, pp. 37–44.

79 Solonari, Vladimir (2015). *Purifiarea naţiunii. Dislocări forţate de populaţie şi epurări etnice în România lui Ion Antonescu*. Bucharest, p. 71.

80 Gold, Rita (2003). *Timpul lacrimilor secate*. Bucharest, p. 69.

81 Hausleitner, Mariana (2009). Der Pakt, die Sowjetisierung und die Folgen, *Osteuropa* (7–8) (Der Hitler-Stalin-Pakt. Der Krieg und die europäische Erinnerung): 203–218.

82 Levin 1976, p. 59.

83 Only in the 1980s did some authors start to claim that Romania was pushed into the alliance with Hitler by the "loss" of Bessarabia and Northern Bukovina. See: Deletant, Dennis (2008). *Aliatul uitat al lui Hitler. Ion Antonescu şi regimul său 1940–1944*. Bucharest, p. 285.

some politicians of different movements in Romania and the Republic of Moldova started to push for the unification of Northern Bukovina and Bessarabia with Romania. In this context, a wave of writings about Antonescu was published after 1992. The Romanian leader became a hero and cult figure for all those who had fought for the annexation of the territories lost in 1940.

Some historians in the Republic of Moldova have underlined the illegitimacy of the separation of Bessarabia and Northern Bukovina. For the first time, the effects of the German-Soviet Non-Aggression Pact were publicly discussed. At the same time, contemporary testimonies were published uncommented. One of these was the already-mentioned report of the actor Pepe Georgescu, which was then cited by many historians. The historians adopted Georgescu's claim that the workers' guards in Czernowitz consisted predominantly of Jews.

In the following, the main Romanian publications that cover the events in Czernowitz in the summer of 1940 are mentioned. In 1992, the military historian Constantin Hlihor and the university professor Ioan Scurtu wrote a book about 1940. From the documents of the Ministry of Interior, they adopted the stereotype of "gangs of members of minorities" who were allegedly infiltrated from the Soviet Union before the invasion to foment unrest. According to Hlihor and Scurtu, Jews abused many refugees who were fleeing to the train station in Czernowitz.[84]

Gheorghe Buzatu, a historian who had been very active in the Ceauşescu era, wrote prolifically about the two eastern provinces. In the 1990s, he was the head of a research institute in Iași belonging to the Romanian Academy and was, until his death in 2013, one of the most active proponents of the rehabilitation of Ion Antonescu. He represented the Great Romania Party (Partidul România Mare) in the Senate from 2000 to 2004. Buzatu discussed the events in Czernowitz in a pamphlet with the provocative title "The way the Holocaust against the Romanian people began." He primarily blamed the Jews for the breakup of the Romanian army in 1940. He based this statement on the comments a general made on June 28, 1940, according to which the "Jewish population

84 Hlihor, Constantin and Ioan Scurtu (1992). *Anul 1940. Drama românilor dintre Prut şi Nistru*. Bucharest, p. 75, p. 114.

perpetrated acts of terrorism and plunder" during the evacuation of Czernowitz.[85] In a book published in 1996, he reprinted some documents from Soviet archives. Among these documents were biographies of individuals who had fled Romania in the summer of 1940 to Soviet Czernowitz, such as the Jewish teacher Chaim Kraft.[86] With such biographies, Buzatu tried to suggest that the Jews had been the main supporters of the Soviet system.[87]

Alex Mihai Stoenescu proceeded in similar fashion in his book *The Army, the Marshall and the Jews* published in large circulation in 1998. The publicist did not hide the fact that he wanted Ion Antonescu rehabilitated. He claimed that three Jews had the three key posts in Czernowitz in June 1940: the photographer Salo Brüll as people's commissar, Glaubach as the mayor, and Hitzig as Glaubach's deputy. Young Jews allegedly attacked Romanians, who fled on trucks, throwing stones at them. The Jews also shot, according to Stoenescu, prison guards and Catholic priests.[88] However, already in July 1940, the German consul in Czernowitz had verified that the shooting of the priest Goebel was a false report.[89] Stoenescu should and could have informed himself better because, as he admitted in 2006, he used to be a long-time collaborator with the security service Securitate.[90]

But in 1994, another former Securitate collaborator offered some evidence against the myth of the Jewish betrayal of June 1940. Mihai Pelin underlined the important impact of the closure of the borders of Romania to the minorities in Northern Bukovina. By closing the borders, Jews and Ukrainians were indeed abandoned by Romania. Only small groups of Jews and Ukrainians had welcomed the Red Army.[91] Pelin's writings appeared without any notes and were mostly ignored by historians. In the

85 Cited in: Buzatu, Gheorghe (1995). *Aşa a început holocaustul împotriva poporului roman*. Bucharest, p. 13.

86 Buzatu, Gheorghe (1996). *Români în arhivele Kremlinuliu*. Bucharest, p. 369.

87 Kuller, Hary (2008). Sionişti sub "lupa" Siguranţei şi Securităţi, *Buletinul Centrului, Muzeului şi arhivei istorice a evreilor din România* 13, p. 197.

88 Stoenescu 1998, p. 83, p. 93.

89 Report of a police inspector of the Suceava region, in Văratic 2001, p. 475.

90 Cronicarul lui Becali, Alex Mihai Stoenescu, a scris şi pentru Securitate, *Evenimentul zilei* (November 1, 2006).

91 Pelin, Mihai (1994). *Legendă şi adevăr*. Bucharest, p. 33f.

expanded reprint of 2008, there is again no indication that many sources were documents from the security services from 1940 to 1941.[92]

For the historian Vitalie Văratic, the Jews, Hungarians, and Slavs were the central reason why Romania could not defend itself in 1940. In the introduction to the collection of documents he published in 2001, Văratic claimed that most Romanian units withdrew without any major problems and that there was major unrest in Czernowitz only because the security forces withdrew too quickly.[93]

In 2004, Mihai-Aurelian Căruntu published his dissertation The Bukovina in the Second World War, which was supervised by Gheorghe Buzatu. Without any critical distance, Căruntu cites the head of the military intelligence service in 1940 according to whom anti-Romanian elements, predominantly Bolshevik Jews, had designed a detailed plan to support the invasion by the Red Army. Here again, the myth of the Jews Sallo Brun (instead of Josef/Salo Brüll) and Glaubach leading workers' units that killed the director of the prison in Czernowitz is reproduced. In fact, the director was killed by the NKVD. Furthermore, it is claimed that all Jews had supported the repressive Soviet regime in 1940–41. The mass murder of Jews during the conquest of Northern Bukovina in the summer of 1941 is presented as a fight against "Jewish partisans."[94] In a contribution to a volume published by Buzatu in 2011, Căruntu names several Jews who allegedly tried to destabilize the non-occupied Southern Bukovina in August 1940.[95]

The Final Report of the International Commission on the Holocaust in Romania published in 2005 included a short chapter on the Jews in Bessarabia and Northern Bukovina in 1940. It is underlined that the majority of the Jews in the two provinces were shocked by the invasion of the Red Army. Not only young Jews but Ukrainians as well were involved in riots against Romanians during the evacuation phase. The accusa-

---

92 Pelin, Mihai (2008). *Săptămîna patimilor 23–28 iunie 1940. Cedarea Basarabiei şi a nordului Bucovinei*. Bucharest.

93 Văratic 2001, p. 130f.

94 Căruntu 2004, p. 80, pp. 110–113, p. 326f.

95 Căruntu, Mihai Aurelian (2011). Sudul Bucovinei în perioada 3 iulie 1940–22 iunie 1941. O regiune disputată în relaţiile româno-sovieto-germane, in Buzatu, Gheorghe and Corneliu Bileţchi (eds.) (2011). *România sub regimul haosului 1919–1989*. Iaşi, pp. 171–195.

tions against "all the Jews of Bukovina," which one finds in some contemporary documents, were, as the Final Report holds, deliberate exaggerations in order to justify the murder of Jews during the evacuation.[96]

Today, only fringe anti-Semites spread the enemy stereotype of Jewish gangs. Here, I mention only the writer Paul Goma.[97] In 2003, Goma published the booklet *The Red Week. 28 June–3 July 1940. Bessarabia and the Jews*. He simply retells, without indicating the sources, the constructions spread out in the documents of the military authorities. To make them even more dramatic, Goma claims that People's Commissar Sallo Brunn (instead of Brüll) and his deputy Glaubach hunted down fleeing Orthodox priests and theological students.[98]

It is now possible in Romania to proceed legally against such pamphlets. Goma preempted this by denouncing his critics of defamation but lost the trial in 2013. This result raises hopes of a future Romania where such fabricated stories about marauding and murderous Jewish gangs no longer have a place. But the debate on the Internet in the context of the passage of bill 217/2015 on July 27, 2015, which bans the paying of tributes to Fascist legionnaires, underlines that there are still some right-wing radicals left in Romania.

---

96 Final Report 2005, p. 82f.

97 He was one of the few dissidents in Romania and lived in France since his expulsion from Romania due to his criticism of the regime in 1977. He was originally from Bessarabia, and his father was deported by the NKVD.

98 Goma, Paul (2003) *Săptămâna roşie, 28 iunie–3 iulie 1940. Basarabia şi evreii.* Chişinău, p. 72, p. 46.

Henry L. Eaton

The Story Created Afterward: Iaşi 1941

The first victims of the Romanian Holocaust were 311 men, women, and children executed at a place called Stînca Rosnovanu in northeastern Moldavia on June 27, 1941. The second massacre of several thousand Jews began the next evening, June 28, in the nearby city of Iaşi. These killings occurred as Romanian and German military units (Army Group South) were beginning their assault on the Soviet Union, Romania having declared war on June 22, 1941, and, with Germany, crossed the Prut River into Soviet territory in the early morning hours of July 2. The murders were harbingers of what was to come. They were also a culmination of the violent recent past of Romanian anti-Semitism. Five months earlier, the Iron Guard (legionnaires) murdered at least 120 Jews in Bucharest (January 21–23, 1941); two months before that legionnaires murdered eleven Jews in Ploieşti (November 22, 1940), and some five months earlier Romanian soldiers forced by the USSR to vacate Bessarabia and Northern Bukovina murdered well over a hundred Jews in the city of Dorohoi and nearby towns and villages (late June, early July 1940).

In the immediate aftermath of these last murders, some carried out with unspeakable brutality, the killers were turned into victims of a humiliating retreat, bullied out of the area without a fight and in the face of Jews allegedly pleased to see them go. The sympathetic Romanian Christian public showed its support for these soldiers and their crimes in the days following their retreat by committing a rash of murders, commonly shooting Jews or throwing them from moving trains (see Mariana Hausleitner's contribution in this volume).[1] Lucreţiu Patraşcanu put it this way: the "total humiliation" born of the Soviet takeover was cured in a rebirth of nationalism that "meant being anti-Semitic." And the form taken by this nationalism and anti-Semitism: "Bloody hooliganism, officially adopted and accepted as state policy."[2]

1 Stanciu, S. (ed.) (1991). *Martiriul Evreilor din România 1940–1944. Documente şi Mărturii.* Bucharest, pp. 25–39.

2 Patraşcanu, Lucreţiu (1945). *Problemele de Bază ale României.* Bucharest, p. 170.

For the mass killings at Stînca Rosnovanu and Iaşi, we have a number of documents by Romanian military and police officials that tell us something about what happened, but they often are distortions of the truth or outright fictions. One such fiction is Ion Antonescu's communique about the Iaşi pogrom of June 28–29, 1941. The next day, June 30, he announced that 500 Judeo-Communists had been executed for shooting at German and Romanian soldiers in Iaşi. In fact Iaşi Jews did no shooting that day, shot at no one.

On that same day, more than a thousand Iaşi Jews died in the stifling heat of one of the two death trains, murdered by Romanian and German officials and military officers and soldiers who sealed them into crowded boxcars in a train that took some eight hours, on a hot summer day, to travel the 18 miles from Iaşi to Podu Iloaiei. At the same time, hundreds more were dead and dying on the other train as it began a week-long meandering journey south to Călăraşi. Also on June 30 in Iaşi, Romanian soldiers pulled eighteen Jews from a building on I. C. Brătianu St., forced them to lie on the side of the street, and machine-gunned them, including a child and its parents. German soldiers at the scene assisted by killing those who were only wounded.[3] On June 29, the day before Antonescu's announcement, the day of the alleged execution of 500 Jews, many hundreds of Jews were murdered on the streets of Iaşi and in its municipal police station. Clearly, Antonescu's communique was a grotesque lie. But his message was clear: Jews are an enemy and will be eliminated from Romania and its territories, by murdering them if necessary.

The Story Created Afterward applies to any number of official reports made by Romanian military and police officials engaged in the ethnic cleansing of Romanian territory. I came across the phrase near the end of the war crimes indictment issued by the Romanian Public Prosecutor's Office in 1947. Fifty-seven men are listed therein and charged with crimes against "the people" (i.e., Jews) of the city of Iaşi and the Bessarabian towns of Sculeni and Mărculeşti in June and July 1941. The particular "story" has to do with the Romanian 6th Cavalry Regiment's efforts to capture the town of Mărculeşti. In reporting the matter to his 14th Infantry Division superiors, regimental commander Colonel Ermil Matieş created the fiction that the town's Jews were mainly responsible for his

3 Carp, Matatias (1996). *Cartea Neagră* (2nd ed., vol. 2, Pogromul de la Iaşi). Bucharest, p. 153.

unit's losses, which in fact largely resulted from the actions of Soviet troops and mistakes made by his own men. Based on that fiction Matieş justified executing the town's whole Jewish community.[4]

Several days before the mass execution at Mărculeşti, the same men who committed that crime murdered the Jews of Sculeni at a place called Stînca Rosnovanu. Here also Matieş concocted a fiction to justify mass murder. On June 23, a day after Romania declared war on the Soviet Union, units of the 6th Cavalry Regiment joined troops of the German 305 Infantry Regiment in a foray across the Prut River into Soviet Bessarabia, establishing a bridgehead in the town of Sculeni. When Red Army troops pushed back two or three days later, the Germans and Romanians retreated into Romania taking with them the Sculeni townspeople. At a place called Stînca Rosnovanu, Jews were separated from Christians, a work overseen by Gheorge Cimpoeş, a former mayor of Sculeni, "borrowed" from the nearby 27th Artillery Regiment for the purpose.[5] That done, Captain Ioan Stihi and Lieutenant Eugen Mihăilescu took the Jews' valuables, put some of the men to work digging trenches, and then lined all the Jews along these ditches. A witness hidden nearby said he saw "Captain Stihi say something to the Jews who were standing in front of the graves, to which they threw up their arms and shrieked."[6] Then they were machine-gunned. Colonel Matieş ordered the execution, and Stihi, Mihăilescu, Sergeant Mihailov, and the soldier Epure carried it out.[7]

In reporting the execution to the 14th Infantry Division on July 20, 1941, Colonel Matieş claimed he ordered the killing because Sculeni Jews had signaled his troop locations to the Soviets resulting in "many casualties." He also reported that a number of his officers and men had been treacherously shot from behind and from houses and gardens by Jews. To prevent this state of affairs, he reports, "I ordered Capitan Stihi

4 Republica Populară Română, Parchetul Curţii din Bucureşti, Cabinetul Criminalilor de război, dos. Nr. 5260/1947, "Rechizitor [...] pentru cercetarea crimelor săvârşite asupra populaţiei din oraşul Iaşi, Stânca Rosnovanu ş Tg. Mărculeşti în luna iune 1941," in Yad Vashem (YV) Record Group 0-11/73, War Crimes Indictment, p. 49.

5 YV: Indictment, p. 46.

6 The United States Holocaust Memorial Museum Record Group (USHMM RG) 25.004M, reel 46, dos. 108233, vol. 120, Ioan Petraru 1948.

7 Carp 1996, pp. 74–83; YV: Indictment, pp. 44–46.

[...] to arrest and execute all suspect Jews from Sculeni." In this and another report, Matieş claims his order to execute was "in conformity with superior orders."[8] After the war, Matieş said he had nothing to do with either the evacuation or execution of Sculeni Jews and knew nothing about Mărculeşti except what he read in the newspapers. His own official reports and eyewitness testimony proved otherwise.[9]

If Colonel Matieş had superior orders to carry out the execution of the Sculeni Jews on June 27, these orders likely came directly or indirectly from his superior, 14th Infantry Division commander General Stavrescu. The general himself knew beforehand what was to happen to the Jews at Mărculeşti. He arrived there on or about July 16, 1941, just as Captain Stihi and Lieutenant Mihălescu were about to begin the killing. He tried but failed to persuade a young girl to separate herself from the condemned, then left as the shooting began. Some 400 or more Jews were stripped of valuables and outer clothing, lined up ten at a time, and machine-gunned. Men were first, then women and children, their jewelry and money safely stashed in a suitcase Captain Stihi brought for the purpose.[10]

It was no accident that the 6th Cavalry Regiment was stationed close to the Bessarabian towns of Sculeni, Gura Căinari, and Mărculeşti, whose Jewish populations were its first victims, or that the former mayor of Sculeni was nearby. The reason for this hinges on Ion Antonescu turning the Soviet-dictated expulsion of Romania from Bessarabia and Northern Bukovina into a national humiliation that called for revenge. So, when preparing for the invasion of the USSR, he arranged his military units such that those officers and soldiers who had been expelled and humiliated would return the way they had had been forced to leave, men like Stihi, Mihălescu, and Sculeni's former mayor. For these men, the war became a personal vendetta. This was also the case with soldiers of the Romanian 16th Infantry Regiment. During that unit's retreat from Bukovina, its commander, Major Valeriu Carp, encouraged his men to torture and murder several Jews from the village of Ciudei. When Carp's unit returned a year later, during the invasion, his men murdered the rest of

8 Carp 1996, p. 75f.
9 YV: Indictment, pp. 44–51.
10 Ibid., pp. 47–55; USHMM RG 25.004M, reel 48, vol. 25.

the community, some 500 or more Jews.[11] Regarding the Sculeni massacre, Lieutenant-Colonel Mureşanu testified in 1947 that he learned from officers of Matieş' 6th Cavalry Regiment that it was the officers themselves who proposed to Colonel Buck, commander of the German 305 Infantry Regiment, that he authorize a joint attack on Sculeni for the express purpose of revenging themselves on the Jews who had humiliated them, and Colonel Buck agreed.[12]

Here, I want to turn to the Iaşi pogrom, looking at its preparation and then the reports of Iaşi officials to their superiors about the events of June 27–30, 1941. But first, here are some short excerpts from the postwar testimonies of two of those superiors, Professor Mihai Antonescu, vice president of the Romanian Council of Ministers during the war, and Eugen Cristescu, wartime intelligence chief of SSI (Serviciul Special de Informaţii).

> M. Antonescu: I would never claim that the Marshal [dictator Ion Antonescu] was a philosemite. [...] But he did not have in mind the physical destruction of Jews. [...] I know that on the eve of the war, or even at its beginning, in Iaşi there occurred serious incidents. SS military units intervened [...] and legionnaires [...] against the Jews. [...] I must tell you it was not an act organized by the government, nor the army, and not Marshal Antonescu[...] this I say with absolute conviction.[13]
> Cristescu: The S.S.I. did not have, either before or on the days [of the pogrom] 29 and 30 June, a single member in Iaşi.[14]

We do not know precisely when Ion Antonescu decided to begin the campaign of eliminating Jews from Romanian territory. Certainly before June 18, 1941, when a convoy of 160 SSI agents, including its commander Eugen Cristescu, left Bucharest for Iaşi in order to ignite a pogrom in the city. Assisting the enterprise was Colonel Radu Dinulescu, Cristescu's immediate superior and chief of military intelligence (Section II of the Supreme General Staff). Ion Antonescu commanded both agencies. The "Special" 160-man SSI echelon was divided into four teams. Grigore Pe-

11 Mircu, Marius (1945). *Pogromurile din Bucovina şi Dorohoi.* Bucharest, p. 26; Ancel, Jean (ed.) (1986). *Documents Concerning the Fate of Romanian Jewry During the Holocaust (VI).* New York, p. 147.

12 Carp 1996, p. 74f.

13 USHMM RG 25.004M, reel 34, vol. 45, p. 15f.

14 Carp 1996, p. 46.

trovici, whose team arrived first in Iaşi, went to the municipal police station (*Chestura*) most likely to meet with Chief Inspector Chirilovici. On June 26, Lieutenant-Colonel Micandru (chief of SSI's Romanian-German liaison section) and his German partner, Major von Stransky, an *Abwehr* (German military intelligence) agent and member of the German legation in Bucharest, met with General Stavrescu at 14th Infantry Division headquarters. The presence of Stransky almost certainly means that General Salmuth, German commander of the 30th Army Corps, also headquartered in Iaşi, was also informed about the SSI operation.

That legionnaires were to have a role in the operation is indicated by a disturbance in the city on June 27 that brought out the city's garrison commander Colonel Lupu. On his approach, a group of men fled leaving behind several carbines and a machine gun. Two men in civilian clothes, who remained, explained to Lupu they were military officers assigned to prepare legionnaires for rear-area security once the invasion of the Soviet Union began. The two later presented themselves, dressed in military uniforms, to Lupu in his office, embarrassed it seems, for not keeping their mission a secret. In fact the two were SSI officers, Major Tulbure, who headed one team, and Captain Balotescu, who belonged to another.[15] According to the postwar testimony of Lieutenant-Colonel Traian Borcescu, chief of SSI secretarial services, these two officers were especially important in directing the massacre. For its planning, Borcescu points to Junius Lecca, chief of the Counter Intelligence Center in Iaşi, who compiled detailed information about the city's Jewish population, based on which Cristescu "together with Section II of the Supreme General Staff [military intelligence] and with the German command elaborated the plan to carry out the massacre in Iaşi."[16] That the mission of SSI in Iaşi was to assist in the destruction of the city's Jewish community is indicated by its larger mission. After Iaşi, it moved eastward with the invading Axis armies to Kishinev, Tighina, Tiraspol, and Odessa assisting in the destruction of the Jewish communities in those cities.

The arrival in Iaşi of SSI agents coincided with the first murders there. The city was bombed on June 24 and again, this time with much greater effect, on June 26. That same Thursday of the second bombing, on the pretext that signals intended to guide Soviet pilots to their targets came

15 Ibid., p. 55f., p. 63.
16 Ibid., p. 52.

from a Jewish residence, three men were hauled from it, one of whom, Herşcu Wolf, had been injured in the bombing, and escorted by Sergeant Mircea Manoliu and Corporal Nicolau of the 13th Infantry Regiment to the 14th Infantry Division headquarters where they were briefly questioned by two officers and returned to their escort to be taken home. Instead Manoliu and Nicolau took them to an isolated area and Manoliu shot at them, killing one, wounding Wolf, and the other escaping. On the night of June 27–28, Manoliu and Nicolau took five Jews to a military railyard to identify the locations of unexploded bombs and afterward murdered them. On the morning of June 28, Manoliu with other Romanian and some German soldiers began terrorizing residents in a Jewish neighborhood, breaking into and looting homes on the pretext that they were searching for a radio transmitter used to communicate with the enemy. Manoliu was only arrested when a number of police and military officials acted together. He was placed in the custody of 14th Infantry Division Pretor Major Scriban who kept him for a short time and then let him go.[17] Matatias Carp speculated that Manoliu, a legionnaire, had the mission of committing outrageous acts of violence to "test the reaction of those authorities who would not be privy to all the secret preparations."[18] Special mission or not, Manoliu's case and the mass killing by Romanian soldiers, hours before, of Sculeni Jews, including some 45 children, signaled the beginning of state-sponsored genocide.[19]

On this same Saturday, June 28, the city's top police and military officials, or their representatives, having been given some information by SSI agents about what was about to happen, began gathering in the evening at the municipal police station or *Chestura*: Police Chief Chirilovici, his Deputy Inspector Leahu, and other police officers; Colonel Barozzi and Major Scriban (chief pretoral officers of the Romanian 3rd Army and 14th Infantry Division); garrison commander Colonel Lupu; prefect of Iaşi District Colonel Captaru; and others. That they did not know what the SSI planned in every detail is suggested by calls made that day by Deputy Inspector Leahu to District 2 Police Commissioner Sprinceană (and probably to other district commanders as well), first to have the police disarm, later to have them keep their weapons, and later still, not to

17 Ibid., pp. 70–73, p. 90, p. 119.
18 Ibid., p. 20.
19 Ibid., p. 20, pp. 81–83.

interfere in what the army was about to do throughout the city, "be it good or bad."[20] These officials commanded a significant amount of policing power. General Stavrescu, commander of the 14th Infantry Division, had a company of military police in his division as well as combat troops should he need them. Because Iaşi was a staging area for troops preparing to invade Soviet territory (on July 2), the general was chiefly responsible for maintaining order in the city. Next in line of authority was garrison commander Colonel Lupu, whose force numbered several hundred gendarmes. Municipal police chief Chirilovici commanded 451 active and 167 reserve policemen. District Prefect Captaru must also have had a sizable number of gendarmes. That they met on the evening of June 28 and again twice on June 29 indicates their need to cooperate. The question is, cooperation to what end? If it was to orchestrate violence such that Jews would be murdered or evacuated by the thousands and military units kept safe, that was done. Not a single soldier was wounded or killed, it seems.[21]

About 9:30 Saturday evening, June 28, one or two planes launched flares over the darkening city, artificial lighting blanketed or turned off due to the threat of air raids. What follows are very condensed selections of city officials' reports about what was happening in the city:

Regional Inspector of Police E. Giosanu's June 29 telephone call to the director general of police [Leoveanu]:

> Signs of disorder began on the morning of 28 June when Sgt. Manoliu, a legionnaire of the 13th Infantry Regiment, and other Romanian and German soldiers, told by Manoliu that radio signals were being sent out from a Jewish neighborhood, began aggressively searching houses there and severely treating residents. Various top officials and city police arrested Manoliu and the other Romanian soldiers and delivered them to the 14th Infantry Division Pretor [Scriban] for his investigation. Thus calm was restored to the city.
>
> At 10 p.m. on 28 June [following the aerial flares and air-raid sirens] police were informed of automatic weapons' fire all along the most important troop routes and all local military units were so informed, especially Gen. Stavrescu who sent out reinforcements to units already on patrol. Despite the intense fire from automatic weapons and searches conducted by police, soldiers, and Germans, not one Jew was discovered shooting. At daybreak, conforming to Stavrescu's order a search of Jewish residences was undertaken without finding any hostile weapons.

20 Ibid., p. 69.

21 Ibid., pp. 62–64, p. 65, pp. 89–91, pp. 123–25.

> In the meantime German and Romanian troops were attacking and plundering Jews. Of those not murdered, some 2,500 were arrested and taken to the Chestura, General Stavrescu intending to evacuate them from the city. Germans said Jews should be killed. Everyone claimed they were Communists capable of helping the Russians. Some Germans said if the shooting continued Jewish districts would be bombed. There is urgent need [complains Giosanu, probably wanting Col. Lupu replaced] for a superior authority to establish order that will calm people down.

Giosanu's second telephone call on June 29 to the director general of police [Leoveanu]: at 10:30 in the evening of June 28–29:

> Jew-Communists, with a very weak contingent of Romanian Communists, fired many automatic weapons in Iaşi with a two-fold aim of provoking panic and disrupting troops on the march. At present 1,000 persons, almost all Jews, have been arrested. A few are dead and a few wounded.

Giosanu's report to the director general on July 2:

> Much shooting the night of 28–29 June, presumed to be the work of Judeo-communists. Despite the intense all-night search for shooters none were found. In the morning Gen. Stavrescu ordered that Jews be sent to prison camps, assuming they had caused the panic in the service of the USSR. The order was executed by District Prefect [Captaru], Garrison Commander [Lupu], and numerous police. On the morning of 1 July I reported to the Director General that the trains carrying Jews stopped in Tg. Frumos and Podu Iloaiei. So far there are hundreds of dead Jews and those gravely wounded in Iaşi suffering without medical care in freight cars. German soldiers are joined by Romanian soldiers in killing Jews. Murdering and robbing also carried out by Public Guardians [police]. Arrest of Jews was ordered by the Division [Gen. Stavrescu], carried out by organs of the Chestura [Iaşi police], and their transport by rail. It was a complicated operation under German pressure. German troops are mixed up in everything. What we can affirm is that on the night of 28–29 June a fierce hostility towards Jews grew first among Germans and later among Romanian soldiers in the belief Jews were in league with the Russians. I do not know how many died on the trains. We could not prevent the operation.[22]

Deputy Inspector of Iaşi Police Gheorghe Leahu, "Declaration" on July 2, 1941:

22 Ibid., pp. 71–73, p. 86f., pp. 109–111.

> Because of the bombing of 26 June, the destruction, public agitation, and blackout at night, soldiers and police patrolled the streets. Germans especially hostile towards Jews: shooting, robbing, beating. The general hostility towards Jews is born of Romanian contact with Germans. In the city were Romanian military units in transit as well as individuals who had abandoned their mission and given themselves to mistreating those being taken to the Chestura, or shooting them in the street. Civilians also attacked them, convinced Communists and Jews had begun the shooting. Germans were especially angry that some taken to the Chestura were freed. Jews were bludgeoned and robbed at the Chestura gates. A formation Todt [Death's Head unit] stationed itself there robbing, clubbing, and shooting Jews as they were bought in. There were about 3,500 Jews in the Chestura when the Germans began to massacre them.[23]

Prefect of Iaşi District Colonel Dumitru Captaru, note to General Stavrescu, June 29, 1941, marked "urgent":

> Sgt. Manoliu of the 13 Infantry Regiment has murdered 6 Jews "without orders from above". Please inquire and notify the Prefect in order that it be known to the Minister of Internal Affairs.

Captaru to minister of internal affairs, June 29:

> Lots of shooting alarming German and Romanian units and the civil population, producing a great panic. One German soldier badly wounded. The culprits are not found. I believe the shooting is the work of some organized persons who want to cause panic as much among German and Romanian units as in the city's population. Up until now indications are that certain persons have tried to throw suspicion on the city's Jews aiming to arouse German and Romanian units and Christians against them leading towards their mass murder. Sgt. Manoliu and Corp. Nicolau, known legionnaires, have murdered 6 Jews without any authority from above.

Captaru to minister of internal affairs, July 2:

> First, regarding events of 28–29 June, much shooting throughout the night; German officers and soldiers angered by nearby shooting. Shots have come from Jewish residences and Jews using blankets have signaled enemy planes. In one such instance Sgt. Manoliu with a number of soldiers under his command searched the houses but failed to catch the guilty. Also information has come to the Chestura about signal lights appearing in areas where Jews live, probably intended to contact enemy agents and signal enemy planes. On 29 June people (Jews mostly) taken to the Chestura from houses from which shots were fired. By firing weapons they intended to produce panic in both German and Romanian units and in the city's population aiming to benefit the enemy. In conclusion: the trouble of 28–29 June was provoked

---

23 Ibid., pp. 115–118.

by Jews, most of whom are Communists, and a few Christian Communists. Their aim was to cause disturbance in the area near the front and thus aid the enemy.

Captaru, extract from a court deposition of May 20, 1947, regarding the death trains:

I asked the Minister of Interior to send strong units of infantry and cavalry to Iaşi to maintain order and at the same time to replace the Garrison Commander [Lupu] with a more competent officer. On 29 June at 2 p.m. Chirilovici told me that the Germans had occupied the Chestura and said it was urgent that the Jews be evacuated from Iaşi especially those arrested, believing that otherwise they would all be shot. I took this course [arranging the evacuation] because of what I believed the Germans were capable. I was with General Stavrescu at the Chestura and saw stretched out along the courtyard wall a large number of Jews who had been shot to death. Evacuation of those at the Chestura was made on the basis of the decision of Stavrescu and by order of the Minister of the Interior and because of the threatening attitude of the Germans who would have shot all those arrested and held in the Chestura. I told Mihai Antonescu that regarding the Jews I had not found proof of guilt and it is necessary to be diligent to prevent their arrests. I believe the rebellion was organized by Germans augmented also by legionnaire elements.[24]

General Gheorghe Stavrescu, commander of the 14th Infantry Division, headquartered in Iaşi at the time of the pogrom, and having final authority in the city over military and police matters, to the minister of interior by telegram on June 29, 1941:

Some 40 enemy planes shot down [air raid on 26 June?] and among the captured pilots are two from Iaşi. Others have probably come down safely and made contact with Judeo-Communists in the city and it is these who, about 8 p.m. on 28 June began to terrorize townspeople, firing revolvers and machine-pistols but without visible effect; shooting continued until 9 a.m. without there being even three victims. German soldiers and Romanian gendarmes have pulled Jews out of houses from which shots were fired and hauled them to the Chestura where the guilty have been executed on the spot. I have put a stop to the killing in the Chestura.[25]

General Stavrescu's postwar deposition July 7, 1945:

Military duties made it impossible for me to carry out my garrison duties. Germans were mainly responsible for searches and arrests and they took over the Chestura. I went to the Chestura and stopped the brutality there and got Gen. Salmuth to pull German soldiers out. When I visited the Chestura I saw those trying to leave shot. I

24 Ibid., p. 71, pp. 89–91, pp. 104–108, pp. 123–125.

25 Ibid., pp. 64–66, p. 67, pp. 102–104.

> told the personnel there that it was not a good idea to crowd so many Jews into the Chestura and to release all those who are within the law. On that day of 29 June I was three times at the Chestura. When I asked some of my own soldiers convoying prisoners, who gave them the order to do that, they said Germans. I saw corpses in the Chestura courtyard. I intervened to stop a German from beating an old man and invited the Germans to leave and some did. I went to Salmuth to make sure his orders for Germans to leave the Chestura were followed. Also I ordered that those being held there illegally be freed.[26]

The director general of state security, General Emanoil Leoveanu, was ordered by Ion Antonescu to personally investigate the events in Iaşi, policing in particular, for the period June 27 to July 1. There are two such reports dated July 2, 1941, numbered 53, and bearing the same signature, Leoveanu.

Leoveanu report of July 2 (original, earlier version?):

> I. History of Events: 1) On 28 June, about 9:30 p.m. were heard the firing of arms in different parts of Iaşi. The shooting continued until 7 the next morning. 2) During the night policemen began investigating an area with other Romanian units merging on Lăpuşneanu St. where they came under a similar attack with the same effect (the troops under attack exchanging fire). They immediately formed a team of police, agents, and guardians plus the 14th Police Company of the 14th Division, a strong assembly with which to search the area from which the shooting came. On this occasion they arrested and took to the Chestura Jews found hidden in cellars. Some of the Jews who resisted and made trouble were executed by German soldiers at the location and on the streets going towards the Chestura. 3) On 29 June at 8:30 p.m. the Chestura organized Jews to be moved to the train station by a detachment of 20 policemen. At the station they were loaded on the train and sent towards the town of Roman. 4) During the days of June 30 and July 1 there was a bit of shooting in different parts of Iaşi, but of no importance.
> II. Findings: German Captain Hoffmann affirmed to me that some 20 German non-commissioned officers and soldiers have been wounded or killed, shot by Jews.
> III. Conclusions: 1) These attacks have been organized and executed by the Jewish population for revenge. 2) Police officials and their subordinates did excellent work.[27]

Leoveanu, July 2, 1941, report (later, claimed authentic by Leoveanu?):

> I. History of Events: 1) On the morning of 28 June Iaşi police were informed that Romanian and German soldiers were searching and mistreating people in the [mainly Jewish] district of Tătăraşi. Police Chief Chirilovici and Garrison Commander Lupu went there and found 8 to 10 gravely injured Jews who were taken to the hospital. It

26 Ibid.

27 USHMM RG 25.004M, reel 45, dos. 10823, vol. 64.

> was established that Sgt. Mircea Manoliu and other soldiers of the Romanian 13th Infantry Regiment joined by soldiers of the 24th Artillery Regiment had searched and badly treated the Jews there, aided by a German unit on the pretext of locating a radio transmitter. At this time it was discovered that this Sgt. Manoliu, a legionnaire from Dorohoi, had shot 5 Jews near the firing range of the Iaşi Garrison and let free after an inquiry by [Major Scriban] Pretor of the 14th Infantry Division. The sergeant must be tried by a Military Court.
> II. Findings. 1) No wounded or dead among Romanian units and no evidence of bullets striking walls of houses or breaking windows. 2) German Captain Hoffmann, said there were 20 German officers and soldiers who had been killed or wounded but that it was not permitted for a foreigner to inspect the places where this happened. However, Major Fărcaş, the Romanian liaison officer with the German 189th Division told me that had there been such casualties Gen. Rötti would have certainly informed the Chestura.
> III. Conclusions. 1) I don't think any Germans were killed or wounded, the attacks having been simulated with stage-prop weapons, which the evidence supports, and with fire crackers to simulate automatic weapons' fire. I believe the attackers were legionnaires and thieves who aimed at producing panic in order to pillage. They easily vanished in the dark and organized their attacks in Jewish districts. 2) Regarding the actions of the Police I believe they acted entirely as duty required.[28]

Leoveanu: declaration before a public prosecutor on July 7, 1945, regarding his investigation of events in Iaşi at the end of June 1941:

> On 29 June 1941 the Interior Minister told me that in Iaşi some very grave events had occurred caused by the police who set going a pogrom against the Jewish population and that Gen. Antonescu has ordered me to go to Iaşi immediately to make an inquiry and establish the guilt of those who were the cause. I left immediately, arriving on July 1 and began an inquiry. From it I concluded that this was a provocation planned by the Germans who staged an attack on the military. This is indicated by cartridges found on the street, those used in the kind of pistol called Flobert which cannot fire further than 3 to 4 meters. Furthermore, not one soldier was killed or even slightly wounded. I noted that Jews were dragged from their houses and taken to the Chestura on the days of the massacre, carried out by the city police together with garrison troops in the city and led by commanding officers. After my inquiry I concluded with certainty that in the pogrom carried out against the Jewish population legionnaires were also involved, legionnaires who cooperated with the police and with other groups in the city.

Leoveanu: "Declaration in reference to the massacre of June 1941 in Iaşi. Given on 17 May 1948":

28 Carp 1996, pp. 118–121.

> I. On 2 July 1941 I was in Iaşi to make an inquiry ordered by the Leader [Ion Antonescu] through the Minister of Interior [D. Popescu] with a view of establishing the actions of the police in the massacre [...]. The duration of the investigation was 3.5 hours, the German commander having ordered me to leave Iaşi. The conclusions arrived at in this brief time [...] are precisely that: THE JEWS DID NOT ATTACK GERMAN AND ROMANIAN TROOPS.
> II. From 2 July 1941 until the present; from what has been learned [...] I am left with the following impressions. [...] 1) The massacre in Iaşi in 1941 could not have taken place without approval of the top leadership of the state [...] Gen. I. Antonescu [...] and Vice President Mihai Antonescu [...] who tried to justify it based on the communique of the President of the Council of Ministers [Ion Antonescu] on 1 July 1941 [announced on 30 June and published in Monitorul Oficial , #153, 1 July 1941, that 500 Iaşi Judeo-Communists had been executed for firing on German and Romanian troops] whereby Jews bear the guilt of the massacre; could not have taken place without actions by the Germans and their Nazi doctrine which calls for the extermination of Jews, and without the collaboration, probably, of the [...] Special Information Service whose chief was Eugen Cristescu. 2) Carrying out the massacre presumes the participation of legionnaires and deserters from the front; locals who were convinced that Soviet pilots were guided by signals, from Jews, to bomb Christian districts; German troops and Death's Head units; probably some police units from other localities [Bessarabia and N. Bukovina from which they were expelled in June 1940], waiting to follow the troops in the event of their advance eastward, and hooligans who profited from the chaos in Iaşi by plundering.
> III) Responsibility. Principally responsible are the cadres belonging to the superior organs of leadership listed above. Local authorities: District Prefect [Col. Captaru] and Garrison Commander [Col. Lupu] are guilty. Alternatively, those who had prior knowledge of the organization of this massacre, they are totally guilty. I suppose those who did not have this prior knowledge are totally responsible if they did not do something when they witnessed the first massacres, whatever their condition: indolence, apathy, even disabilities.[29]

The first (June 29) local official reports of the Iaşi pogrom generally cast Jews or Judeo-Communists as instigating panic and disrupting troop movement through the city in order to assist the Russians. Later reports tend to shift the blame increasingly toward German soldiers, angry at being shot at and convinced Jews were an enemy, and to a lesser degree toward legionnaires, motivated by hatred and the chance to pillage. In postwar depositions, city officials generally claim they tried to maintain order and stop the killing, and fault other officials for their own failings. Perhaps their most lasting misrepresentation was accusing Germans and their legionnaire toadies as the principal villains. This became the standard myth. Not least in promoting this idea was the court that tried

29 USHMM RG25004M, reel 44, dos. 108233, vol. 53.

these officials. Germans were responsible for the pogrom; Romanian officials failed to stop them, or at worst helped pave their way.

Police Inspector Giosanu reported that the fierce hostility toward Jews grew first among Germans and later among Romanian soldiers. He expresses concern for Jews on the train to Podu Iloaiei but claims he could not prevent their murder.

Prefect Captaru appears at first to realize that the initial shootings in the city were intended to throw suspicion on Jews and to bring about their mass murder, which had to be prevented by any means. He also wanted the murderer Sergeant Manoliu arrested. But in a later report Captaru claims Jews were using blankets and lights to signal enemy planes and Sergeant Manoliu acted properly trying to catch them. In his postwar testimony, the prefect claims he managed the evacuation of Jews to save them from being murdered and because he had no proof of their guilt. He shifted blame for initiating the crisis from Jews to Germans and legionnaires. But that he was dedicated to saving Jews by evacuation is hardly credible. He had 50 freight cars available for the first train of 2,530 Jews (51 per car) but used only 35 (72 per car), and for the second train, he had 34 cars for 1,902 Jews (56 per car) but used only 18 (105 per car). Approximately, of the 4,432 Jews entrained, 2,713 died.[30]

General Stavrescu said he could not keep order in the city because of his military duties. He did not point out in his postwar defense, however, that he contributed to the disorder by publishing an incendiary piece in the Iaşi paper *Prutul* on June 27, the day after Soviet bombers hit the city hard. He asked citizens to help authorities catch malefactors and alarmists and warned that "those in the service of the enemy will receive capital punishment." Every Iaşi reader would have known that Jews were the target of his remarks. That same day he ordered the city's Jewish leaders to meet with Police Chief Chirilovici to be told that the general accused their community of signaling enemy planes, and benefited thereby, and required them to turn in to police any equipment that could be used to help the enemy.[31] Stavrescu did visit the *Chestura* three times on June 29 but his claim that he stopped the killing there is not true.

The postwar court that tried the general made a distinction between those who "effectively realized" (planned and ignited) the pogrom (e.g.,

30 YV: Indictment, pp. 36–44.

31 Carp 1996, p. 67f.

SSI agents and their superiors) and those, like Stavrescu, who "effectively participated in accomplishing it." The general failed to maintain order, allowed his own soldiers to compete with Germans and legionnaires in terrorizing Jews, and continued to plague Jews with searches for weapons though none were found and not one German or Romanian soldier was either wounded or killed. In this way, reads the indictment, General Stavrescu fostered the massacre and brought the Hitlerist aims of exterminating Jews to Iaşi.[32] The court apparently did not believe the visit of top SSI officers with the general before the pogrom made him one of their partners, placing him also in the "effectively realized" group.

Regarding the two July 2, 1941, reports of the director general of state security Emanoel Leoveanu, Jean Ancel proposes that the original was reported at the time and the revised created later (during 1944) to better serve government leaders facing the possibility of postwar trial. Another example are two July 2 reports by Police Chief Chirilovici both numbered 99,[33] one a copy of the original that surfaced after the original had been destroyed, and the other a forgery. Ancel claims Ion Antonescu initiated the scheme of forgeries and suggests that SSI chief Cristescu may have been the principal author of the bogus reports. Ancel also proposes that other July 2, 1941, reports, those by Chirilovici, Leahu, Giosanu, and Captaru, are doctored versions, the originals successfully destroyed. The key problem for the administration was how to shed responsibility for the Iaşi pogrom. In his "authentic" July 2 report, Leoveanu claimed Jews "organized and executed" the attacks that began the pogrom. That lie worked in 1941 but would be counted absurd in a postwar courtroom.

According to Ancel, General Antonescu made up a story that legionnaire soldiers (Sergeant Manoliu comes to mind) influenced by German troops and urged on by legion sympathizers among civilians as well as criminals initiated the massacre with the participation of some isolated Romanian soldiers acting on their own. Romanian officials' efforts to prevent the massacre were stymied, so the story goes, by the Germans. Official records that played a different tune, those of SSI, for example,

32 YV: Indictment, p. 16f.

33 Carp 1996, p. 87, p. 111.

were destroyed. [34] The edited story didn't save Antonescus or the Governor of Transnistria Alexianu or Deputy Interior Minister Vasiliu from executions. It may have substantially reduced the punishment of other mass murderers. Those who didn't die in prison were released by 1962.[35]

What the edited story did serve successfully was the idea that Romania was not responsible for the mass killing of Iaşi Jews and by extension the Jews in territories it governed during the war: Bukovina, Bessarabia, and Transnistria (the area between the Dniester and Bug rivers). It was adopted by national leaders, school teachers, historians, and deniers generally to keep alive the idea that Romania had no Holocaust. I witnessed this denial in the National Theater building in Iaşi in late June 1991 where Elie Wiesel gave a memorial address on the 50th anniversary of the Iaşi pogrom. He had spoken a few words when a woman in the front row called him a liar. He waited until she was escorted out and then continued.

The woman was not out of place in that building. Like many monuments in Iaşi, the National Theater has its connection to anti-Semitism. It is named after the poet-playwright Vasile Alecsandri, one of Romania's founders, respected for his poetry and regarded as the father of Romanian drama. His play *The Village Bloodsuckers* was being performed in Bucharest in 1866 when lawmakers there were creating a constitution for the newly emerging Romania state. Among their concerns was whether or not the law should grant citizenship to resident Jews. Mihail Kogălniceanu, one of the most important fathers of the new state, advised those lawmakers to see Alecsandri's play and to deny citizenship to Jews, and deny they did. This rejection of citizenship is the grandfather of Romania's anti-Semitic legislation. Alecsandri's bigger-than-life statue fronts the Iaşi theater building. There is, on the other hand, a life-sized pedestal-mounted bust of Avram Goldfaden, "father" of Yiddish theater, among the statues of prominent Romanian theater artists that ring the building. It is a reminder that the city once had a large and lively-spirited Jewish population.

---

34 Ancel, Jean (2005). *Preludiu la assasinat: Pogromul de la Iaşi, 29 Iuni 1941*. Iaşi, p. 415f.

35 Ioanid, Radu (2000). *The Holocaust in Romania*. Chicago, p. 287.

Alti Rodal

A Village Massacre: The Particular and the Context

The Borivtsi massacre

Etti (Yitte) and Iosif (Yossel) Preminger, a young Jewish couple, survived the July 1941 massacre that took the lives of some 150 Jews from their village Borivtsi and the adjoining village Kyseliv in the Kitsman district (rayon) of Northern Bukovina, near the border with Galicia, about 44 kilometers northwest of Czernowitz/Chernivtsi (hereafter Chernivtsi). In this massacre, they lost their parents, siblings, and extended family, which included the three grandparents of this author. Armed Ukrainians, whom they knew personally, appeared at their door in the late afternoon and ordered them to step outside. They were escorted to a small lake in the midst of fields on the outskirts of the village, where groups of Jews had already been assembled. There they were shot. Etti was hit by a bullet in the leg, just as she saw her 18-year-old friend, Tontze, fall into the water, lifeless. An uncle (who along with his wife and four of his children did not survive the massacre) is remembered shouting just before he collapsed, "Run, children, run!" Though wounded, Etti did run to the surrounding fields. She will later discover that her husband and two others also escaped.

Etti hid in the tall grasses until nighttime and then began walking, bloodied and in a daze. At dawn, she overheard one of the Ukrainians who had herded the Jews toward the lake ask a local girl if she has seen any Jews in the vicinity. Etti's memories, described in 2001, are of being engulfed by a thick cloud, and then soaked by a heavy downpour. A young Ukrainian in a wagon drove her to the village of Verechanka, about 8 kilometers away, where her aunt lived, but she found the house empty and all the furniture piled up outside. Two Ukrainians then brought her in their wagon to Zastavna, the next town, to the home of her cousins (the parents of this author), to whom she relayed the news that their parents, siblings, and extended family had been massacred. Shortly thereafter, her husband Iosif joined her. They stayed with the cousins for three months, before all were deported to camps in Transnistria, where, with the help of many small acts of kindness from local peasants, they somehow survived three harsh winters, hunger, typhus, and more.[1]

Etti and Iosif lived to bear witness to the July 1941 massacre of the Jews of Borivtsi at a military tribunal trial of three of the alleged perpetrators in December 1944 in Chernivtsi. Both at the pretrial interrogations and at the trial itself, they had to confront the three defendants, whom they knew well from the village. Etti's testimony also appears in a July 4, 1945, document of the Soviet Extraordinary State Commission to Investigate Crimes of Nazi Invaders and Their Collaborators (henceforth ESC). Attached to this document are lists of the victims of the massacre.[2]

Scope of this study and sources used

The purpose of this contribution is threefold: (a) to provide an account of the specific events and circumstances related to the massacre of almost all the Jews in the village of Borivtsi in July 1941; (b) to consider whether the 1941 events in Borivtsi reflect a pattern characteristic of similar events across rural Northern Bukovina at that time; and (c) to treat the role of the Organization of Ukrainian Nationalists (OUN), alongside Romanians and Germans, or otherwise, in these events.

This article draws to a significant degree from Soviet sources, including ESC records; highly detailed records of interrogations conducted in

---

1 The Premingers shared their tale of survival with this author on a number of occasions since the late 1960s, including in a videotaped interview in Yiddish in 2001. The interview notes and video are in the author's personal archives.

2 State Archive of the Russian Federation (GARF), 7021-79-76-0065, ark. 39–39ob. The ESC records—which include lists of perpetrators and victims, maps of massacre sites, and records of interrogation of alleged perpetrators and witnesses—were eventually stored in Fonds 7021 of the GARF in Moscow. Yad Vashem microfilmed these records in 1990. The United States Holocaust Memorial Museum (USHMM) obtained copies of the Yad Vashem microfilms on 27 reels and created a town index to 1,450 localities in 1995. In 2008 the USHMM acquired an additional large body of documentation relating to pretrial interrogations and trials in Soviet Ukraine in 1944–45. Research for this article has focused largely on the latter records relating to events in Borivtsi, held at the Archives of the Security Services of Ukraine for the Chernivtsi region (AUSBUChO). These documents are also available at the USHMM Archives, RG-31-018M, Reel 85. Archivists at the USHMM were not able to confirm whether a similar body of documentation exists for the adjoining village Kyseliv.

connection with the 1941 events in Borivtsi by Soviet officials with fourteen alleged perpetrators, three Jewish witnesses and five Ukrainian witnesses (described as "Soviet activists"); and the records of Soviet military tribunal trials in which seven of the alleged perpetrators of the Borivtsi crimes were convicted and sentenced.

An important question relates to the reliability of the Soviet sources. Might the Soviet officials who conducted the interrogations or prepared the documents have entered false information into the records in order to incriminate particular Ukrainian nationalists viewed as a political threat to the regime? A critical approach to Soviet sources is indeed warranted, given the nature of Soviet interrogation techniques and motivations.[3] To address this concern, research for this article has included the following measures: (a) a critical textual analysis of the documents to identify inconsistencies and other signs of doctoring of records, as well as details unlikely to have been invented; (b) cross-referencing with other sources that may either corroborate or raise questions about the accounts in these documents—including memoirs and oral testimonies of survivors and other witnesses;[4] and (c) comparing the circumstances, events, and actors described in these documents with other relevant accounts for the region more broadly, such as *Yizkor* (memorial) books[5] for nearby towns

3 On the history and workings of the Extraordinary Commission: Sorokina, Marina (2005). People and Procedures: Toward a History of the Investigation of Nazi Crimes in the USSR, *Kritika: Explorations in Russian and Eurasian History* 6(4): 797–831. Sorokina argues that the Commission's primary purpose was to deflect attention from the Soviet Union's own war crimes and to publicize Nazi atrocities, as part of a Soviet propaganda campaign.

4 In addition to oral interviews with the Premingers and other surviving family members, this author conducted videotaped interviews with Christian villagers in Kyseliv and Borivtsi in July/August 2001 (five years before the French priest, Patrick Desbois, adopted a similar approach in order to identify mass grave sites in Ukraine and elsewhere in Eastern Europe). The videotapes of these interviews are in the author's personal archives and have also been donated to the Yahad–In Unum archives in Paris.

5 In the 1950s, survivors who settled in Israel or the West, with the help of their *Landsmanshaften*, embarked on a project to create books to commemorate their destroyed communities. Many of these Yizkor (Memorial) Books ("Yizker bikher" in Yiddish) for Ukraine have been translated into English and may be accessed through the Jewish genealogy website: http://kehilalinks.jewishgen.org/Ukraine.html. Yizkor books and memoirs consulted for this article include those for Horodenka (20 km from Borivtsi)—*Sefer Hordenka* by Meyer Sukher; *My Walk Through Seven Levels of Hell* by Reuben Prifer; and *In the Time of Murder* by Chaim Karl Kaufman.

and villages (as none exist for these particular two villages), and with authoritative, published research on the broader context and patterns of violence for Northern Bukovina in the summer of 1941. Such research and writing has deepened significantly and expanded since the mid-2000s, following the publication of the Final Report of the International Commission on the Holocaust in Romania and the territories Romania controlled, and new research by Ukrainian and Western scholars, based on documentation in Ukrainian archives that has become accessible since the 1990s.[6]

The documentary record

There are two sets of Soviet documents relating to the Borivtsi events: the interrogation and trial records (dated May 1944 to January 1945) and

6 International Commission on the Holocaust in Romania (2005). *Final Report*. Iași. Other published works consulted for this article include: Ancel, Jean (2011). *The History of the Holocaust in Romania*. Lincoln/Jerusalem; Fostii, Ivan (2000). Diial'nist' OUN na Bukovyni u 1940–1941rr. [Activities of the OUN in Bukovina in 1940–1941], *Z arkhiviv VUChK-HPU-NKVD-KGB* 2–4: 454–471; Fostii, Ivan (2005). *Pivnichna Bukovyna i Khotynshchyna u Druhii svitovii viini* [Northern Bukovina and the Khotyn Region during the Second World War]. Chernivtsi; Geissbühler, Simon (2014). "He spoke Yiddish like a Jew": Neighbors' Contribution to the Mass Killing of Jews in Northern Bukovina and Bessarabia, July 1941, *Holocaust and Genocide Studies* 28(3): 430–449; Geissbühler, Simon (2013). *Blutiger Juli: Rumäniens Vernichtungskrieg und der vergessene Massenmord an den Juden 1941*. Paderborn; Golczewski, Frank (2008). Shades of Grey: Reflections on Jewish-Ukrainian and German-Ukrainian Relations in Galicia, in Brandon, Ray and Wendy Lower (eds.). *The Shoah in Ukraine: History, Testimony, Memorialization*. Bloomington/Indianapolis, pp. 114–155; Himka, John-Paul (1997). Ukrainian Collaboration in the Extermination of the Jews during the Second World War: Sorting Out the Long-Term and Conjunctural Factors, www.zwoje-scrolls.com/zwoje16/text11.htm (originally in *Studies in Contemporary Jewry* 13/1997: 170–189); Ioanid, Radu (2000). *The Holocaust in Romania: The Destruction of Jews and Gypsies under the Antonescu Regime, 1940–1944*. Chicago; Solonari, Vladimir (2007). Patterns of Violence: The Local Population and the Mass Murder of Jews in Bessarabia and Northern Bukovina, July-August 1941, *Kritika: Explorations in Russian and Eurasian History* 8(4): 749–787; Solonari, Vladimir (2010). *Purifying the Nation: Population Exchange and Ethnic Cleansing in Nazi-Allied Romania*. Washington/Baltimore; Struve, Kai (2012) Rites of Violence? The Pogroms of Summer 1941, *Polin* 24: 257–274; Struve, Kai (2013). Tremors in the Shatter-Zone of Empires: Eastern Galicia in Summer 1941, in Bartov, Omer and Eric D. Weitz (eds.). *Shatterzone of Empires*. Bloomington, pp. 463–484; Struve, Kai (2015). *Deutsche Herrschaft, ukrainischer Nationalismus, antijüdische Gewalt. Der Sommer 1941 in der Westukraine*. München.

ESC records (July 1945). The latter indicate that a small number of Germans and Romanians were involved in the 1941 massacres in the entire Kitsman district, Chernivtsi region (which includes Kyseliv, Borivtsi, and Zastavna). A German commander named Hess is described as being in charge of an SS unit responsible for the execution of nineteen Soviet "peaceful citizens" in the town of Kitsman (22 kilometers southeast of Borivtsi); eleven Romanian gendarmes of various ranks are said to have been responsible for assisting or participating in various executions in the area, of whom two are accused of beating and torturing residents of Kyseliv and Borivtsi. One of the two is further accused of leading the execution of forty-six residents of Kyseliv. The ESC document also lists thirty-five Ukrainians, of whom eleven are said to have rounded up, tortured, or participated in the killings of the residents of Kyseliv. Another ten are named as having participated in the massacre of forty-five people in Borivtsi; and nine as having been involved in the round-ups and execution of seventeen residents of Kitsman.[7]

A related ESC document states that the execution of the Soviet activists in Borivtsi took place on July 27, 1941, and that the massacre of the Jews took place on the night of July 29–30, 1941. These dates correlate neither with the dates indicated in the records of interrogation nor with the witness and survivor testimonies, all of which place the crimes three or four days after the Soviets retreated from the area around July 3. These and several other inconsistencies may be due to errors (deliberate or not) in the ESC documents, or they may reflect changed perspectives—a shift from detailed information-gathering by interrogators, very shortly after the return of Soviet authorities to the region in preparation for specific trials, to an emerging postwar perspective colored by new priorities, which included playing down both the ethnicity of the victims and the role of local collaborators.

The ESC documents, however, do contain several handwritten lists of victims of the executions of the massacres in Kyseliv and Borivtsi, which clearly indicate Jewish surnames. The different lists overlap to some extent and include variations in spelling and the number of victims

7 "Act of the Extraordinary State Commission, 9 July 1945," in USHMM Archives, RG-22-002M, reel 15, folder 76, pp. 15–19.

listed. A consolidated list adds up to approximately 150 Jewish and 5 non-Jewish Ukrainian victims.[8]

In contrast with the ESC documents, the interrogation and trial records yield a detailed and largely coherent picture of the July 1941 events, offering insights into both the external factors and the internal dynamics at the local level that led to the massacre. Reconstructing a narrative based on these records, however, is challenging. One needs to wade through hundreds of pages of statements and follow a maze of names of some fifty alleged perpetrators. Of these, fourteen were interrogated multiple times. Their statements are not always consistent. Different perspectives are found in the testimonies of the "Soviet activists" (who were also local non-Jewish Ukrainians) and the few Jewish witnesses. The task is to extract from the dispersed fragments of information a coherent story that also captures significant details and nuances.

There are four main lines of questioning in the records of interrogation, prioritized as follows: (a) What connection did the alleged perpetrators have with the OUN and what were the practical activities of the OUN in the region? (b) Who planned and carried out the July 1941 execution of the Soviet activists? (c) Who planned and carried out the July 1941 massacre of the Jews of Borivtsi? And (d) what happened to the property of the Jewish victims?

A representative sample of the responses to the aforementioned questions, from the perspectives of the Jewish witnesses, the alleged perpetrators, and other non-Jewish witnesses, is set out below. This sample offers a glimpse into the questioning techniques of the Soviet interrogators and the inherent drama, as interrogations with individuals are interspersed with in-person confrontations between the alleged perpetrators themselves as well as with the main witnesses.

8 Handwritten versions of these lists are at the GARF, f. r-7021, op.79, d.76, l.64, l.66. Interviews with the two survivors and extended family of the Borivtsi victims since the late 1960s suggest that these are partial lists, as the names of a number of known victims are not included.

Testimony of the Jewish witnesses, 1944–45

Etti and Iosif Preminger were interrogated separately by Soviet officials in Chernivtsi in June and November 1944 in connection with the investigation of three alleged perpetrators—Dmytro Bakhur, Todor Fedoriak, and Stepan Prodanchuk. Etti described the July 1941 events as follows:

> In July 1941, on the fourth day [according to Iosif's testimony, it was the third day] after the retreat of the Red Army from Borivtsi, Ukrainian nationalists organized the killing by shooting of the Jewish population of the village. I know this because on the day of the shooting, at around 5 in the afternoon, the following men armed with guns entered our house: Stepan Korbashevs'kyi, Todor Bakhur, Todor Fedoriak, Ivan Hordii and Heorhii Kravchuk. They ordered my husband and me to follow them and did not allow us to take any belongings. As we exited the house, I noticed Prodanchuk standing near the rock, armed with a gun. After that, these men led us to the outskirts of the village. When my husband and I came within sight of the lake Bul'bon, we saw that several Jewish families were already gathered there. Others continued to arrive from all sides, escorted by armed men, their hands tied with barbed wire or a cord. After a group of about 23 of us had been gathered, we were escorted to the shore of the lake by armed individuals, including Ivan Grevul', Mykola Fedoriak, Todor Fedoriak, Petro Bakhur, Stepan Prodanchuk, and others whose names I cannot remember. On the way to the lake, I asked Todor Fedoriak: "Where are you taking us? Let me go. What bad have I done to you?" He responded: "Go to Stalin. You wanted Soviet government." The Jews were ordered to stand facing the lake. I heard those who were escorting us say jokingly: "Yids, go drink some water." And then, following an order, they opened fire. As a result, 19 people in our group were killed and four escaped, among them my husband and I.[9]

In responses that echo the testimony of survivors from other locations in Eastern Europe, both Etti and Iosif told the interrogators that they knew the alleged perpetrators and that their relations with them prior to these events had been good. Etti added that this may explain why she and her husband were not tied up like the others before the shooting and therefore were able to escape.[10]

Excerpts from Etti's earlier testimony, given on June 17, 1944 (included in the case files of two alleged perpetrators, Dmytro Bakhur and Dmytro Soreiko), name fifteen Ukrainians, armed with rifles and sticks,

---

9 AUSBUChO, prosecution case file of S. Prodanchuk, T. Fedoriak, and P. Bakhur, ark. 78ob–79.

10 Ibid., ark. 80–81.

who guarded the Jews by the lake, as well as another twelve individuals described as present at the massacre.[11]

Another Jewish person, Salia Wurenbrandt, provided the Soviet officials with information she received from her brother, Natan Shekhner, a survivor of the massacre, when they met in a concentration camp in Transnistria. Their father was among those shot in Borivtsi. During an interrogation in December 1944, Salia stated that Natan was at the house of the Engel family when Todor Bakhur, Ivan Grevul', Mykola Fedoriak, and Dmytro Fedoriak tied up their hands with barbed wire and forced them to go to the grasslands outside the village and then to the lake where the massacre took place. The documents provided by Salia include the names of twenty-three alleged perpetrators of the massacre.

It is noteworthy that only ten of the names on Salia's list overlap with the names provided by the Premingers.[12] It is also noteworthy that a number of additional names that figure prominently in the interrogations do not appear on either the Premingers' lists or Salia's list. The discrepancies between the different lists raise questions—whether these reflect sloppy record-keeping by officials or only partial recollections by those providing the names or possible doctoring of the documents by Soviet officials intent on implicating particular Ukrainians in the crimes.

The July 1941 events as described by the alleged perpetrators in 1944–45

The sequence of the July 1941 events as described by the alleged perpetrators themselves may be summed up in the following composite account: Within a few days of the retreat of Soviet troops from the region, Stepan Korbashevs'kyi, Todor Bakhur, and Heorhii Kravchuk returned to the village after a period of hiding during the Soviet occupation. Korbashevs'kyi, described as the local OUN leader, soon called a meeting at the home of Mykola Fedoriak, attended by up to thirty people, where he set out a plan, which was almost immediately carried out, to execute four (or five by one account) local non-Jewish Ukrainian officials (referred

---

11 AUSBUChO, prosecution case file of D. Bakhur, ark. 11-11ob, 23; and prosecution case file of I. Korbashevs'kyi and D.Skoreiko, ark. 36.

12 AUSBUChO, prosecution case file of S. Prodanchuk, T. Fedoriak, and P. Bakhur, ark. 85–86ob.

to as "Soviet activists"), who had administered the village during the Soviet occupation. (Their execution is described in great detail by several of those interrogated.) A few days later (July 7, 1941) Korbashevs'kyi convened a second meeting of local Ukrainian nationalists on the outskirts of the village (referred to as the grasslands), at which he announced that the nationalists had taken power in Borivtsi and that an order had been given by the Hungarian military authorities to kill the Jews in Borivtsi and Kyseliv. The men were then divided into several groups and set out to round up the Jews of Borivtsi, killing on the spot Avrum Prostak, who resisted. They then forcefully escorted the Jews of the village (men, women, and children) on foot and in carts (for those unable to walk) to a small lake named Bul'bon, on the outskirts of the village and shot them into the lake. Estimates of the number of victims vary in the statements of the alleged perpetrators. As described in one such statement: "They apprehended four families and brought them to the village council, where about 76 Jews were gathered, screaming and pleading for their lives."[13] Two statements mention that several days later the bodies came to the surface; when this was brought to the attention of the village elder Ivan Korbashevs'kyi (brother of Stepan), he ordered that the corpses be hauled out of the water and buried nearby. Several stated that after the massacre, Ivan Korbashevs'kyi distributed the property among the participants of the massacre, some receiving homes, others a cow or a horse; he kept a few wagons for himself.[14]

Between May and October 1944, fourteen of the alleged perpetrators of the massacres were arrested. All fourteen were subjected to multiple interrogations in connection with military tribunal trials held for seven of them between December 4, 1944, and January 31, 1945. Six received sentences of twenty years' hard labor; one was sentenced to death, but his sentence was commuted to twenty years' hard labor. Reviews of several of the case files in the 1990s (see Diana Dumitru's contribution in this volume) did not result in the "rehabilitation" of any of these individuals.

Not included among those arrested in 1944 were two alleged leaders of the execution and massacre, Stepan Korbashevs'kyi and Heorhii Kravchuk. Korbashevs'kyi, identified by Heorhii Kushnirek in a May 1946 interrogation as the leader of the OUN for the Kitsman district of Northern

13 AUSBUChO, prosecution case file of Oleksandr Skoreiko, ark. 17–19ob.

14 Ibid., ark. 51–54.

Bukovina, was reportedly arrested by the Soviet authorities and sentenced to ten years of hard labor; Kravchuk, described as a member of the OUN, reportedly died in prison.[15]

Beyond a description of the events, the interrogation records offer clues to the motivations of the perpetrators, ranging from assertion of the *Żydokomuna* motif (that the Jews collectively supported Soviet power); to indoctrination in the ideology of integral nationalism, prevalent in Galicia and Bukovina at the time, which promoted ethnic cleansing; to social and familial networks supportive of radicalized action; to petty greed and opportunism—and, likely, combinations of the above.

Among the first to be interrogated in May and June 1944 were Stepan Farus and Ivan Grevul', both named by the Premingers as participants in the massacre. Both were surprisingly forthcoming with information about who committed the crimes. One may speculate that they were promised immunity from prosecution in exchange for such information, apparently a technique that often yielded results for the Soviet interrogators.[16] According to the interrogation records, Farus, along with several other alleged perpetrators, named Stepan Korbashevs'kyi, Heorhii Kravchuk, and Todor Bakhur as the organizers of both the execution of the Soviet-appointed non-Jewish local officials and the massacre of Borivtsi's Jews. Farus also named twenty local Ukrainians who were present at the massacre of the Jews, including Dmytro Bakhur, Petro Bakhur, and Todor Fedoriak, as well as himself, and indicated which of these individuals was armed.[17] In separate interrogations, Grevul' listed twenty-two men who were present at the meeting in the grasslands and who subsequently took part in the massacre.[18] Excerpts from their interrogation records were inserted, therefore, in the prosecution case files connected with the trials of Stepan Prodanchuk, Todor Fedoriak, Petro Bakhur, Ivan Korbashevs'kyi, and Dmytro Skoreiko.

---

15 Haluzevyi derzhavnyi arkhiv Sluzhba bezpeki Ukraïny (HDA SBU) [The Branch State Archive of the Security Services of Ukraine], f. 13, spr. 372, t. 4, ark.292-294. Also online: http://avr.org.ua/getPDFasFile.php/arhupa/hdasbu-13-0-372-4-023.pdf.

16 Instances of the successful use of this technique in the interrogations of OUN members are described in Fostii 2000, pp. 456–461.

17 AUSBUChO, prosecution case file of S. Prodanchuk, T. Fedoriak, and P. Bakhur, ark. 101–102.

18 Ibid.

The brothers Bakhur

The interrogation records of the three Bakhur brothers offer a representative sample of the detailed responses the interrogators received from the alleged perpetrators relating to the main issues of interest that guided their questioning—membership in the OUN, involvement in the execution of the Soviet activists and the massacre of the Jews, and the disposition of the Jews' property.

A native of Borivtsi born in 1910, Petro Bakhur was interrogated at least seven times between September 9 and November 30, 1944. In initial interrogations he denied membership in the OUN and involvement in the massacres. Eventually, he admitted that he guarded Jewish property after the massacre, on the orders of Heorhii Kravchuk, but that he personally received nothing.[19] In the course of the next two interrogations, he admitted that he was a member of the OUN and that he was recruited by his brother Todor. He continued to deny involvement in the massacres but admitted that he and Mykola Fedoriak attempted to apprehend Avrum Prostak and family, but Prostak resisted and was shot by Fedoriak. He also stated that Prostak's family escaped.[20] The interrogator then confronted him with Iosif Preminger's testimony that when the Jews were gathered on the grasslands outside the village, it was Petro, along with Fedoriak, and Dmytro Bakhur, who brought the family of his brother Avrum Prostak—including his wife and three children; and that when other nationalists asked Petro about the whereabouts of Prostak, Petro gestured to show that Prostak had already been killed. Preminger stated further that Petro was among the participants of the shootings and that his wife Etti, who had escaped, later learned from Christian teenagers in Borivtsi that Prostak was murdered by Petro and Fedoriak. Petro then admitted involvement in the murder of Prostak, but denied participation in the shootings by the lake.[21]

Petro did not seem to be aware that his brother Todor had also been arrested and interrogated a number of times in July 1944, and that he had provided detailed information regarding the OUN in Borivtsi, the ex-

19 Ibid., ark. 2, 9–9ob, 12–15.

20 Ibid., ark. 16, 17ob.

21 Ibid., ark. 24.

ecution of the four Ukrainian Soviet officials in the village, and the massacre of the Jews. Todor had described in detail the strategy for eliminating the "Soviet activists" devised by Stepan Korbashevs'kyi, and how these local officials were pursued and killed, including the fact that when one was found to be still alive after the shots, Stefan Farus finished him off with the dull side of an axe.[22]

When interrogated about the murder of the local Jews, Todor described the second meeting of nationalists convened by Korbashevs'kyi on the grasslands, at which Korbashevs'kyi announced that an order had been received from the Hungarian military authorities to gather and kill all the Jews from the two villages. At that meeting, Korbashevs'kyi described Jews as adherents of Soviet power and severely castigated those who refused to fulfill the order to kill the Jews as traitors to the Ukrainian cause.[23] This is one of several instances documented in the interrogation records that indicate the role of ideological indoctrination, peer pressure, and intimidation in persuading individuals to participate in the crimes.

A third, older brother, Dmytro Bakhur, was arrested by Red Army counterintelligence SMERSH in Kozel'sk (Russia) on September 25, 1944—he was in the Red Army at the time. Charges included membership in the OUN and participation in the killings of Jews and Soviet activists in July 1941. He was interrogated twelve times between September 27 and November 21, 1944. Initially, he claimed not to know where his two brothers, Petro and Todor, were or anything about the OUN in Borivtsi—seemingly unaware of his brothers' disclosures.[24] Nor did he seem to know that two other soldiers then in Kozel'sk had given testimonies implicating him in the crimes—Mykhailo Repets'kyi, identified by Etti Preminger as a participant in the massacre of the Jews, and Dmytro Biloholovka, a resident of Borivtsi described as a "Soviet activist," who stated that Dmytro Bakhur threatened to kill him, "just like other Communists and Jews." Biloholovka also claimed that the three Bakhur brothers had been members of the OUN at the start of the war and described

22 Ibid., ark. 95–95ob.
23 Ibid., ark. 96–96ob.
24 AUSBUChO, prosecution case file of Dmytro Bakhur [No.20990], ark. 2, 7–8ob.

seeing them stroll around the village in July 1941, armed with rifles and wearing blue and yellow armbands and the trident badge.[25]

Dmytro Bakhur acknowledged that the four Soviet activists, whom he named, had been executed, but claimed not to know who killed them, denying his own involvement. When presented with testimony from Ivan Prysiazhniuk (a village official under the Soviet occupation who managed to escape at the start of the attack), Dmytro admitted that the three main organizers of the massacres were indeed members of the OUN, but continued to deny that he participated in this action or in the massacre of the Jews, even after the interrogator confronted him with the testimony of his brother Todor and Etti Preminger.[26]

Questioned about who appropriated the property of the murdered Jews, Dmytro responded that the property was assembled in the courtyard of the village council, but claimed not to know what happened to it afterwards. He stated that Jewish homes were given over to local residents and that he himself moved into the house of Leon Engel, but denied participation in the massacre. The interrogator did not believe him, noting that the houses and property of the Jews were given to active participants of the massacre. Dmytro denied this, saying he did not get the house for free, but made regular payments for it.[27]

In a later interrogation, Dmytro was confronted with statements made by Mykola Fedoriak and Stefan Farus in May/June 1944, which implicated him in the massacre of the Jews. Confrontations were also arranged between Dmytro and Biloholovka, Repets'kyi, and Prysiazhniuk individually. The latter three claimed that Dmytro was a member of the OUN who had participated in the massacre of Soviet activists and Jews.[28] Prysiazhniuk also described how he escaped when the local nationalists began to attack the appointed village officials, but then was caught by Romanian gendarmes, who brought him back to the Borivtsi village council building. When Dmytro saw him, bound and lying on the floor, he began to beat him in the chest, stopping only when a Romanian gendarme intervened. After the return of Soviet power in 1944, Petro

---

25 Ibid., ark. 28–32ob.
26 Ibid., ark. 8–10ob.
27 Ibid., ark. 11–11ob.
28 Ibid., ark. 45–49.

Bakhur invited Prysiazhniuk to his home, where he met Todor and Dmytro. After some vodka, Dmytro asked him to forgive him for the beating and pleaded that he not betray him to the Soviet authorities. When Todor asked Prysiazhniuk for advice on how to conceal their participation in the massacres, he suggested they join the Red Army and promised not to betray them.[29] Dmytro eventually admitted to guarding the Jews assembled at the village council building and escorting them outside the village, but not to participating in the shooting. At his trial in late December, however, he finally admitted to participating in shooting the Jews, saying that Stepan Korbashevs'kyi forced him to do so.[30]

The same story, with only slight variations, emerges from the interrogations of Stepan Prodanchuk (interrogated at least five times between September 4 and December 9, 1944) and Todor Fedoriak (interrogated at least four times between September 10 and November 2, 1944). Both were confronted by the Premingers in person on November 30, 1944. Fedoriak eventually admitted that he was a member of the OUN, recruited by Todor Bakhur in 1940, and that he was present at the meeting at the grasslands during which Stepan Korbashevs'kyi called upon the residents of the village to support Ukrainian statehood and to assist in the execution of the Jewish population.[31] These accounts and those relating to Stepan's older brother, Ivan Korbashevs'kyi (interrogated at least five times between October 21 and November 17, 1944) and Dmytro Skoreiko (interrogated at least seven times between October 26 and November 30, 1944) further corroborate the core story regarding the events. Again, most responded initially by denying involvement in the crimes, and progressed to partial acknowledgments, offering alibis or minimizing spins. Some tried to shift blame to others, including to those known to have evaded arrest in 1944 or who had died since the 1941 events.

Strewn across the interrogation records are random but evocative details relating to the July 1941 events, such as the statement that many of the local men mobilized to round up the Jews did not have weapons—

29 Ibid., ark. 43ob, 44.

30 Ibid., ark. 54, 73.

31 AUSBUChO, prosecution case file of S. Prodanchuk, T. Fedoriak, and P. Bakhur, ark. 39–44ob.

only stones, scythes, and sticks.[32] Another fact, with far-reaching repercussions, is contained in Prysiazhniuk's statement that the whole village knew about the massacre and talked about it openly, including about the looting of the property of the victims by the nationalists and the distribution of the victims' houses and belongings among the village residents.[33] That these events were widely discussed and had entered the collective consciousness of the village was evident in the 2001 interviews with residents of Borivtsi. Sixty years after the events, the elderly retained vivid memories of the violent roundup of the Jews and the massacre, while younger people were able to relate stories they heard from their parents and grandparents.

While not dismissing the possibility of tampering with the information recorded in the interrogation documents, the suggestion that these documents are all or mostly Soviet fabrications is not credible. The repeated descriptions of key aspects of the July 1941 events—such as the nature of the two meetings of local nationalists convened by Stepan Korbashevs'kyi at which the executions of the Soviet activists and the Jewish population were planned, and the details relating to the execution and the massacre—are fairly consistent across the interrogation records, even while including discrepancies in the lists of alleged perpetrators and victims, as well as variances in emphasis and nuances that would be unlikely in a fabricated account. These accounts are also consistent with how the events were remembered and recounted by two survivors of the massacre over several decades since the late 1960s, as well as by the elderly villagers interviewed in 2001. Their remembrance is based on personal experience, not on the interrogation records.

The OUN network in Borivtsi

In addition to establishing the facts regarding the crimes committed, the Soviet interrogators were interested in extracting information about the organizational structures and activities of Ukrainian nationalists. These documents are, therefore, rich in detail concerning processes of recruitment and secret meetings of the OUN in rural Bukovina in 1939–41 as

32 AUSBUChO, prosecution case file of O. Skoreiko, ark. 14–16ob

33 AUSBUChO, prosecution case file of D. Bakhur, ark. 41–42ob.

an underground organization and the OUN's methods of taking power and garnering popular support after the Soviet retreat in early July 1941.

Most, if not all, of the alleged perpetrators interrogated in connection with the Borivtsi crimes, at one point or another, admitted to being members of the OUN, or were described by others as such. As the OUN was a suppressed illegal organization, a number had gone into hiding after the establishment of Soviet rule in Northern Bukovina, in particular after the NKVD (People's Commissariat for Internal Affairs) arrested several members in 1940–41. They returned to the village immediately following the Soviet retreat. This was the case for the three who led the Borivtsi execution and massacre—Stepan Korbashevs'kyi, Heorhii Kravchuk, and Todor Bakhur.[34] The sense of danger and need for secrecy during the Soviet occupation is a recurring theme in these accounts—for example, Prysiazhniuk's statement that during this period the local OUN underground functioned under the cover of the drama circle.[35] Several of the alleged perpetrators had enlisted in the Red Army in 1940–41, gained experience in the use of firearms, and then deserted following the Soviet retreat. Some were arrested by the Romanian authorities in 1943 because of their membership in the OUN—Stepan Korbashevs'kyi, Heorhii Kravchuk, and Todor Fedoriak among these.[36] Several were in the Red Army after the war at the time of their arrest in the summer/fall of 1944, perhaps, as suggested in testimonies, following advice that such service might camouflage their OUN connection and preempt arrest for past crimes.

The OUN's recruitment methods and organizational structures are also described in these records. Todor Bakhur, who recruited several other Borivtsi natives into the OUN, was himself recruited in 1939 by another Borivtsi resident, Vasyl' Peleshatyi. The latter, described in these records as a leader of the OUN's station (*stanytsia*) for Borivtsi, also recruited Korbashevs'kyi, Kravchuk, the Skoreiko brothers, and the Zhukovs'kyi brothers. The argument Peleshatyi is said to have presented in recruiting Todor Bakhur and others was that Ukrainian independence would greatly improve their economic situation. Bakhur stated that

---

34 AUSBUChO, prosecution case file of O. Skoreiko, ark. 14

35 AUSBUChO, prosecution case file of D. Bakhur, ark. 41–42ob.

36 Ibid., ark. 41–44; AUSBUChO, prosecution case file of S. Prodanchuk, T. Fedoriak, and P. Bakhur, ark. 100.

Peleshatyi persuaded him to recruit others and lead the local cell (the "Seven"), and that he did so. He also stated that Peleshatyi was among those arrested in 1940–41, which led several others to go into hiding.[37]

A fuller account is provided by the Ukrainian historian Ivan Fostii, whose finding is that Peleshatyi was persuaded after his arrest to divulge information that exposed most of the OUN network in the Zastavna district. From him, the Soviets also learned about the close contacts between the OUN leadership in Bukovina and Galicia. As observed by Fostii: OUN leaders who fell into the hands of the NKVD or NKGB (People's Commissariat for State Security or the Soviet secret police) frequently forgot about their "Decalogue" (ten commandments of the Ukrainian nationalist) and exposed the participants of the clandestine network known to them.[38] Todor Bakhur appears to have been among these.

Questioned about the OUN, Oleksandr Skoreiko stated that the organization was headed by Andrii Mel'nyk; that he swore allegiance to the OUN in December 1941 together with Heorhii Skoreiko, in the house of Stepan Prodanchuk; and that the latter read the text of the oath and they repeated it. He also described meetings of the cell, which took place regularly and at which cell leader Todor Bakhur and later Prodanchuk would read from nationalist literature; and mentioned sessions dedicated to military training.[39]

The interrogation accounts indicate that the Ukrainian nationalists in Borivtsi were closely linked to the wider regional OUN network, in particular in Galicia; that their links were primarily with the Melnykite faction, though some also identified with the Banderites; and that the village had a core group of intensely active OUN members, suffused with the radical ideology that characterized a segment of the Galician nationalists. In the course of his interrogation, Todor Bakhur described the regular meetings and activities of the local OUN members under the Romanian occupation in the late 1930s, mentioning that Stepan Korbashevs'kyi would bring him nationalist literature—such as the magazine *Rozbudova natsii*, and the newspapers *Krakivs'ki visti* and *L'vivs'ki visti*—which he would read and then return to Korbashevs'kyi, presumably for further circulation.[40]

---

37 Ibid. ark. 93–95, 104; AUSBUChO, prosecution case file of D. Bakhur, ark. 25–26.

38 Fostii 2000, p. 461.

39 AUSBUChO, O.Skoreiko prosecution case file, ark. 11–13.

40 AUSBUChO, prosecution case file of S.P rodanchuk, T. Fedoriak, P. Bakhur, ark. 98.

As recent research has shown, these OUN-affiliated publications, produced by radicalized OUN ideologues in Galicia, carried profoundly anti-Semitic articles in the 1930s and early 1940s on a regular basis.[41] There are also indications in the interrogation records that the local nationalists received external guidance on how to organize and engage the population in the nationalist enterprise. A communal celebration that took place in the village shortly after the massacre of the Jews was likely organized by Borivtsi's OUN members in support of Ukrainian statehood, in a manner similar to mass events of this type orchestrated at the time by the OUN in various locations in Galicia.[42]

A noteworthy pattern discerned in these records is that of brothers (or cousins) recruiting each other into the OUN and/or participating together in the massacres. The stories and lists of alleged perpetrators for Borivtsi feature, in addition to the Bakhur brothers, Stepan and Ivan Korbashevs'kyi; Todor, Mykola, and Volodymyr Fedoriak; Dmytro, Heorhii, Vasyl, Oleksandr, and Iu. Skoreiko; Dmytro, Stepan, and Ivan Hordii; and Dmytro, Vasyl, and Heorhii Zhukovs'kyi. The phenomenon of siblings encouraging each other to radical action, prompted by strong familial mutual trust and support as well as shared perspectives, has been studied more recently in connection with modern-day mass violence and may offer a partial explanation of the Borivtsi events.

An important question is the extent to which external actors and the broader context influenced events in this particular locality. The interrogation records for Borivtsi make no mention of the presence of Germans or Romanians during the massacre of the Jews. Stepan Korbashevs'kyi's announcement regarding orders from the Hungarian military to carry out

---

41 For examples of anti-Semitic items in these publications see: Carynnyk, Marco (2011). Foes of Our Rebirth: Ukrainian Nationalist Discussions about Jews, 1929–1947, *Nationalities Papers* 39(3), pp. 315–352, here p. 321; Kurylo, Taras (2013). "Jewish Question" in Ukrainian Nationalist Thought of the Interwar Period, *Polin* 26, here pp. 237ff.

42 AUSBUChO, prosecution case file of D. Bakhur, ark. 17, 17ob. This topic is treated by Oleksandr Melnyk in a not-yet-published thesis in which he notes that "the primary functions of such events—which typically featured speeches by functionaries of the OUN, prominent members of local communities, and representatives of the Greek Catholic Church in front of parading militias and local residents dressed festively in traditional garments—was to legitimate the Stets'ko government, foster perception of its own strength among the Ukrainian population and to intimidate political opponents" (chapter 2, "The Nationalist Challenge and Legitimacy Contests," p. 109).

the massacre is repeated by several of the alleged perpetrators, including Ivan Grevul', Todor Bakhur, and Todor Fedoriak.[43] However, this may suggest simply that Korbashevs'kyi's was their common source for this claim, rather than confirming that there was in fact such a command. There is no other mention in the interrogation records or in authoritative historical accounts that Hungarians were in the area at the time, other than in Horodenka, 20 kilometers away.[44] To identify external actors and events that influenced the crimes committed in Borivtsi, there is more to be gleaned from broader historical accounts about the OUN in the Chernivtsi region and in Galicia and the wave of anti-Jewish violence that swept across Northern Bukovina and Bessarabia in the summer of 1941.

The OUN network in Northern Bukovina

The findings of this micro-study of events in Borivtsi are largely consistent with authoritative published accounts relating to both the wider OUN network and the patterns of violence in July 1941 in Northern Bukovina.

A glorifying history of Bukovyns'kyi kurin' (Bukovinian Battalion)—a militant nationalist organization affiliated with the OUN that was staffed primarily by Ukrainians from Bukovina but fought in various locations and for various causes—provides a detailed description of the OUN network in Bukovina during the Soviet occupation. Included in this history is a statement that on the eve of the Soviet-German war, the central leadership of the OUN issued instructions to form armed formations that would take control of the towns and villages and create state structures.[45] This is precisely what the three OUN leaders in Borivtsi were doing immediately after the Soviet retreat from the area.

In a book and an article, the Ukrainian historian Ivan Fostii provides a region-wide context for the OUN in Northern Bukovina, as well as information that bears directly on the July 1941 events in Borivtsi. Fostii

43 AUSBUChO, prosecution case file of S.Prodanchuk, T.Fedoriak, and P.Bakhur, ark. 96–96ob, 103, 119–123.

44 Pohl, Dieter (1996). *Nationalsozialistische Judenverfolgung in Ostgalizien 1941–1944*. München, p. 49.

45 Duda, Andrii and Volodymyr Staryk (1995). *Bukovyns'kyi kurin' v boiakh za Ukraïns'ku derzhavnist' 1918, 1941, 1944*. Chernivtsi, p. 56.

describes the structure, leadership, and operations of the OUN in Bukovina beginning in the 1930s, relying on a range of sources, including Soviet records similar to those used for this chapter, which in his view are most reliable and precise when it comes to factual, chronological, and personal aspects of the OUN's history. He describes the OUN's conflicted relationship with the Romanian regime until June 1940 and the repressions it experienced under the Soviet occupation that followed. He notes that the OUN was of particular interest to the Soviet regime because of its large clandestine network, perceived as capable of leading armed resistance to establish an independent Ukrainian state.

Fostii's account of the career of Petro Voinovs'kyi, an OUN leader based in Chernivtsi, is of particular relevance for understanding the July 1941 events in Borivtsi. Voinovs'kyi's predecessor as OUN leader for the Chernivtsi region was Viktor Kulyshir, who was arrested by the Soviets in November 1940 but released from prison in exchange for revealing the structure of the regional OUN organization. From Kulyshir the interrogators learned the names and numbers of activists in Bukovina, their links with the OUN organizations in Bucharest and Galicia, and that those under the command of Voinovs'kyi collected weapons.[46] According to Fostii, the information divulged by Kulyshir and several others led to the exposure of almost the entire OUN network in the Zastavna district, leading a number of activists to go into hiding. Fostii concludes that this development strengthened the inclination of the OUN leadership in Northern Bukovina to cooperate with the Germans, alongside, of course, the widespread discontent with the Soviet occupation and the hope (which proved illusory) that Germany would aid in the establishment of an independent Ukrainian state.

As OUN leader for the Chernivtsi region, Voinovs'kyi cooperated with the occupying Germans, and, according to Fostii, possibly also with the NKVD—not an unusual instance of double collaboration.[47] During the Soviet occupation, Voinovs'kyi had coordinated the activities of the OUN cells in the region and organized sabotage actions against Soviet targets. Then, as soon as the Soviets retreated, he organized a string of massacres of Jews in Bukovinian villages, described by Fostii as follows:

46 Fostii 2000, p. 459f.

47 Fostii 2005, p. 130.

> To demonstrate support for the anti-Jewish policy of Hitler, Voinovs'kyi had planned a series of attacks on Jews in Bukovinian villages to be staged immediately upon the withdrawal of Soviet forces. [...] The first victims were residents of the village Miliyeve. On 5 July Voinovs'kyi's band, re-enforced by some 20 volunteers armed with rifles, pistols, sawed-off guns, spikes and agricultural instruments, attacked the village. Divided into several units of 5 to 7 men each, Voinovs'kyi and his group rushed to the homes of local Jews, whom they characterized as the backbone of Soviet power in Bukovina. Voinovs'kyi personally took part in the attack, firing revolver shots at still living victims. [...] According to the perpetrators of the massacre, altogether they shot some 120 people.
>
> On the same day Voinovs'kyi and his group attempted a similar attack in the village Ispas. But the then chairman of the village, Ivan Heorhiyovych Denys, categorically prohibited them from harming the local Jews, despite pressure exerted by Voinovs'kyi. Similar deadly attacks on Jewish communities on the orders of the OUN leadership also took place in Banylov, Karapchev, Shyshkivtsi, Luzhany, Napolokivtsi, Vaslovtsi and other villages in the region.
>
> On 7 July, on orders of the regional leader of the OUN (M) Stepan Korbashevs'kyi, district leader of the OUN Heorhii Kravchuk, and sub-district commander Todor Bakhur, the nationalist fighters killed 45 Jews in Borivtsi and 54 in Kyseliv.[48]

Fostii then mentions the execution of the Ukrainian village officials who had served in Borivtsi during the Soviet occupation, and observes that the murders of innocent people alienated many people. However, Fostii does not clarify the connection between Voinovs'kyi and Korbashevs'kyi, nor does Voinovs'kyi's name appear in the ESC or interrogation records examined for this chapter. While these gaps call for further research, Fostii's account suggests that Voinovs'kyi as regional OUN leader would have directed Korbashevs'kyi, the Kitsman district OUN leader, to organize the execution and massacre in Borivtsi.

Fostii goes on to describe Voinovs'kyi's subsequent recruitment of volunteers and the creation of the Bukovinian Battalion, and the movement of this battalion from Sniatyn, where it split into two factions—Banderites and Melnykites, to Horodenka, and Kamianets-Podilskyi, where Voinovs'kyi left 25 of his subordinates to staff the police. The battalion then went on to Kiev, passing Zhmerynka, Vinnytsia, Zhytomyr, and Berdychiv on the way. In each of these towns, according to Fostii, Voinovs'kyi left behind his representatives to work in the Ukrainian police, in the guards' service, or as interpreters with German commandants; in late September 1941 the battalion reached Kiev (in time for the Babyn Yar

48 Fostii 2000, p. 466; Fostii 2005, p. 132.

massacre), where its members experienced disappointment because the Germans did not allow the creation of a Ukrainian national army. The battalion was then dissolved and some of the cadres went on to serve in the Ukrainian police in Kiev, as well as in neighboring district centers. Others went to the 115th and 118th battalions of the German *Schutzpolizei* or *Schutzmannschaft*.[49]

Massacres in Northern Bukovina, Bessarabia, and Galicia

The broader context for the 1941 anti-Jewish violence in the Chernivtsi region is shaped by the crossing of German and Romanian troops into Northern Bukovina and Bessarabia on July 2, 1941. Massacres of Jews in these territories began shortly before and intensified during the first few days of the offensive. The perpetrators of these massacres, who were mostly Romanian soldiers and gendarmes, were carrying out a deliberate policy of the Antonescu regime to ethnically "purify" the reconquered territories that had been part of Romania during the interwar years but were seized by the USSR in late June 1940 through a secret agreement with Nazi Germany. Ion Antonescu himself had communicated to the military on June 30 clear instructions to kill Jews as "enemy agents," and special death squads were created for this purpose. The Romanian gendarmerie—manned by many of the same officers who had served in Bukovina and Bessarabia before June 1940 and who were therefore adept in identifying Jews within the local population—played a key role in the massacres. In Bukovina, however, some did not enforce the "cleansing" order as zealously as others.[50]

Accounts of the anti-Jewish violence in Northern Bukovina and Bessarabia generally refer to the power vacuum following the Soviet retreat

49 Fostii 2000, p. 466f.; Fostii 2005, p. 129; Duda/Staryk 1995, pp. 84–92, pp. 120–150. The presence of members of the Bukovinian Battalion in Kiev in time for the Babyn Yar massacre (September 29–31, 1941) is a matter of current research and controversy. In his memoir, Vasyl' Veryha indicates that the Bukovinian Battalion was also in Kamyanets-Podilskyi at the time of the first large-scale mass murder of Jews on August 27–28, 1941 [Mel'nyk, Kost' et al. (eds.) (1985). *Na zov Kyieva: Ukrains'kyi natsionalizm u II svitovii viini. Zbirnyk statei, spohadiv I dokumentiv*. Toronto/New York, p. 111].

50 Solonari 2007, pp. 755–760.

from the area, which lasted several days and enabled various anti-Semitic forces—mostly radical Ukrainian and Romanian nationalists—to organize pogroms and mass executions of Jews. In some locations in these two territories, the massacres were carried out by German troops and members of *Einsatzgruppe* D. In other cases, elements within the local Romanian and Ukrainian populations carried out pogroms and mass murders on their own, in many instances before the arrival of the German or Romanian troops—this was especially the case in rural areas. An estimated 43,500–60,000 Jews were murdered in this wave of violence.[51]

The widespread violence occurring in the region and beyond would have had an impact on those who orchestrated the massacres in Borivtsi and Kyseliv. They certainly would have heard about the massacre and chaos two days earlier in Chernivtsi, the capital of Bukovina. Romanian and German forces reoccupied Chernivtsi on July 5, 1941, with precise orders from the Antonescu government to punish Jews for "supporting the Soviet occupation"—an accusation central to the propaganda campaign in the region. In fact, the Jews of Bukovina suffered no less than others under the Soviets, with some 3,000 (or more) Chernivtsi Jews deported to Siberia. Within the first 24 hours after the entry of Romanian and German forces into the city, between 2,000 and 3,000 Jews were murdered in house-to-house operations (including the chief rabbi of Bukovina, the chief cantor, and leaders of the community). The iconic Jewish temple was torched. Pogroms and massacres also occurred at this time in other Bukovinian towns and rural areas, as well as in neighboring Bessarabia and Galicia.

The events in Stanestii de Jos, a village east of Chernivtsi, parallel the events in Borivtsi. As recounted by Simon Geissbühler, a Ukrainian nationalist committee was formed after the Soviet withdrawal and before the arrival of Romanian troops. Its first action after taking over control in the village was to direct its members, some armed only with hammers and agricultural tools, to round up and murder the local Jews. When the

51 This summary account of the broader regional context draws from published works listed above by Jean Ancel, Simon Geissbühler, Radu Ioanid, Vladimir Solonari, and Kai Struve.

commander of the Romanian gendarmes arrived, he halted the bloodbath but by then between 80 and 130 Jews had been killed.[52] Similar massacres involving local perpetrators are described by Geissbühler for other towns and villages in Northern Bukovina, including Banila/Siret, Vyzhnytsia, Banila/Cheremosh, Milie, Sadagura, Nepolokivtsi, Kitsman, Kyseliv, and Boian.[53]

In relation to this wave of violence, a distinction should be made between *pogroms*, defined as spontaneous acts of anti-Jewish violence by local non-Jews, and an organized region-wide program of ethnic cleansing by means of mass murder, or, indeed, genocide. Pogroms did occur in the region in 1941, often in response to news that plunder and attacks on Jews would be permitted for a specified time. However, the events in Borivtsi and many other locations in Bukovina and Bessarabia were of a different order of mass violence, as entire Jewish populations of towns and villages were rounded up with the intent of total annihilation. Such massacres should be considered localized instances of genocide—and, because they occured in the summer of 1941, an integral part of the Holocaust in Ukraine, whether carried out by German and Romanian invaders, or by locals. The historian Vladimir Solonari presents a similar argument in his study on the patterns of violence in 1941 in Bukovina and Bessarabia.[54]

The widespread violence against Jews in the first days of July throughout the two territories would have made it seem timely and legitimate (in the sense that it was sanctioned by the authorities and common practice) to initiate similar actions locally, especially when re-enforced by ideological and political arguments. This leads to the key question: What

52 Geissbühler 2014, p. 434; Solonari 2007, p. 763.

53 Geissbühler 2014, pp. 434–436.

54 Solonari 2007, p. 764f. "'Pogrom' is a generic term profusely used after World War II to describe popular violence against Jews in Bessarabia and northern Bukovina. Indeed, in what was then happening in almost all localities of these two provinces, many characteristics of what are usually understood as 'pogroms' were discernible: the breakdown of law and order, chaotic mass participation, and the plunder of property compounded by indiscriminate beatings and the occasional killings of victims. [...] But the term 'pogrom' obscures serious differences in the patterns of popular violence: while in some places pogromists concentrated on plunder and beatings without engaging in *systematic* murder, in others they systematically and purposefully *killed* Jews."

were the ideological, political, and other factors that contributed to raising the violence toward Jews in this region to a genocidal level?

Since the mid-1990s, an increasing number of scholars have focused attention on the wave of anti-Jewish violence in the summer of 1941 in Galicia, Northern Bukovina, and Bessarabia. They have produced detailed accounts of the events in various localities, based on a range of sources, including German, Soviet, and local records, as well as written memoirs and oral testimonies of survivors and witnesses.[55] Their accounts provide compelling evidence regarding the critical role of radical nationalist Romanian and Ukrainian groups in escalating the violence to genocidal actions and the participation of segments of the local population. The following is a consolidated summary of the factors that led to the violence, drawn from analyses offered in several broad-based accounts, and observations on the specific story of Borivtsi.

Traditional anti-Semitism—such as perceptions of Jews as Christ-killers or economic exploiters—was a marginal factor, not a trigger of the 1941 wave of violence. Such perceptions were present in Ukrainian religious and folk culture (as in Christian Europe more broadly), fed by socioeconomic antagonisms in previous centuries and the precarious position of Jews as a vulnerable minority that tended to identify with the dominant cultures and ruling peoples—in particular, Poles and Russians, whom Ukrainians regarded as their oppressors. Despite such negative perceptions, Jews and non-Jews lived together for the most part normally over extended periods. One can conclude, therefore, that traditional anti-Semitism did not cause the genocidal violence, though it may have facilitated it—either by lessening inhibitions on the part of some individuals to murder Jews, or more readily condoning such actions when carried out by others. Likewise, greed and sadism may have motivated some perpetrators, but would not have generated genocidal acts on their own.

A more powerful factor relates to the emergence of radical nationalist groups in Galicia and Bukovina, and within the OUN in particular, prepared to use any means to achieve the goal of an independent Ukrainian

55 These include, for Bukovina, published works by Ivan Fostii, Simon Geissbühler, and Vladimir Solonari, as well as studies focused on the 1941 pogroms in L'viv and western Ukraine by (in alphabetical order): Tarik Cyril Amar, Omer Bartov, Franziska Bruder, Marco Carynnyk, John-Paul Himka, Jeffrey Kopstein, Christoph Mick, Dieter Pohl, Alexander Prusin, Per Rudling, Timothy Snyder, and Kai Struve.

state, thought of in the dominant spirit of the time as one that should be ethnically homogenous. These nationalists had taken lessons from two failed Ukrainian statehood experiments in the 1917–21 period and became radicalized by political violence in the two decades that followed. By 1941, OUN ideologues had codified and supplemented traditional anti-Semitic beliefs with the *Żydokomuna* slogan, which equated Jews with Communism—a slogan intensively propagated by German and Romanian propaganda to target both Jews and the Soviets, and adopted by the OUN ideologues, even though they regarded the Soviets/Russians, not the Jews, as their primary enemy.[56]

Inherent in the *Żydokomuna* equation was the insinuation that Jews were collectively responsible for Stalinist crimes. This notion proved to be highly potent in inciting anti-Jewish violence in the area at the time and persisted despite the obvious reality that the vast majority of Jews were not in fact Communists and had suffered alongside others during the Soviet occupation (in deportations, expropriations, and suppression of national organizations and expression) and regardless of the fact that chairmen of village and town councils during the Soviet occupation were almost invariably local non-Jews and that those responsible for the painful experience of mass deportations in June 1941 were also not Jews. The prevalence of this insidious argument is recorded in numerous survivors' memoirs and interviews for the region, including for Borivtsi, as is evident in Etti Preminger's testimony: When she asked a perpetrator who escorted the Jews to the site of the massacre, "What bad have I done to you?" his response was: "Go to Stalin. You wanted Soviet government."[57] It is hard to believe that he would have been unaware that she and virtually all the Jews of Borivtsi were in fact not Communists but rather apolitical, religiously observant Jews, preoccupied with daily life struggles during the difficult period of Soviet rule.

Kai Struve connects the adoption of the *Żydokomuna* accusation by the radical nationalists in western Ukraine with strategic calculations "to utilize the favourable opportunity afforded by the German invasion in order to achieve the long-term goal of the "ethnic cleansing" of their territory

56 Himka 1997.

57 AUSBUChO, prosecution case file of S. Prodanchuk, T. Fedoriak, and P. Bakhur, ark. 78ob–79.

with regard to the Jews."[58] Support for this finding may be found in a guideline given by leaders of the OUN's Banderite faction to the administrations and militias following the Soviet retreat—to cleanse Ukrainian territory of enemy minorities, specifically, "Muscovites, Poles, and Jews."[59] As proof that the OUN was not involved in the anti-Jewish violence of the summer of 1941, some have pointed to an April 1941 OUN-B resolution, which warned against pogroms so as not to distract the masses' attention from the real enemy—Moscow. Struve points out, however, that this resolution nonetheless highlights the "Muscovite-Bolshevik" connection, and that together with the earlier instruction to cleanse the territory of enemy minorities, it "paved the way for the involvement of local militias and OUN supporters in anti-Jewish violence."[60]

The geopolitical situation was clearly a major factor in the mass violence in early July 1941. While German and Romanian forces were carrying out massacres of Jews in some parts of Bukovina, in other parts a political vacuum existed for several days after the retreat of the Soviets, which the Ukrainian nationalist underground was able to fill with its own organs of local power.[61] A related and crucial factor was the competition between Romanian and Ukrainian nationalists for control over Northern Bukovina, while ingratiating themselves with the Germans. As Ivan Fostii observed, Voinovs'kyi and his band organized the massacres of Jews in rural Bukovina as a way of demonstrating support for German anti-Jewish policy.[62] Vladimir Solonari echoes and amplifies this observation regarding Ukrainian nationalists in Northern Bukovina: "The actions they undertook in early July 1941 were in pursuit of the strategy of taking power and presenting Romanians with a *fait accompli*. Cleansing the territory of Jews was obviously part of that strategy… [Doing so before the arrival of the Romanian authorities] in their minds was a sign that they were in control. Besides, they tried in this way to curry favor with the Germans."[63]

58 Struve 2012, p. 273.
59 Cited in: Struve 2013, p. 469.
60 Ibid.
61 Solonari 2007, p. 768.
62 Fostii 2000, p. 466.
63 Solonari 2007, p. 769f.

Commitment to creating an ethnically homogenous state characterized the competing nationalist aspirations of both the Romanian regime and the OUN leadership in Bukovina. The former set out to "ethnically purify" Bukovina and Bessarabia and to integrate these territories into Greater Romania; the latter adopted the radical Galician nationalists' agenda of integral nationalism and ethnic cleansing. In pursuit of their respective and common goals, radical Romanian and Ukrainian nationalists advocated and then implemented genocidal ethnic cleansing actions, when the opportunity to do so presented itself in early July 1941.[64]

Perspective of Borivtsi residents, 2001

Interviews with elderly Borivtsi residents in 2001 corroborated the central fact around which the 1944 interrogations revolved—that local villagers were involved in the 1941 massacres in Borivtsi and Kyseliv. A question about who the perpetrators were, which was framed to imply that responsibility for the crimes lay with the Germans or Romanians, elicited the following unequivocal response from several interviewees: "No, no, it was our own bandits who did it." Several of the interviewees were witnesses to the roundups and the massacre. Though they were teenagers at the time, they retained vivid memories sixty years later of their Jewish neighbors being forcibly escorted out of the village. Some were witnesses of the massacre and were able to point out exactly where the shooters stood, what their own vantage point was, and what they saw. They were surprisingly open in sharing accounts of the horrors they witnessed and the disturbing scenes, such as villagers rushing into a Jewish home right after its occupants were taken away in order to take hold of what they could of the meager possessions inside. Younger interviewees

64 The euphemistic term "ethnic cleansing" refers to the removal of a designated segment of the population defined on an ethnic basis, whether by means of nonviolent pressured emigration, organized population transfers, forced deportation, or mass murder. Where the means used is deliberate mass murder with intent to annihilate that segment of the population in a particular region, the ethnic cleansing is genocidal. In the latter case, the concepts of ethnic cleansing and genocide merge. As described by Norman Naimark, "literally and figuratively, ethnic cleansing bleeds into genocide, as mass murder is committed in order to rid the land of a people." See: Naimrak, Norman (2007). Theoretical Paper: Ethnic Cleansing, in *Online Encyclopedia of Mass Violence*.

were able to relate stories they heard from parents and grandparents about specific brutal actions as well as acts of extraordinary compassion on the part of some villagers at the time.

The elderly interviewees offered several stories of attempts to shelter Jews, which they had witnessed, and the special case of a Ukrainian woman in the village who hid two small Jewish children and then raised them as her own. The need for such stories, which offer a ray of light in a very dark period in the village's history, is understandable. That there were in fact such instances in this village is also credible. The Premingers stated in 1944 (according to the interrogation records) and repeated in interviews decades later that relations in the prewar years between the Jewish inhabitants of the village and their Christian neighbors, including with some of the alleged perpetrators, were good. This is echoed in reminiscences of other former Jewish residents of the village who had moved from Borivtsi to nearby Zastavna and Kitsman in the late 1930s, including this author's parents and the survivor Miriam Strassberg.[65] Similarly, the elderly non-Jewish residents in the village described close friendships with Jews in the village (whom they named) and how they were warmly received in Jewish homes. The sense of injustice, pain, and regret evoked by remembrance of the crimes committed against the village's Jews is contained in a strange and surprising assertion made by several of these interviewees—that the 1986 Chernobyl disaster, whose toxic clouds traveled all the way to Kyseliv and Borivtsi, was "punishment for what we did to the Jews."

A monument erected in 2001 by family of the victims at the site of the massacre was found vandalized in 2008. In 2015, a village administrator told the author that children swimming in the lake, which had in part reappeared at the site with the 2010 floods, came out of the water holding human bones. Scars from the 1941 events remain.

Conclusion

The massacre of the Jews in the village of Borivtsi in Northern Bukovina in early July 1941 is one instance of a region-wide ethnic cleansing operation—planned and organized by the OUN leadership in Chernivtsi, in

65 www.youtube.com/watch?v=hRlqBso_Ng8&context=C39cfdf2ADOEgsToPDsklina6r0jiTMGkt6tvZkFtW (2:41–2:55).

line with a broader plan devised by radical members of the OUN in Galicia in anticipation of the German invasion. The OUN leaders in Borivtsi implemented this plan in the village by recruiting some thirty local men, mostly OUN members, to quickly round up the Jews and carry out the massacre. The lingering sense of injustice and remorse expressed many decades later in the 2001 interviews suggests that most of the villagers were likely not in favor of the killings and not involved in perpetrating them, though they may have felt a collective shame about appropriating looted property and standing by as their Jewish neighbors were murdered by a group of local young men.

The findings regarding events in this one small village fit the patterns identified by authoritative scholars in evidence-based accounts for western Ukraine more broadly. These scholars continue to contend, however, with an opposing school of thought and policy that is protective of the OUN's reputation, that minimizes the OUN's involvement in wartime crimes, that dismisses all evidence from Soviet sources as tainted, and that considers witnesses' memory unreliable. The crimes committed are instead attributed to Romanians, Germans, other non-Ukrainians, or local hooligans, not to OUN members as such.[66]

And so does the past shape the future, illuminating it, or haunting it…

66 John-Paul Himka discusses the views of proponents of this school of thought, such as the memoirist Yevhen Nakonechny and the historian Volodymyr Viatrovych, in "The Reception of the Holocaust in Postcommunist Ukraine." See: Himka, John-Paul and Joanna Beata Michlic (2013). *Bringing the Dark Past to Light. The Reception of the Holocaust in Postcommunist Europe*. Lincoln/London, pp. 635–640.

Kai Struve

Anti-Jewish Violence in the Summer of 1941 in Eastern Galicia and Beyond

During the first days and weeks after the German attack on the Soviet Union on June 22, 1941, the Jews in the newly occupied territories were hit by a wave of violence originating from different groups of perpetrators. Specifically, it included early on mass executions by units of the German police, primarily the *Einsatzgruppen* of the Security Police, and by other units of the German police and armed forces. A second main source of violence against Jews were anti-Soviet insurgents and non-Jewish civilians in those borderland areas between the Baltic and the Black Sea that had been only recently annexed by the Soviet Union, that is, in September 1939 and in June 1940, based on the agreements of the Molotov-Ribbentrop Pact of August 23, 1939.

This contribution summarizes the main results of a larger study on anti-Jewish violence during the first weeks after the German attack in the mostly Ukrainian region of eastern Galicia.[1] The focus is on the character and context of the violence from the side of the local population and their interaction with German activities. After outlining the events in eastern Galicia, the contribution compares this region with others in that strip of territory between the Baltic Sea and the Black Sea that had been ruled by the Soviets during the previous twelve to twenty-one months.

Thereby, the chapter addresses a problem that received considerable attention in research and in the public in the wake of Jan Tomasz Gross' book on the pogrom in the town of Jedwabne in northeastern Poland on July 10, 1941.[2] In contrast to the mostly Polish regions, the fact

1 Eastern Galicia is defined here as the southeastern regions of the Polish state that had belonged to the Austrian Crown Land of Galicia until 1918 and that became a part of the Soviet Union after September 1939. Struve, Kai (2015). *Deutsche Herrschaft, ukrainischer Nationalismus, antijüdische Gewalt. Der Sommer 1941 in der Westukraine*. Berlin.

2 Gross, Jan T. (2001). *Neighbors. The Destruction of the Jewish Community in Jedwabne, Poland*. Princeton.

that pogroms had taken place in other parts of the western Soviet borderlands had already been known since the beginning of the war and was subsequently debated controversially. Especially, this was true for the Ukrainian case.

In the Ukrainian case, the controversies pertained not only to the number and scale of pogroms, local participation and its reasons, but mostly to the role of Stepan Bandera's Organization of Ukrainian Nationalists (Orhanizatsiia ukraïns'kykh natsionalistiv, OUN-B). While its leading postwar activists and historians, sympathizing with them, denied their involvement and responsibility,[3] others ascribed to them an important role.[4] The controversy was fueled by the fact that the Soviet Union had engaged in a fierce propaganda campaign against the Ukrainian nationalists since the Soviet reoccupation of western Ukraine in 1944. This was a part of the war against the Ukrainian Insurgent Army (Ukraïns'ka povstans'ka armiia, UPA) that had been founded by the OUN-B at the end of 1942. The propaganda campaign also continued after UPA's final defeat at the beginning of the 1950s. The main goal of this campaign was to present the Ukrainian nationalists as fascist collaborators with the Germans and as their henchmen.[5] However, Soviet writings tended to ignore the crimes committed by the Ukrainian nationalists against Jews, presenting the Ukrainians instead as German-sponsored executioners of the Ukrainian population.[6]

From the point of view of large segments of the population in western Ukraine and among Ukrainian exiles, Soviet propaganda was immensely cynical not only because it provided the ideological cover for the brutal suppression of Ukrainian resistance against Soviet rule but also because it was part of the denial of Soviet crimes committed in the days after the

3 Most prominently: Stets'ko, Iaroslav (1967). *30 chervnia 1941. Proholoshennia vidnovlennia derzhavnosty Ukraïny.* Toronto, p. 239f.; for a more recent example from historiography see: V'iatrovych, Volodymyr (2006). *Stavlennia OUN do ievreïv. Formuvannia pozytsiï na tli katastrofy.* L'viv, p. 59f.

4 See, for example: Friedman, Philip (1958/59). Ukrainian-Jewish Relations During the Nazi Occupation, *Journal of Jewish Social Science* 12: 259–294, here pp. 274–276.

5 Weiner, Amir (2001). *Making Sense of War. The Second World War and the Fate of the Bolshevik Revolution.* Princeton, pp. 165–169; Rossolinski-Liebe, Grzegorz (2014). *Stepan Bandera. The Life and Afterlife of a Ukrainian Nationalist. Fascism, Genocide, and Cult*, Stuttgart, pp. 362–383.

6 See as a blatant example: Beliaev, V. and M. Rudnytskii (1954). *Pod chuzhimi znamenami.* Moscow, pp. 54–68.

German attack on the Soviet Union. When the Soviets started to retreat, they murdered inmates of prisons who had been arrested for political reasons. These murders were committed on an especially large scale in western Ukraine, apparently because the German advance here was slower than in other parts of the front. In eastern Galicia, between 7,500 and 10,000 prison inmates were killed.[7]

While in the Ukrainian case, primarily, the question of the role of the OUN-B and its collaboration with the Germans were controversial, for the last one and a half decades, the discussion on the pogroms of the summer of 1941 has been enormously influenced by Jan Gross' study on the Jedwabne case. On the one hand, Gross' small book and the ensuing debate have produced important new insights, especially with respect to a differentiated evaluation of relations between Jews and non-Jews in the period of the Soviet occupation and the increase in anti-Semitism. On the other hand, it also seems to have reinforced some misleading assumptions about the character of anti-Jewish violence in the summer of 1941 both in Polish and other territories. Gross' study emphasizes an image of the pogroms as a largely spontaneous, murderous, and massive outbreak of anti-Semitic hatred where, as he summarized in his description of the events in Jedwabne, "half of the population [...] murdered the other half," referring to the fact that about one half of Jedwabne's inhabitants were Christian and the other half Jewish.[8] The critical point here is that such a generalization in fact distracts from attempts to look

---

7 For a discussion of numbers, see: Struve 2015, pp. 214–216. Other authors mention higher numbers. For example: Oleh Romaniv and Inna Fedushchak estimate the number of murdered prison inmates in Western Ukraine at about 22,000, among them 17,000 in eastern Galicia. Romaniv, Oleh and Inna Fedushchak (2002). *Zakhidnoukraïns'ka trahediia 1941*. L'viv, p. 63. Krzysztof Popiński mentions 20,000–24,000 murdered inmates for eastern Poland, among them 14,000–18,000 for eastern Galicia. Krzysztof Popiński (1997). Ewakuacja więzięń kresowych w czerwcu 1941 r. na podstawie dokumentacji "Memorialu" i Archiwum Wschodniego, in: *Zbrodnicza ewakuacja więzień i aresztów NKWD na Kresach Wschodnich II Rzeczypospolitej w czerwcu-lipcu 1941 roku*. Warsaw, pp. 71–77. See also: Musial, Bogdan (2001). *"Konterrevolutionäre Elemene sind zu erschießen." Die Brutalisierung des deutsch-sowjetischen Krieges im Sommer 1941*. Berlin, pp. 98–142.

8 Gross 2001, p. 7.

for answers about who the actual perpetrators were and what their political and organizational background was.[9] Attempts to exterminate the whole Jewish population in larger towns such as Jedwabne were rare exceptions among the large number of localities where acts of violence against Jews took place. Furthermore, as was the case also in Jedwabne, closer examination clearly shows that the actual perpetrators were a smaller, organized group whose actions are not adequately described as a largely spontaneous outbreak of deadly violence, as will be discussed in further detail below.

In the following part of the contribution, I outline the results of the study of anti-Jewish violence in eastern Galicia before comparing them with other regions.

Plans and expectations before June 22, 1941

Concerning the question of whether the Germans had made preparations to instigate pogroms alone or jointly with the help of Ukrainian or other nationalist groups, a central document is the often-cited cable that Reinhard Heydrich, head of the *Reichssicherheitshauptamt* (Reich Main Security Office), sent to the commanders of the *Einsatzgruppen* on June 29, 1941. Here, Heydrich ordered his police forces to secretly support "self-cleansing activities of anti-Communist and anti-Jewish circles" in the newly occupied territories and to instigate local pogroms. He referred to a meeting with officers from the *Einsatzgruppen* on June 17, 1941, where he had already given similar instructions.[10] In fact there are more documents to prove that there were widespread expectations on the German side that violent reckonings with "Jews and Communists" in the newly occupied territories would take place after the Soviet armed forces had left. This was seen as a good and healthy phenomenon that should be supported.[11]

---

9 See for an early, partly similar critique of Gross' approach and conclusions: Stola, Dariusz (2003). Jedwabne. Revisiting the Evidence and the Nature of the Crime, *Holocaust and Genocide Studies* 17: 139–152.

10 The cable is published in: Klein, Peter (ed.) (1997). *Die Einsatzgruppen in der besetzten Sowjetunion 1941/42. Die Tätigkeits- und Lageberichte des Chefs der Sicherheitspolizei und des SD*. Berlin, p. 319.

11 Kangeris, Karlis (2004). Die nationalsozialistischen Pläne und Propagandamaßnahmen im Generalbezirk Lettland 1941–1942, in Gaunt, David et al. (eds.). *Collaboration*

But there are no further documents that indicate any kind of concrete preparation or preplanning in cooperation with Ukrainian or other local forces. Apparently, Heydrich sent the cable because he (and most likely also Heinrich Himmler) believed that, so far, the *Einsatzgruppen* had put too little effort into instigating pogroms. Heydrich may have had in view especially *Einsatzgruppe* B, while the activities of *Einsatzgruppe* A in Lithuania could have provided input for his instructions on how his police forces should proceed. [12] Until the date of Heydrich's cable, *Einsatzgruppe* C, which had been active in the Ukrainian territories in eastern Galicia and Volhynia, had not had many opportunities to instigate pogroms because of the slow advance of German troops here during the first days of the invasion. However, this would also indicate that there had not been any thorough planning and preparation except for a discussion at the meeting on June 17, 1941. Here support for violent reckonings was only one among many subjects that were discussed regarding the deployment and tasks of the *Einsatzgruppen*.[13]

Another argument against the existence of the joint planning and more concrete and detailed preparation of pogroms against Jews consists in the fact that the instigation of pogroms was an aim of the German police forces. Deep mutual distrust existed between them and Stepan Bandera's OUN. The OUN had cooperated with the Germans since its foundation in 1929 with an interruption between the end of 1933 and 1937–38 (the period of German-Polish rapprochement) in the same way as its predecessor, the Ukraïns'ka viiskova orhanizatsiia (UVO) (Ukrainian Military Organization) had during the 1920s. However, in this period, the OUN already had the support of the German military intelligence, the

and Resistance During the Holocaust. Belarus, Estonia, Latvia, Lithuania. Bern, pp. 161–186, here p. 169; Quinkert, Babette (2009). *Propaganda und Terror in Weißrussland 1941–1944. Die deutsche "geistige" Kriegführung gegen die Zivilbevölkerung und Partisanen*. Paderborn, pp. 56f.

12 Rossino, Alexander B. (2003). Polish "Neighbours" and German Invaders: Anti-Jewish Violence in the Białystok District during the Opening Weeks of Operation Barbarossa, *Polin* 16: 431–451, here p. 443.

13 On the meeting of June 17, 1941: Wildt, Michael (2002). *Generation des Unbedingten. Das Führungskorps des Reichssicherheitshautptamtes*. Hamburg, p. 557f.; Ogorreck, Ralf (1996). *Die Einsatzgruppen und die "Genesis der Endlösung"*. Berlin, p. 58f.

Abwehr, while the German political police, the *Gestapo*, and the *Außenpolitisches Amt* (Foreign Political Office) of Hitler's NSDAP, headed by Alfred Rosenberg, preferred cooperation with other Ukrainian groups.[14]

The distrust was only aggravated by the split in the OUN in 1940 when Bandera's followers separated from the organization's leadership under Andrii Mel'nyk. Finally, the conflicts within the OUN resulted in an interruption in cooperation with Bandera's organization by the *Abwehr* in November 1940. However, the *Abwehr* resumed cooperation in the spring of 1941 in the context of the preparation of the attack on the Soviet Union. The reason for this was that with the split, the Mel'nyk leadership had lost the support of most of the organization in the German-occupied part of Poland as well as contact with the underground organization in the Soviet-occupied territories of eastern Galicia and Volhynia. As a result of the split, practically only the Bandera-OUN was able to provide the German *Abwehr* with intelligence from the Soviet territory and, probably even more importantly, to prepare an insurgency in the Soviet territories of western Ukraine that were to start with the German attack on the Soviet Union.[15] Furthermore, Bandera and his followers seemed to have avoided closer contacts with the German Security Police because they knew the hostile attitude of the Security Police toward them and probably feared that it could prevent them from implementing their plans to build a Ukrainian state.

In contrast, Andrii Mel'nyk's OUN not only cooperated with the *Abwehr* but there also seems to have existed some form of cooperation between Mel'nyk's OUN and the German Security Police.[16] After June 22, 1941, people linked to the Mel'nyk faction could be found as translators or in other capacities both within *Einsatzgruppe* C and in the so-called *Einsatzkommando Lemberg* that was sent from the *Generalgouvernement* to eastern Galicia to establish structures of the German Security Police.[17] Apparently, not only the *banderivtsi* kept distance but also

---

14 For the earlier cooperation, see the comprehensive study by Golczewski, Frank (2010). *Deutsche und Ukrainer 1914–1939*. Paderborn.

15 On the Ukrainian underground in the Soviet territory and the OUN-B's preparation of an uprising, see: Patryliak, Ivan K. (2004). *Viis'kova diial'nist' OUN(B) u 1940–1942 rokakh*. Kiev.

16 On the preparations for the war by both factions of the OUN, see: Struve 2015, pp. 172–209.

17 Ibid., p. 227f., p. 299.

the Security Police preferred the more docile Mel'nyk followers to the *banderivtsi*. The Security Police mistrusted the *banderivtsi* because of their activist, defiant attitude.

The result was that the German police forces that had been assigned the task of instigating pogroms cooperated with a Ukrainian organization that had lost nearly all connections to the Ukrainian underground in the Soviet areas and, thus, prior to the German attack on June 22, 1941, would not have been able to prepare pogroms. On the other hand, the Ukrainian organization that had strong underground forces in the Soviet territory cooperated with the *Abwehr* and the German army that had other tasks and priorities than preparing acts of anti-Jewish violence.

The perception of Jews as supporters and beneficiaries of Soviet rule

However, both the Germans and the Ukrainian nationalists shared the view that the Jews were the main supporters and beneficiaries of Soviet rule—both generally and especially in the period of 1939–41 in the newly acquired Soviet territories. The perception of Jews as the "biological substance" of Soviet rule, as Klaus-Michael Mallmann has argued, formed the rationale for the mass executions of Jews by the German police forces during the weeks after June 22, 1941.[18] While, during the war with Poland in September 1939, the main enemy had been the Poles, with the Jews being seen rather as an undesirable group of the population, in this new war they appeared as a core group of the Soviet enemy. In another letter to the *Einsatzgruppen* on July 1, Heydrich explicitly wrote: "It is obvious that the cleansing activities have to extend first of all to Bolsheviks and Jews."[19] While most of the Bolsheviks fled before the Germans arrived, most of the Jews stayed. By the end of July, the German police units targeted Jewish males, primarily from the intelligentsia, because they were seen as especially pro-Soviet and as a security risk. The attempt to annihilate the whole Jewish population began only later.

---

18 Mallmann, Klaus-Michael (2000). Die Türöffner der "Endlösung" Zur Genesis des Genozids, in Paul, Gerhard and Klaus-Michael Mallmann (eds.). *Die Gestapo im Zweiten Weltkrieg. "Heimatfront" und besetztes Europa*. Darmstadt, pp. 437–463, here p. 443f.

19 Klein 1997, p. 320f.

The perception of Jews as supporters and beneficiaries of Soviet rule had also spread widely among the non-Jewish population in the territories occupied by the Soviet Union in September 1939 and June 1940.[20] The radical Ukrainian nationalists shared it, too. In May and June 1941 the leadership of the Bandera-OUN wrote down extensive instructions for the beginning of the German-Soviet war. They described the organization's main aim as the installation of local administrations and militias in localities where the Soviet troops were about to leave as soon as possible and preferably before the German troops arrived. This would provide the basis for Ukrainian state-building and demonstrate to the Germans the strength of the Ukrainians' will and ability to establish such a state. Despite repeated efforts, the OUN-B was unable to receive any clear assurances from the German side that a Ukrainian state would be founded as a result of the war against the Soviet Union.

One of the tasks that Stepan Bandera's OUN assigned to its combat groups and local militias was to cleanse the territory of "hostile elements," that is, remnants not only of Soviet troops and NKVD officials but also more generally of supporters of Soviet rule.[21]

A number of documents show that within the OUN-B, primarily, Jews were seen in this role. But also with respect to the foundation of a Ukrainian nation-state, Jews were considered to be an undesirable group. The head of the OUN-B's structures in the Soviet territories, Ivan Klymiv, interpreted these tasks in an especially radical way in two leaflets that he had written already before the beginning of the German attack and that were widely distributed in western Ukraine in July 1941. One of the leaflets exhorted its readers: "People! Know! Moscow, Poland, the Hungari-

20 See on the image of Jews as pro-Soviet in Western Ukraine: Mick, Christoph (2007). "Only the Jews do not waver..." L'viv under Soviet Occupation, in Barkan, Elazar et al. (eds.). *Shared History–Divided Memory. Jews and Others in Soviet-Occupied Poland, 1939–1941.* Leipzig, pp. 245–262. The question if such a perception was based on real attitudes among Jews or on older prejudices has been especially intensely discussed for the Polish case, see on that debate: Struve, Kai (2008). Geschichte und Gedächtnis. Polen und Juden unter sowjetischer Herrschaft 1939–1941, *Jahrbuch des Simon-Dubnow-Instituts* 7: 495–530.

21 Veselova, O. et al. (eds.) (2006). *OUN v 1941 rotsi* (part 1). Kiev, pp. 58–176, here p. 93; see also: Carynnyk, Marco (2011). Foes of Our Rebirth: Ukrainian Nationalist Discussions about Jews, 1929–1947, *Nationalities Papers* 39, pp. 315–352, here p. 329f.

ans, the Jews [*zhydova*]—these are your enemies. Destroy them." In addition, Klymiv introduced Military Revolutionary Tribunals with the power to apply the death penalty and to ascribe "collective responsibility" to families and nations for all offences against the Ukrainian army and state.[22]

This describes the framework of orders and instructions that the local and regional commanders of the OUN-B insurgency received. Their aim was to build a Ukrainian state—which the Germans tried to prevent.

Contexts of anti-Jewish violence in eastern Galicia

A close analysis of acts of anti-Jewish violence in about 30 cities and small towns as well as a number of villages in eastern Galicia during July 1941 with the participation or at the instigation of local people enables the distinction to be made between three main contexts of the violence.[23]

The retrieval of murdered prison inmates

In a number of localities acts of violence against Jews took place in the context of the retrieval of the corpses of prison inmates who the Soviets had killed before their retreat. The best known case here are the events in the western Ukrainian capital L'viv on July 1, 1941.[24] In L'viv, as in several other cities where murdered prison inmates were found, the German military authorities ordered the Ukrainian militia to bring Jews to the prisons as workers for the retrieval of the corpses in order to allow relatives to identify and to bury them. It was part of the usual procedure of the German army to use primarily Jews as forced laborers for all kinds of work after German troops had occupied a certain locality. Ukrainian militias established themselves based on the underground structures of the

---

22 Kraievyi provid Ukraïns'kykh natsionalistiv na MUZ (Matirni ukraïns'ki zemli), "Ukraïns'ke narode!", in Dziuban, Orest (ed.) (2001). *Ukraïns'ke derzhavotvorennia. Akt 30 chervnia 1941. Zbirnyk dokumentiv i materialiv.* Kiev, pp. 126–129; Nachal'nyi kom[andant] Ukr[aïns'koï] nats[ional'noï] revoliuciinoï armiï, leitenant Liegenda, "Hromadiane Ukraïns'koï derzhavy!", in: ibid., pp. 129–131; see also Carynnyk 2011, p. 332.

23 The following section is a summary of a micro-analysis of anti-Jewish violence of which the details can be found in: Struve 2015, pp. 216–667.

24 See on L'viv also: Himka, John-Paul (2011). The Lviv Pogrom of 1941: The Germans, Ukrainian Nationalists, and the Carnival Crowd, *Canadian Slavonic Papers/Revue canadienne des slavistes* 53: 209–243.

OUN-B in all these localities and nearly everywhere else in eastern Galicia closely before or after the arrival of German troops in line with the OUN-B's plans for state-building as from May 1941.

The fact that Jews were forced to retrieve the corpses of the prison inmates confirmed in the eyes of the non-Jewish population the already widespread perception of Jews as supporters and beneficiaries of Soviet rule and that they also bore responsibility for the Soviet mass murder. The work with the decomposing bodies itself was already a form of punishment. Mocking and beatings while they worked added to their humiliation. In other instances they were arrested on the streets or forced from their apartments to do that work. Sometimes this escalated to murder. In L'viv and in other localities residents joined the militia in bringing Jews to the prisons. The violence was most intense around the prisons where many people seeking relatives or friends who had been arrested by the Soviets had gathered. As many scenes from the L'viv pogrom show, the violence there was also part of—and this is also true for other localities—the public displays that celebrated the reversal of the previous social order by publicly punishing the Jews for their alleged earlier transgressions.

In nearly all localities German forces were present at the prisons and controlled the entrances. They supervised the retrieval of the bodies and usually after some hours also stopped the violence. In many instances, members of the German police or armed forces participated in the violence. During the pogrom in L'viv, the largest single murder case consisted of the execution of about a hundred Jews by members of *Einsatzgruppe* C in the yard of the Brygidki prison. There are strong indications, though no clear proof, that the *Einsatzgruppe* also contributed to the fact that many more Jews were brought to the prisons than could work there. In at least two of the three prisons, they seem to have encouraged local civilians to commit acts of violence. In the case of Boryslav, there is more clear evidence that a unit of the German police under the command of the Higher SS and police leader Friedrich Jeckeln encouraged violence. In this city, a fierce pogrom with many acts of murder developed on July 3 and 4. Also here a number of the victims were shot by the German police unit in the yard of the local prison building. In Drohobych, a bloody pogrom unfolded immediately after German troops occupied the city and corpses of murdered inmates were found. In Zolochiv and in Ternopil', the retrieval of murdered prison inmates was a scene of anti-Jewish violence. The events here, however, were primarily part of another context, that is, of a series of violent excesses committed by parts of the "Viking" division of the *Waffen-SS* as will be discussed below.

However, Soviet massacres of prison inmates did not always produce deadly anti-Jewish violence. Apparently, the attitude and the procedure of the local German military or police authorities had an influence here. For example, in Stanislaviv (today Ivano-Frankivs'k), Stryi, and Zhovkva, the Soviets also killed prison inmates. In Stanislaviv, Jews had to retrieve the dead, but this did not become a public ritual of humiliation and punishment of the Jews. It seems that only enough workers were brought to the prison who could actually work there. Stanislaviv was occupied by Hungarian troops. In those localities where Hungarian troops were present, they usually prevented the murder of Jews, though not all acts of violence. Stryi and Zhovkva were occupied by German troops and here too the retrieval of the corpses was not accompanied by violence. In the case of Stryi, the sources do not allow conclusions to be drawn as to who had to retrieve the corpses of the murdered prison inmates. Jews had to prepare a mass grave for them and were threatened and beaten during that work. There were also some mocking and physical attacks on Jews by Ukrainian youths in the streets of the city, but no one seems to have been killed. In Zhovkva, Soviet POWs had to take out the murdered inmates from the NKVD building. Shortly after the occupation of the city, German troops burned down the synagozgue, and, for several hours, groups of Ukrainian youths attacked Jews and smashed windows in streets inhabited by Jews. But here as well no Jews were killed.[25]

Punishments and executions by OUN-B insurgents

As described above, the instructions of the OUN-B for the initial phase of the German-Soviet war allowed for "cleansing the territory of hostile elements" and described Jews in a very general way as supporters of Soviet

25 The retrieval of corpses in Zhovkva that has not been treated more extensively in my book is shown in a short sequence of a film made by an officer in the staff of Army Corps IV, for information on the film: www.filmarchives-online.eu/viewDetailForm?FilmworkID=d59811dd19f2c01abba0a6174ee8b8be (accessed on May 2, 2016). On attacks on Jews, see: Gerszon Taffet, Archiwum Żydowskiego Instytutu Historycznego (AŻIH) 302/141, p. 9f.; Józef Hochner, ibid., 301/1892.

rule. Ivan Klymiv's leaflets had radicalized these instructions even more, especially his order to introduce Military Revolutionary Tribunals and their power to impose collective punishments on families and national groups. That seems to have been the central context of deadly violence in small towns and many villages over which the German and Hungarian troops did not have full control during the first days and weeks of their occupation. Usually, the violence took place without the knowledge of the German or Hungarian military authorities. Such punishment could take very different forms and often affected not only Jews but also Ukrainians and Poles. However, the "punishment" of Ukrainians was usually milder and less deadly, and concerned specific individuals who had served in the Soviet village administration, supported the foundation of kolkhozes, or had allegedly informed on others. In the case of Jews, often whole families were killed, and the murder of Jews seems to have been much more widespread than among other nationalities. It can be assumed that this was the result of the stereotypical perception of Jews as supporters of Soviet rule. Poles were also sometimes killed for allegedly having supported Soviet rule, informed on Ukrainians, or because they were seen as enemies of the Ukrainian state.

In this context, the violence could take on very different forms, however. For example, in the village of Dychkiv, near Ternopil', local OUN activists arrested nine to twelve Jewish males, led them out of the village, and executed them there on July 6, that is, about three days after the Red Army had retreated from this area.[26] In the village of Perevoloka, near Buchach, local OUN-B activists arrested at least ten men already before German troops had arrived, among them eight Ukrainians and two Jews, and executed them. In addition, they killed one Jewish family. The morning after the killings, they declared during a public meeting that an independent Ukrainian state had been founded, apparently referring to the declaration of the foundation of a Ukrainian state by Bandera's deputy Iaroslav Stets'ko on the evening of June 30, 1941, in L'viv that had also been announced via the L'viv radio station.[27]

In other localities, for example the small towns of Ulashkivtsi and Otyniia, several dozen Jews were killed out of a Jewish population of several hundred or about one thousand. In the memoirs of surviving

26 Struve 2015, p. 534f.
27 Ibid., pp. 515–518.

Jews, these acts of violence appear as a pogrom in the sense of a spontaneous, wild outbreak of excessive violence. In fact, closer examination of sources and the context of events in other localities suggest that the acts of murder were targeted killings of a number of Jewish families by local insurgent groups of the OUN-B.[28] In the small town of Kosiv, near Chortkiv, and the village of Nezvys'ko, near Obertyn, the punishment of the Jews became an attempt to exterminate the whole Jewish population, with 80 to 115 victims in Kosiv and about 60 in Nezvys'ko.[29]

Violent excesses by units of the Waffen-SS

Parts of the "Viking" *Waffen-SS* division were responsible for the bloodiest pogroms in eastern Galicia. This unit of the *Waffen-SS* was part of the combat troops subordinated to the German armed forces and had no police tasks. The division had been newly deployed before the German attack on the Soviet Union. Most of the soldiers of this ideologically highly motivated unit, which saw itself as an elite military formation of the national socialist state, had had no battle experience when they moved through eastern Galicia. They were part of a second line of troops that had not, or only to a small degree, taken part in the intense fighting in the border area. There were some skirmishes with Soviet troops also east of L'viv, but in major combat activity the "Viking" division became involved only in the northeast of Ternopil' and at the former Polish-Soviet border near Husiatyn. Apparently, they started their war against the Soviet Union by shooting Jews whom they met on their way to the front line.

Parts of the division had a central role in the violent excesses committed in Zolochiv, Zboriv, Ozerna, Hrymailiv, Skalat, and most of all in Ternopil'. In all these localities, local Ukrainian militias and inhabitants also participated in the violence. But most of the victims—between 8 and 30 percent of the Jewish population of these cities and towns—were clearly the result of the involvement of the *Waffen-SS* troops. They combed these localities for Jewish men and shot them "as if it was a hunting expedition," as one Jewish witness described what he saw in Ternopil'.[30] Or they assembled Jews at certain places—for instance in Zolochiv at the NKVD prison, where the Jews also had to retrieve the

28 Ibid., pp. 551–554, pp. 638–643.

29 Ibid., pp. 545–548, pp. 654–662.

30 Otto Schorman: The Brown Terror, AŻIH 302/295, p. 7.

bodies of murdered inmates—and shot them there. In Ternopil', the largest city where a pogrom by this unit took place, probably between 2,300 and 4,000 Jews were killed. This was violence on a much larger scale and with a very different character than the violence in other localities.[31]

For nearly all localities with high numbers of deaths, the sources give different or only very rough numbers. In some cases it is possible to discount some numbers in the sources or assumptions in the literature as unlikely, based on descriptions of the violence or on data about the Jewish inhabitants. Nevertheless, every estimate of the total number of Jews killed in acts of violence with the participation of local inhabitants for the whole of eastern Galicia contains a high uncertainty. The sources are often vague, and there may have been acts of violence in villages that are not documented in any sources. However, my estimate of the number of Jewish victims in localities for which we have documents is between 7,300 and 11,300. These numbers do not include mass executions by German police forces, of which the largest in eastern Galicia took place in L'viv on July 5, but they do include the massacres in those localities where the *Waffen-SS* "Viking" division was involved. However, about 60 percent of the victims were killed in pogroms in which the *Waffen-SS* "Viking" division played a central role.[32]

Nevertheless, in terms of local perpetrators, at the core of all cases of deadly violence that I could examine there were clearly or very likely insurgents of the OUN-B or local militias founded by them. This was the case in those localities where Jews were brought to the prisons to retrieve murdered inmates. The role of the OUN-B groups is even clearer in those localities where the violence consisted mostly of targeted killings of certain individuals or families.

In summary, it can be stated that there was no uniform "pogrom scenario" but that the anti-Jewish violence consisted of different segments that, however, often overlapped. They were interconnected by the perception of Jews as supporters and beneficiaries of Soviet rule. The results of the close analysis of anti-Jewish violence also show that understanding it as a massive, spontaneous outbreak of anti-Semitic hatred is to a certain degree misleading. There can be no doubt that anti-Jewish attitudes strongly increased during the period of Soviet rule and that

31 On the massacres of *Waffen-SS* division "Viking": Struve 2015, pp. 561–630.

32 For a more detailed discussion of the number of victims, see: ibid., pp. 668–671.

there was a general atmosphere of hostility toward Jews in the summer of 1941. However, these anti-Jewish attitudes alone only rarely seem to have resulted in deadly violence. There were two other preconditions for deadly violence on a larger scale perpetrated by the local population. Such acts of violence took place where they were encouraged by the German authorities or where acts of murder were perpetrated by local militias or combat groups. In both cases, from the local side, nationalist insurgents played a central role. For them the acts of violence were part of the change of rule and of state-building.

Beyond eastern Galicia

Comparison of eastern Galicia with other regions of the western Soviet borderland confirms the finding that deadly violence against Jews perpetrated by the local population emanated mostly from insurgent groups who aimed at the removal and the punishment of alleged supporters of Soviet rule and at establishing their own nation-states. Among these regions, the situation in Volhynia was very similar to that in eastern Galicia because in Volhynia too a strong OUN-B underground existed that acted according to the same instructions as the underground in eastern Galicia.[33]

Except for Volhynia, the events in eastern Galicia resemble most strongly those in the Baltic countries, primarily in Lithuania. After the Soviet Union had occupied Lithuania, Latvia, and Estonia in the summer of 1940, in all three countries an anti-Soviet, nationalist underground developed that had connections with exiled groups in Germany. As in the Ukrainian case, during the first months of 1941, the German *Abwehr* established, with the help of the exiled organizations, connections to the underground that served to obtain intelligence from Soviet territory and to support the preparation of uprisings for the initial phase of the German-Soviet war.[34]

---

33 On anti-Jewish violence in Volhynia in the summer of 1941, see: Spector, Shmuel (1990). *The Holocaust of the Volhynian Jews 1941–1944*. Jerusalem, pp. 64–79; Ivan Kachanovs'kyi (2014). OUN(b) ta natsysts'ki masovi vbystva vlitku 1941 roku na istorychnii Volyni, *Ukraïna moderna* 20: 215–244.

34 Kangeris, Karlis (1994). Kollaboration vor der Kollaboration? Die baltischen Emigranten und ihre "Befreiungskomitees" in Deutschland 1940/1941, in Röhr, Werner (ed.).

The underground seems to have been strongest and most active in Lithuania. Because of the direct border with Germany, the connections between the underground and the exiled groups in Germany were also the closest. The most important Lithuanian organization in exile was the Lithuanian Activist Front (Lietuvių Aktyvistų Frontas, LAF) that was founded in November 1940 in Berlin by representatives of different political groups. In the months before the German attack on the Soviet Union, the LAF issued and distributed a number of leaflets and instructions to the underground in Lithuania on how to prepare for the anti-Soviet uprising and the reestablishment of the Lithuanian state. Even more strongly than in the case of the OUN-B's instructions and leaflets, those of the LAF were characterized by the identification of Jews as supporters and beneficiaries of Soviet rule. Accordingly, Jews also appeared prominently among those who were to be called to account for Soviet rule. Similar to the OUN-B's instructions, they tended to submit Jews to harsher punishments than non-Jews.[35] In contrast to the Ukrainian case, documents of the Lithuanian anti-Soviet resistance explicitly stated that the expected change of rule should be used as an opportunity to drive out as many Jews as possible from Lithuania as punishment for their alleged support of Soviet rule. They asserted that by spreading terror and fear, the Jews should be made to escape together with the Soviets.[36]

Unlike western Ukraine where the German troops faced fierce resistance by strong Soviet forces during the first days of the war, in Lithuania the Red Army quickly retreated without much fighting. They left the Lithuanian capital already on June 23 while German troops arrived there only in the late afternoon of June 24. Simultaneously, with the Soviet retreat and before the arrival of the German troops, underground Lithuanian insurgents emerged and established a Lithuanian government led by the LAF. Already on June 23 the Lithuanian insurgents, usually known as "partisans," had started with arrests of those whom they considered

---

Okkupation und Kollaboration (1938–1945). Beiträge zu Konzepten und Praxis der Kollaboration in der deutschen Okkupationspolitik. Berlin, pp. 165–190.

35 One leaflet even stated that Lithuanian "traitors" could rehabilitate themselves by proofing that "they had liquidated one Jew." On the instructions for the Lithuanian underground and on this controversially discussed leaflet, see: Dieckmann, Christoph (2011). *Deutsche Besatzungspolitik in Litauen 1941–1944* (Bd. 1). Göttingen, pp. 246–252.

36 Ibid., p. 253.

to be supporters of Soviet rule and enemies of the Lithuanian state. They were primarily Jews. Also, attacks on Jews took place on the streets, which had been encouraged by broadcasts from the local radio station that had been taken over by the insurgents.[37]

When the commander of *Einsatzgruppe* A, SS-Brigadeführer Franz Walter Stahlecker, arrived in Kaunas in the morning of June 25, he immediately began work on intensifying anti-Jewish violence from the local side. As he later reported, this had required some effort. He talked with different leaders of the Lithuanian insurgent groups, but apparently was only able to convince one of the leaders, Algirdas Klimaitis—who may have been a member of the radical fascist "Iron Wolf" movement—to participate in his plans for extending the anti-Jewish violence.[38] During the nights of June 25–27, Klimaitis' men entered the primarily Jewish quarter of Vilijampole and killed, as Christoph Dieckmann estimates, between 600 and 1,000 Jews there.[39] However, in his report from October 1941, Stahlecker mentions much larger numbers: 1,500 killed during the nights of June 25–26 and 2,300 more during the following nights until June 28.[40] There were also other places in the city where acts of anti-Jewish violence or murder took place, but on a much smaller scale.[41]

Arrests of alleged Soviet supporters also continued during these days. About 90 percent of those who had been arrested by the beginning of July were Jews, the other 10 percent, about 360 people, were Lithuanians, Russians, and Poles. Beginning on June 29, the Jews among those who had been arrested were brought to the so-called Fort VII, a nineteenth-century fortification, and incarcerated there. During the following days, more Jews were brought there. By July 6, most of them, about 5,000 men and women, had been killed by members of the Lithu-

37 Ibid., pp. 313–315; Szarota, Tomasz (2000). *U progu zagłady. Zajścia antyżydowskie i pogromy w okupowanej Europie*. Warsaw, pp. 217–225.

38 Dieckmann 2011, p. 317f. For Stahlecker's report see: "Einsatzgruppe A: Gesamtbericht bis zum 15. Oktober 1941 (Doc. 180-L)," in *Trial of the Major War Criminals before the International Military Tribunal, Nuremberg 14 November 1945—1 October 1946*. Nuremberg 1949 (vol. 37), pp. 670–701, here p. 672, p. 682.

39 Dieckmann 2011, pp. 319–321.

40 "Einsatzgruppe A: Gesamtbericht...," in *Trial of the Major War Criminals* (vol. 37), p. 682.

41 Szarota 2000, pp. 226–264.

anian insurgent forces supervised by the *Einsatzgruppe*. After complaints from the Wehrmacht about the brutal murders, the German Security Police had the killings stopped. Instead *Einsatzkommando* 3, a part of *Einsatzgruppe* A that remained in Lithuania after Stahlecker and the other parts had left for Latvia, organized the so-called Rollkommando under SS-Untersturmführer Joachim Hamann, whose members were mostly Lithuanians recruited from Klimaitis' men. During the following months, this unit shot several tens of thousands of Jews in Lithuania and neighboring regions.[42]

The character and extent of anti-Jewish violence in other, smaller localities in Lithuania has not been researched very thoroughly so far. However, it seems that there too acts of anti-Jewish violence originated primarily from insurgent groups or new local administrations and militias that they established. They arrested or killed those whom they considered to be enemies of the Lithuanian state or who had allegedly collaborated with the Soviets—in the view of the Lithuanian insurgents, primarily Jews.[43]

A comparison of the events in Lithuania with those in western Ukraine shows three main differences:

a) In Lithuania, the scale of murders of prison inmates by the Soviets was much smaller than in western Ukraine. Altogether, about 400 inmates of prisons and about 700 other civilians were killed during the Soviet retreat. The largest Soviet massacre took place in Pravieniškės, but here the corpses were found only on June 28 when the large public acts of anti-Jewish violence in Kaunas had for the most part already finished.[44]
b) The commander of *Einsatzgruppe* A, Franz Walter Stahlecker, much more actively instigated anti-Jewish violence than *Einsatzgruppe* B and C. Therefore, it seems to be quite likely that his activities in Kaunas provided inputs to Heydrich's above-cited letter of June 29. For Heydrich, Stahlecker's activity in Kaunas

42 On this unit see: Stang, Knut (1996). *Kollaboration und Massenmord. Die litauische Hilfspolizei, das Rollkommando Hamann und Ermordung der litauischen Juden*. Frankfurt am Main.

43 Dieckmann 2011, pp. 361–379.

44 Ibid., p. 301f.

probably was an exemplary procedure that other *Einsatzgruppen* had to follow.

c) In contrast to the other *Einsatzgruppen*, Stahlecker recruited, already during the first days of the war, local units from among the insurgents that then carried out a large part of the actual executions of Jews and others during the following months.

Stahlecker followed a similar procedure in Latvia. When German troops occupied Riga on July 1, as in Kaunas, they were greeted by Latvian insurgents who had also been involved in clashes with the retreating Red Army units. Here, on the same day, about hundred corpses of murdered inmates of the Riga prison were found.[45] On July 1 and during the following days, the Latvian insurgent forces arrested in close cooperation with the *Einsatzgruppe* a large number of people who they claimed had supported Soviet rule. Also, in Riga they seem to have arrested primarily Jews. There were also some attacks on Jews in the streets or in places where Jews were brought as forced laborers. However, apparently this did not have a similar dimension as in a number of western Ukrainian cities or as in Kaunas.[46]

In Riga Stahlecker began to build his own local Latvian police force immediately after his arrival. As in Lithuania with Algirdas Klimaitis, he

---

45 Angrick, Andrej and Peter Klein (2006). *Die "Endlösung" in Riga: Ausbeutung und Vernichtung 1941–1944*, Darmstadt, p. 72f.; Felder, Björn M. (2009). *Lettland im Zweiten Weltkrieg. Zwischen sowjetischen und deutschen Besatzern 1940–1946*. Paderborn, p. 225.

46 The scale of violence and the question who initiated the arrests is controversial in the literature. Andrej Angrick and Peter Klein (2006, p. 73, pp. 78–84) emphasize the Latvian initiative. For Katrin Reichelt this seems to be less clear: Reichelt, Katrin (2011). *Lettland unter deutscher Besatzung 1941–1944. Der lettische Anteil am Holocaust.* Berlin, pp. 82–84. Andrew Ezergailis does not see independent actions of the Latvian forces also for the first days after the Soviet retreat, but describes them as having been totally under German command: Ezergailis, Andrew (1996). *The Holocaust in Latvia 1941–1944. The Missing Center.* Riga, pp. 210–221; see also: Ezergailis, Andrew (2004). "Neighbors" Did Not Kill Jews!, in Gaunt, David et al. (eds.). *Collaboration and Resistance During the Holocaust. Belarus, Estonia, Latvia, Lithuania.* Bern, pp. 187–222, here pp. 217–221. On the arrests see also: Felder 2009, pp. 225–227. Felder's interpretation here follows Ezergailis', but some of the sources that he cites seem to support rather the argument that in the initial phase of occupation the Latvian police forces arrested Jews to a high degree on their own initiative based on the view of Jews as Soviet supporters."

recruited them with the help of a person who seems to have been rather on the margins of the Latvian insurgents, the former Latvian police officer Viktors Arājs who headed one of the insurgent groups in the city. Arājs soon formed a Latvian unit that, as *Hilfssicherheitspolizei*, would carry out together with parts of the *Einsatzgruppe* most of the mass executions of Jews during the following months in Latvia. During the evening and night of July 4, Stahlecker organized with the help of Arājs' men a pogrom in Riga. According to the reports of the *Einsatzgruppen*, 400 Jews were killed and synagogues were burned down.[47] Clearly, this was not a spontaneous outbreak of violence, but a preplanned massacre by a certain group of perpetrators who acted on Stahlecker's instructions.

The large majority of Latvia's Jews lived in Riga. Therefore, no major acts of anti-Jewish violence by Latvian insurgents seemed to have occurred in other localities. However, as in other regions, here as well insurgents who transformed into local police forces or helped to establish local Latvian administrations arrested and sometimes executed individuals who had supported Soviet rule or whom they considered to be traitors. Those arrested were handed over to the German police forces that executed them or had them executed by the Arājs command.

Basically, the events in Estonia were similar to those in Lithuania and Latvia, but with the difference that no major acts of anti-Jewish violence took place. Clearly the reasons for this were that there was only a very small Jewish community in Estonia and that after the occupation of Latvia, the German advance slowed down and only completed the occupation of Estonia toward the end of August 1941. This allowed most of Estonia's Jews to escape. Only about 1,000 Jews fell under German rule. However, Estonian insurgents too took over local administrations and formed police forces when the Red Army retreated, and they also arrested and executed alleged or real supporters of Soviet rule.[48]

Further comparison with the Belarusian territories confirms the significance of anti-Soviet insurgents for the violence against Jews. There

---

47 Mallmann, Klaus-Michael et al. (eds.) (2011). *Die "Ereignismeldungen UdSSR." Dokumente der Einsatzgruppen in der Sowjetunion* (Bd. 1). Darmstadt, p. 129.

48 Birn, Ruth Bettina (2006). *Die Sicherheitspolizei in Estland 1941–1944. Eine Studie über Kollaboration.* Paderborn, pp. 73–79, pp. 159–171; Weiss-Wendt, Anton (2009). *Murder without Hatred. Estonians and the Holocaust.* Syracuse, pp. 94–107, pp. 123–135.

was no Belarusian anti-Soviet insurgency. Accordingly, for those regions and localities of western Belarus that were inhabited mostly by Belarusians, sources show only a small number of acts of violence against Jews—as it seems, mostly of a non-deadly character. The reason for this was not that general hostility toward Jews here was significantly less than in other regions. Leonid Rein has argued that the readiness to take part in the persecution and murder of Jews, as later phases of the Holocaust show, did not differ here from neighboring regions.[49] The decisive difference with respect to acts of anti-Jewish violence in the summer of 1941 was that no Belarusian anti-Soviet insurgency with a program of assuming power and removing or punishing Soviet supporters existed.

The case that seems to contradict the argument that deadly anti-Jewish violence can be ascribed to a high degree to nationalist anti-Soviet insurgents and their attempt at state-building is the Polish one. A considerable number of acts of deadly anti-Jewish violence occurred in those territories of western Belarus inhabited mostly by Poles.[50] For the Poles, the German invasion was not accompanied by the expectation that a Polish state would be reestablished. Yet here too an active, nationalist anti-Soviet underground movement existed among the Polish population. Polish insurgents also attacked Soviet troops in the days after June 22 and supported the German invasion. As an important recent study by Mirosław Tryczyk clearly shows, in Jedwabne and other towns and villages in the region, the violence emanated primarily from mem-

49 Rein, Leonid (2006). Local Collaboration in the Execution of the "Final Solution" in Nazi-Occupied Belorussia, *Holocaust and Genocide Studies* 20: 381–409, here p. 389f. See also: Cholawsky, Shalom (1998). *The Jews of Bielorussia During World War II*. Amsterdam, p. 271f.

50 A more thorough investigation into acts of anti-Jewish violence began as a reaction to the publication of Jan Tomasz Gross' book *Neighbors* on the pogrom in Jedwabne, see Machcewicz, Paweł and Krzysztof Persak (eds.) (2002). *Wokół Jedwabnego, t. 1: Studia, t. 2: Dokumenty*. Warsaw, and here primarily the articles by Dmitrów, Edmund (2002). Oddziały operacyjne niemieckiej Policji Bezpieczeństwa i Służby Bezpieczeństwa a początek zagłady Żydów w Łomżyńskiem i na Białostocczyźnie latem 1941 roku, in ibid., pp. 273–351; Żbikowski, Andrzej (2002). Pogromy I mordy ludności żydowskiej w Łomżyńskiem i na Białostocczyźnie latem 1941 roku w świetle relacji ocalałych Żydów I dokumentów sądowych, in ibid., pp. 159–271; see also: Żbikowski, Andrzej (2006). *U genezy Jedwabnego. Żydzi na kresach północno-wschodnich II Rzeczypospolitej, wrzesień 1939-lipiec 1941*. Warsaw, pp. 213–231.

bers of the Polish underground who started to punish "traitors" and establish new local administrations and militias. The situation here was especially tense owing to numerous arrests among members of the Polish underground since the summer of 1940, when the NKVD liquidated a major Polish partisan base in the region and obtained lists of the members of the anti-Soviet resistance.[51]

In many localities of the mostly Polish regions of western Belarus, anti-Jewish violence claimed a very high number of victims, also in comparison with most Ukrainian and, as it seems, also Lithuanian localities. Except for the numerous Soviet arrests, there seem to have been two reasons for the scale of violence. Firstly, radical anti-Semitism had had strong roots in this region even before 1939 and became an integral part of the anti-Soviet underground, and secondly, there seems to have been more active and longer-lasting encouragement for anti-Jewish violence by German police units than in other regions. Most of the more bloody acts of violence from the local side, as in the case of the mass murder in Jedwabne, only began ten days after the German occupation or later.

The level of anti-Jewish violence was also very high in Northern Bukovina and Bessarabia, which after July 2 were invaded by Romanian troops. According to Simon Geissbühler's estimate, in Northern Bukovina about 4,500 Jews were killed here by mid-July 1941, that is, about 6.5 percent of the 70,000 Jews living in that region. In Bessarabia the proportion of victims among the Jewish population seems to have been even higher.[52] The high level of deadly violence was clearly the result of the involvement of the Romanian armed forces and police units. In contrast to the other parts of the Soviet borderlands, the invaders and insurgents shared the same national identity and both intended to avenge the humiliation of summer 1940 when the Romanian state and its armed and police forces had been forced to leave the region. Already by then, anti-Jewish pogroms by Romanian armed forces or police units with several hundred victims had taken place.[53] When Romanian troops crossed the

51 Tryczyk, Mirosław (2015). *Miasta śmierci. Sąsiedzkie pogromy Żydów.* Warszawa; on the anti-Soviet underground also Strzembosz, Tomasz (2004). *Antysowiecka partyzantka i konspiracja nad Biebrzą X 1939–VI 1941.* Warsaw.

52 For a discussion of numbers of victims, see: Geissbühler, Simon (2013). *Blutiger Juli. Rumäniens Vernichtungskrieg und der vergessene Massenmord an den Juden 1941.* Paderborn, pp. 114–118.

53 Ibid., pp. 44–47.

border on July 2, their clear aim was to cleanse Northern Bukovina and Bessarabia of its Jewish inhabitants, whom they considered to be supporters of Soviet rule and "traitors." The removal of the Jews was also seen as the attainment of the Romanians' "national liberation."[54]

After the invasion, units of the Romanian armed forces and the gendarmerie began to cleanse localities of "Communists and Jews," which included the murder of the elderly, women, and children. They also incited local inhabitants to acts of anti-Jewish violence. However, in a number of localities, violence had begun already before the arrival of Romanian troops or police units.[55] Apparently, here also, this was part of the change of rule and the assumption of power by new groups, based on anti-Soviet underground structures.

In those parts of Northern Bukovina that were mostly inhabited by Ukrainians, apparently the Ukrainian attempt to take over the local administration before the Romanians arrived or could establish their own state institutions contributed to the fact that acts of violence without the participation of the Romanian military or police seem to have been more widespread than in Bessarabia.[56] The OUN also had a strong underground movement in Northern Bukovina. In contrast to eastern Galicia and Volhynia, the Bukovinian OUN remained loyal to the Mel'nyk leadership after the split in the OUN in 1940. Nevertheless, after June 22, the Bukovinian OUN began an uprising in a similar way as the OUN-B had in eastern Galicia and Volhynia. It created local administrations in a number of localities to prepare for the building of a Ukrainian state.[57] Here too, this attempt at state-building included the arrest or killing of alleged

54 Ioanid, Radu (2000). *The Holocaust in Romania. The Destruction of Jews and Gypsies under the Antonescu Regime, 1940–1944.* Chicago, p. 90f.; Solonari, Vladimir (2006): "Model Province". Explaining the Holocaust of Bessarabia and Bukovinian Jewry, *Nationalities Papers* 34: 471–500, here pp. 485–487.

55 Solonari, Vladimir (2007). Patterns of Violence. The Local Population and the Mass Murder of Jews in Bessarabia and Northern Bukovina, July–August 1941, *Kritika. Explorations in Russian and Eurasian History* 8: 749–787, here pp. 755–766.

56 Ibid., pp. 767–771; Geissbühler 2013, pp. 61–71.

57 Duda, Andrii and Volodymyr Staryk (1995). *Bukovyns'kyi kurin'. V boiakh za ukraïns'ku derzhavnist' 1918, 1941–1944.* Chernivtsi, pp. 55–59; see also: Hausleitner, Mariana (2001). *Die Rumänisierung der Bukowina. Die Durchsetzung des nationalstaatlichen Anspruchs Großrumäniens 1918–1944.* München, pp. 384–386, pp. 417–422.

Soviet supporters, whom the Bukovinian Ukrainians also primarily believed to be among the Jews.

Conclusion

Overall, a comparison of the findings for eastern Galicia with the other regions clearly shows that the core group of perpetrators were anti-Soviet insurgents who were aiming at (re)establishing their nation-states. Only the Polish case is to a certain degree an exception because, for the Polish insurgents, the German attack did not create the expectation of the renewal of statehood. Nevertheless, the Polish insurgents also experienced the German invasion as a liberation from the Soviet threat, which paved the way for a change of local administration. The anti-Jewish violence had spontaneous elements, but at the core of the larger-scale acts of deadly violence in all places were organized groups of insurgents.

Before the beginning of the German attack, there had been joint preparations of the anti-Soviet insurgency by the *Abwehr* and the different nationalist underground organizations. The *Abwehr* expected these groups to have a certain role in the establishment of new local administrations, but there were no clear agreements regarding this issue. Furthermore, there is no indication that there was any agreement on anti-Jewish pogroms. The anti-Jewish violence from the local side resulted mostly from the state-building projects of the insurgent groups that were, however, contrary to the German plans and later in all cases prevented by them.

For the anti-Soviet insurgents, the anti-Jewish violence was part of the punishment of "traitors" or Soviet supporters that also affected non-Jews. But Jews were punished and killed in much higher numbers and more generally because of the stereotypical perception of Jews as pro-Soviet. Nevertheless, the fact that the long-term aim of the nationalist insurgents was to establish an ethnically pure nation-state played a role here. At least in the Lithuanian and Ukrainian cases, the change of rule appeared as an opportunity to rid their country of unwanted minorities. This was also clearly a central factor in the Romanian violence against Jews in Northern Bukovina and Bessarabia.

There may have been some connections, in addition to those of the *Abwehr*, between the German Security Police and underground groups of a fascist orientation in the Baltic countries, where the underground was less unified than in Ukraine. However, at least the research literature gives no indication that this may have been significant for acts of anti-Jewish violence after June 22, 1941. Active incitement to engage in anti-Jewish violence from the German side only started with the activities of different German police units and, in eastern Galicia, also of the *Waffen-SS* "Viking" division after the German attack.

Everywhere a precondition for deadly violence on a larger scale was the involvement of insurgents or clear German encouragement and in many cases both. Spontaneous attacks on Jews that also took place rarely seem to have become deadly outside these contexts.

Witold Mędykowski

The Pogroms in the Former Soviet Occupation Areas in the Summer of 1941

A wave of anti-Jewish pogroms occurred in the summer of 1941 in the former Soviet occupation zone.[1] According to the borders before September 1, 1939, this area consisted mostly of the eastern parts of the Polish Republic. Occupied by the Red Army in September 1939, subsequently annexed by the Soviet Union, following the Ribbentrop-Molotov Pact, these areas retained certain autonomy within the relevant Soviet republics. Until June 22, 1941, documents were checked on the border of these areas, except for Vilnius, which the Soviets returned to Lithuania six weeks after they had taken charge of this region. In the summer of 1940, the Soviet Union occupied the Baltic countries as well as Northern Bukovina, Bessarabia, and parts of Finland.

The aforementioned areas were very diverse geographically, economically, ethnically, and culturally. Although many Russians lived there, these areas were not ethnically Russian. Not part of the Soviet Union in the interwar period, these regions had belonged to independent states. They were inhabited by various ethnic groups some of which had failed to gain independence and create their own states. The German attack together with allied forces gave these groups an opportunity to rebuild old alliances in the hope of gaining independence and getting rid of old enemies. Of course, Germany had different plans and did not intend to give up any territory gained or to create independent states for others. However, the Germans needed local allies not just for political, economic, or military support. Under the guise of promoting the struggle for independence and activities of local nationalist movements, the Germans instrumentalized the local allies' hatred of Communists and Jews to have them carry out some of the dirty work, namely, to murder political opponents and to exterminate the enemy civilian population.

---

1 This text is based on the Polish publication of the book by the same author: *W cieniu gigantów. Pogromy Żydów w 1941 roku w byłej sowieckiej strefie okupacyjnej. Kontekst historyczny, społeczny i kulturowy*. Warsaw, 2012.

At the beginning of the war, the cooperation of the local population was essential. The local collaborators found out later that it was very difficult to withdraw from their uncompromising partnership with the Nazis. Siding with the Germans meant nothing less than crossing the Rubicon, placing the locals in a very specific political and military constellation, determining not only their allies but also their enemies.

During the German invasion of the Soviet Union, in contrast to the local population, the Jews, considered to be the Germans' enemies, automatically became a persecuted population. In addition, some Jews had identified with Communism and the Soviet Union, and the sudden social, political, or professional advance of some of them between 1939 and 1941 was particularly agonizing for the gentile locals since it did not fit their traditional view of the Jews and their role in society. Such a sudden upward mobility, with some Jews appointed to serve at various levels in the state administration and security apparatus, was new, conspicuous, and difficult to accept for many non-Jews in view of their own concurrent "degradation."

The unexpected German invasion of the Soviet Union dramatically changed the situation. The Soviet troops suffered defeat after defeat, and the German army seemed to be invincible. Following the saying "the enemy of my enemy is my friend," many welcomed these developments, which revived their hope of establishing a new order. The German invasion was often accompanied by short interregna, when the Soviet army, police, and administration had already retreated but the Germans had not yet arrived. In this vacuum, some communities in these areas were better organized than others. Depending on the balance of power, some of the locals acted brutally, while others were relatively civilized. If there was chaos, some individuals and groups, who had or could get hold of weapons, would engage in robbery and violence, and it would take time to restore relative order. Local community leaders in positions of authority and influence played important roles, regardless of whether they were armed or not. Due to its rapid advance, the German army was often neither able nor interested in dealing with the local administration, leaving a temporary power vacuum in vast rural areas. However, it was vital for the German army to establish a functioning administration and garrisons or police forces in the big cities due to their strategic, tactical, or economic importance.

Most of the Jews living in these areas had no chance of escaping. Regarded as enemies by both the Germans and the local population, they found themselves defenseless in a hostile environment and exposed to widespread acts of robbery and murder. The perpetrators fell into various groups, sometimes working together: the civilian population, local bands, paramilitary groups, militias, the German army, the German police, and the *Einsatzgruppen*. In L'viv and other cities with a predominantly Ukrainian population, German troops, together with local people, attacked Jews. In other places, the locals acted without the German forces' explicit consent. In eastern Galicia, Northern Bukovina, and Bessarabia, Romanian and Hungarian military units, as the Germans' allies, participated in the invasion of the Soviet Union and sometimes prevented the local population from attacking the Jews.

It is important to investigate the nature of the pogroms and extermination of Jews in this part of Europe with the aim of identifying common features, differences, and mutual influences. Were these acts against Jews part of the Holocaust?[2] If so, the pogroms furthered the Nazis' aim of exterminating all the Jews and helped them to achieve their ultimate goal.[3] However, the discussion of this topic is more complex, since people living in the area wanted to get rid of the Jews at the local level, while the Nazis' objective was much more comprehensive. The locals' assistance reduced the need for Nazi forces to be involved, facilitating the overall German operation.

The murder of prisoners

In the early days of the war, perceiving the need to evacuate these areas, the Soviet authorities faced the additional problem of how to deal with the inmates in prisons located close to the frontlines. This was a critical question for the Soviet regime since prisoners were treated as enemies

2 See the film: *Kovno Ghetto—a Buried History* (1997, directed by Herbert Krosney, with the participation of Martin Gilbert); Yad Vashem Archives (YVA) V–2072; see also: Archiwum Żydowskiego Instytutu Historycznego (AŻIH), 302/105; YVA, M.49.P/105 (O.16.P/105), pp. 22–25; AŻIH, 302/227; YVA, M.49.P/227 (O.16.P/227), pp. 1–4.

3 See the protocol from the Wannsee conference on January 20, 1941, in Arad, Y. et al. (eds.) (1996). ***Documents on the Holocaust: Selected Sources on the Destruction of the Jews of Germany and Austria, Poland, and the Soviet Union***. Jerusalem, pp. 249–261.

of the state and the system, so that, even in times of armed conflict, the possibility of releasing them did not come into consideration. However, in the face of the Germans' rapid advance, the Soviets had to decide the fate of thousands of prisoners from the wave of arrests in eastern Galicia in June 1941, including many activists in the Ukrainian nationalist movement as well as Poles and Jews. In need of an immediate decision, People's Commissariat for Internal Affairs (NKVD) representatives turned to Lavrentiy Beria,[4] proposing the release of prisoners with mild sentences, while those who had committed more severe crimes would be shot. Beria agreed. During the evacuations, the prisoners were treated accordingly, but implementation differed in the various regions in the Soviet occupation zone.

In the Baltic states, most prisoners were evacuated, but some were left behind in the prisons and later liberated by the local population or the German army.[5] In Soviet western Belarus, most of the prisoners were evacuated, and when this was impossible because of sudden attacks, the guards left them in the prisons. However, in some areas of eastern Galicia, the scenario was very different. In many towns, the inmates were liquidated in the prisons or in remote locations, and then NKVD guards would attempt to burn the bodies. The biggest massacres took place in the L'viv prisons.[6] While the total number of prisoners executed in eastern Galicia is not known, it is estimated at well over 10,000 (see Kai Struve's chapter in this volume).

By murdering prisoners in eastern Galicia, the NKVD fomented the sympathy among Ukrainians for the Germans as well as the hatred for the Jews and "the Bolsheviks." This undoubtedly exacerbated the already explosive situation. The Poles were also part of this; on the one hand, they were hated by the Ukrainians, while, on the other, due to their declining position in the social hierarchy, they were rather hostile toward

4 Lavrentiy Pavlovich Beria (1899–1953) was a Soviet politician of Georgian descent and the head of the NKVD between 1938 and 1953.

5 *Zbrodnicza ewakuacja więzień i aresztów NKWD na Kresach Wschodnich II Rzeczypospolitej w czerwcu–lipcu 1941 roku*. Warsaw (1997), p. 74f.

6 In L'viv, the number of murdered Jews was over 4,000. See: Popiński, K. et al. (eds.) (1995). *Drogi śmierci. Ewakuacja więzień sowieckich z Kresów Wschodnich II Rzeczypospolitej w czerwcu i lipcu 1941*. Warsaw, pp. 8–10; Pohl, Dieter (1997). *Nationalsozialistische Judenverfolgung in Ostgalizien 1941–1944. Organisation und Durchführung eines staatlichen Massenverbrechens*. München, p. 55.

the Jews. Both the Poles and the Ukrainians considered the Jews to be Soviet collaborators, despite the persecution of the Jewish political parties, youth movements, social and communal organizations, and religious life by the Soviet authorities. Poles and Ukrainians saw the Jews everywhere: in the militia, the workers' guards, managerial positions, the party, and the NKVD. The Jews, perceived as the enemy number one, became the personification of evil.

Naturally, it was not important whether these myths, nurtured by age-old racial hatred and anti-Semitism, were true or not, but rather how they were perceived by the surrounding society. After murdering the prisoners, the NKVD and the Red Army departed, leaving the Jews without any protection. The various factions, each for their own reasons, concentrated all their hatred on the Jews as the substitute for the defunct Soviet power.

The murder of prisoners was not the only contributing factor to the pogroms. As discussed above, such acts also took place during the power vacuum in small towns where there were no prison murders. In the big cities, however, the NKVD crimes became extremely powerful catalysts for future events: the German gained allies in their quest to murder the Jews. After the withdrawal of the Soviets, the residents immediately broke down the prison gates to set the inmates free, only to find many mutilated and charred bodies.

It is important to note that there were also Jews among the prisoners murdered by the NKVD.[7] In the wave of arrests in June 1941, many Zionist activists as well as Ukrainian nationalists were imprisoned. Although the exact number is not known, in L'viv alone, the list of identified victims indicates dozens of Jewish victims. Of course, German and Ukrainian propaganda did not mention the Jews murdered by the NKVD. Outside eastern Galicia, the number of prisoners killed was limited. When prisoners were evacuated in convoys, some were shot during the transport, but, since these events did not take place in the cities, they did not have a strong impact on the population's mood. In many towns in western Belarus (former Polish areas), there was no time to evacuate the prisoners, so they escaped or were freed.

---

7 Popiński et al. 1995, pp. 228–232.

The power-vacuum period

The pogrom period in 1941 can be divided into several sub-periods, taking into account timing; geographical, political, and military conditions; as well as type of locality. There were also great differences in the organization and other factors affecting the scope and nature of the pogroms, which were carried out over vast territories.

The outbreak of the war played an important role in the pogroms of the summer 1941. Although war was not a necessary condition, it was clearly very favorable to pogroms. The Soviet authorities played an important role in restraining interethnic conflicts in the territories they occupied in 1939–41. After initially flirting with various ethnic groups, they governed by terror and a strong hand. All organizations, even those not openly hostile to the Soviet regime, were considered undesirable and reduced by numerous arrests and deportations of activists, since they did not fit into the framework of a totalitarian state, which only had room for the Communist Party and a single youth organization, the Komsomol. Some nationalists who did not hold leadership positions were co-opted by the new regime and enlisted in the ranks of the local administration and various economic organizations.

Under Soviet rule, in order to survive, nationalism seemed to have entered a state of lethargy. However, it did not disappear, staying particularly strong in the areas of Ukraine close to the *Generalgouvernement*, which allowed a relatively free flow of people and information and supported the activities of Ukrainians on its territory, ranging from education to the political and paramilitary fields.[8] In addition, the Ukrainians, who were much better organized than other groups, strove to create their own independent state. Propaganda by underground organizations was strong and fell on very fertile ground. The division of Poland in 1939 renewed hopes for independence with German assistance. Although these attempts were thwarted by the Soviet invasion in 1939, the desire for national independence remained solid.

An interregnum or an interruption in the continuity of power generally refers to periods between a ruler's death and the election of a new one.

---

8 Torzecki, R. (1972). *Kwestia ukraińska w polityce III Rzeszy, 1933–1945*. Warsaw, p. 194.

With known hereditary successors, such transition periods are less dangerous than when the succession is unclear. The stability of state power is usually endangered in such periods, because they not only give opportunities to fight for power to various pretenders but also because they carry the threat of civil war and of the destruction of social order. While the term "interregnum" suggests a lack of power at the higher levels, this does not necessarily apply to lower levels. Thus, the term "power vacuum" better describes the situation in the vast territories previously occupied by the USSR that were rapidly conquered by the Germans.

A power vacuum is dangerous because it is usually rapidly filled in a more or less random fashion by elements aspiring to exercise power, such as spiritual leaders, prominent and widely recognized intellectuals, or political activists and leaders of political parties. However, a power vacuum is most often filled by military leaders who have weapons and can exercise real force, such as leaders of paramilitary groups or individuals forming armed gangs. Moreover, the impact of such situations is stronger in smaller towns and villages where government authorities are not strong enough to prevent armed groups from taking over power. Often, these groups consist of criminal elements, who are not interested in exercising power but rather in using the situation to plunder and kill.

The term "power vacuum" best describes the situation in the formerly Soviet-occupied areas in the summer of 1941, when there was neither an army nor a functioning administration there. These areas, mainly in today's Ukraine and Belarus, were under the shadow of the great conflict between Nazi Germany and the Soviet Union. Also, in some cities, such as L'viv, the power vacuum was created when the Soviet troops withdrew and the German troops had not yet entered the city, facilitating the temporary takeover by local Ukrainian nationalists who formed militias in an attempt to fill the void.

The swift advance by the German troops was the main factor behind the power vacuum in 1941. The armored divisions that were able to break even the strongest enemy defense lines played an extremely important role. In the first few weeks of the war, the German troops moved tens of kilometers a day. If they met stronger resistance in smaller towns, they would leave them encircled, while the main forces continued to move forward.[9] Thus, smaller enemy units that could not threaten the main German forces were left to be liquidated later. During this period with a relatively unstable frontline, the Soviet administration, party apparatus, activists, and the army panicked, evacuating areas in the face of the rapid German advance, creating enclaves with a power vacuum.

The lack of organized German administration in the newly occupied territories led to uncertainty about the future there. Obviously, Germany had prepared plans, but to win the sympathy of Ukrainian nationalists, of nationalists in the Baltic countries, and of other populations, they fostered the impression that creating independent states or, at least, a broad autonomy in the Third Reich was a real possibility. The fight against the USSR was understood by the local population as a struggle for their liberation from the Soviet yoke. Germany deliberately fomented these rumors and did not immediately disarm the local self-defense groups, partisans, and local militias.[10] This double game was supposed to trick the nationalists. The Germans also documented the locals' hatred of the Jews, disseminating images and films showing anti-Jewish violence, not only to increase support for their rule but also to show that they were not alone in their mission against the Jews and the Communists.[11] Of course, Germany's double game was deliberate, giving a free hand to local nationalists and violent groups known to be anti-Semitic. The collective acts of "justice" against the Jews perpetrated by local nationalists and violent groups served many purposes, first and foremost as a distraction from the collaboration and participation in the Soviet occupation of the same groups. The violence was a kind of self-cleaning ritual.

A power vacuum existed in the Baltic states, especially in Latvia and Lithuania, too. The Estonian case was different because the frontline was stabilized only at the end of July 1941, while in Lithuania and Latvia the uncertainty was shorter. A major difference between the ethnically Ukrainian areas and Lithuania and Latvia was that the Soviet occupation only lasted for a year in the latter. Thus, the Soviet regime was only a brief interlude because all the Baltic states had been independent with

---

9 For example in Drohobycz. See: YVA, O.3/7656, pp. 2–8.

10 Arad, Y. et al. (eds.) (1989). *The Einsatzgruppen Reports: Selections from Dispatches of the Nazi Death Squads' Campaign against the Jews, July 1941–January 1943*. New York, p. 62.

11 Arad et al. 1996, p. 390.

their own extensive administration and system of government before the summer of 1940. After the Soviets left these areas, there was a rapid restoration of a more or less functioning administration without a prolonged power vacuum.

Using the local population's mood to incite pogroms

Local people could not systematically kill Jews due to vastness of the territory, but the locals participated in pogroms and massacres against the Jews. In cases of mass murder and pogroms brought to the courts after the war, perpetrators often claimed to have acted under pressure. However, according to victims' testimonies, most of the individuals, especially civilians, participating in pogroms or *Aktionen* against the Jews together with the *Einsatzgruppen* were not coerced, and there were no penalties for those who did not want to be part of the killings.

The loss of a moral compass was another very important element in the locals' complicity to murder. As victims of persecution and crimes by the Soviet NKVD, they could have tried to justify the massacres of innocents, but, in fact, these crimes could not be considered as retaliatory since the Jewish victims of the pogroms and mass executions were in no way connected to the NKVD arrests, deportations, and crimes. The Jews simply served as a placeholder. Even if political commissars responsible for crimes committed before or during the war had been among the victims, they would have been unlawfully deprived of their POW status, of due process, and of a fair trial.

The *Einsatzgruppen* exploited the local population by granting them permission to discharge their hatred and tensions directed toward the Jews. The authorization to steal from the Jews was also a kind of corrupt German reward for loyalty. The occupiers filmed and photographed crimes committed against the Jews. This material was later used in German propaganda. As stated in an *Einsatzgruppe* report: "It was no less important to create for the future established and proven facts that freed people on their own initiative took the strictest measures possible against the Bolshevik and Jewish enemy without any apparent order from the German authorities."[12]

12 From the *Einsatzgruppe* report dated October 15, 1941, from the Baltic states, in Arad et al. 1996, pp. 389–393.

Pogroms and the Holocaust

The pogroms of 1941 took place in the shadow of armed conflict between Nazi Germany and its allies and the USSR. The sudden German attack on the Soviet Union caused a partial Soviet military defeat in the first few months of the war, before the frontlines stabilized in 1942. The fast successes of the Germans contributed to increased cooperation of the local population and nationalist organizations with Germany. Sympathy for the Germans did not have to be associated with hatred of the Soviet Union and of Communist ideology and vice versa. However, anti-Semitism was another factor that played a key role.

A complex of decisions, factors, and processes led to the Holocaust, including to the pogroms as an essential, but not the most important, element. The wave of pogroms in the summer of 1941, disrupting the tense but relatively peaceful relations between the Jews and the surrounding societies, was followed by a progressive deterioration of the relations between Jews and gentiles. Most pogroms took place after the beginning of Operation Barbarossa, in many places they occurred during the interregnum period, without any German involvement. Pogroms took place throughout German-dominated areas, especially in the Baltic states, Ukraine, the Łomża and Białystok regions, and in Northern Bukovina. From the Jewish point of view, the pogroms are clearly a part of the Holocaust, since they contributed to the extermination of the Jews in Europe.

The activities of the *Einsatzgruppen*, some of which were carried out in cooperation with the German police or the Wehrmacht, the gendarmerie, the Romanian army, and other groups, should be considered separately. The executions by the *Einsatzgruppen* were often aided by local police units. As Martin Dean's research shows, during the so-called second wave of murders of Jews in Ukraine and Belarus in 1942, the ratio of German perpetrators to local militiamen ranged from 1:5 to 1:10 in many places.[13] Clearly, without the cooperation of local police, perpetrating mass murder on that scale would have been severely hampered or impossible. Due to manpower shortage, it would have taken much longer

13 Dean, Martin (1999). *Collaboration in the Holocaust: Crimes of the Local Police in Belorussia and Ukraine, 1941–44*. New York, pp. 161–167.

and might have been much more difficult to kill so many Jews in the eastern borderlands without local help. Possibly, extra troops could and would have been brought in to carry out the extermination of the Jews, but this would have led to significant delays and other difficulties.

The Final Solution was a program to systematically exterminate all the Jews. Under Nazi policies, with the participation of satellite countries and help from collaborators, millions of Jews were killed in the context of what later became known as the Holocaust or Shoah. What was the role of the pogroms in the Holocaust? Were the pogroms a part of the Nazi policy? Did those who participated in pogroms specifically aim at murdering all Jews?

First, it should be noted that racist Nazi ideology had many supporters among other ethnic groups outside of Germany. During the interwar years, particularly in the 1930s, many 'strong' authoritarian leaders advocating anti-Semitic policies came to power in Eastern Europe.

Second, the numerous arrests and deportations as a result of the Soviet policy of direct occupation and persecution of political elites and national activists and the introduction of the Soviet economic system, including collectivization and nationalization, the depreciation of the value of the currency, led to a sharp increase in anti-Soviet sentiment. This is usually underestimated in Eastern Europe due to the long Communist period there, which had a great impact not only on historiography but also on the common understanding of history. In spite of their brutal occupation, the Germans were initially admired for their strength, order, discipline, and organization, even in occupied Poland. During 1939–41, when the Germans invaded the territories that had previously been under Soviet occupation, the residents' expectations initially rose. They saw the Germans as liberators from the Soviet yoke and expected them to make economic changes and help them recover their lost independence. Thus, their expectations and hopes coincided with racism, anti-Semitism, and hatred, and the Jews were the victims in this process. Therefore, it seems reasonable to claim that the Holocaust, the result of wide-ranging processes taking place in Germany and Europe, should include the pogroms.

The issue of responsibility is another theoretical problem: Was the racist policy responsible for the pogroms? What was to role of the Germans in the pogroms? Did the responsibility fall solely on the local population? From the legal point of view, this is a question not only of ideological influences but also of organizational responsibility. Who planned specific activities, took concrete decisions, and was in charge of executing them? In the larger sense, the organizers of crimes bear the main responsibility for them, but, in the strict sense of the word, the perpetrators are responsible.

These arguments were used during the investigation of and later in the research on the events in Jedwabne in Poland. But the documentation is insufficient to resolve the issue of organizational responsibilities. Thus, the question remains: Were commands given, and what were the Germans' expectations? If the Germans were not at the site of the crime or if their presence was minimal, they would not have had control over whether their commands had been faithfully executed. There might be unexpected problems: incomplete or faulty execution of commands, attempts to dodge, escape, evade, or postpone executions. In Wąsosz, there were no such attempts. Similarly, in Jedwabne, Radziłów, and many other places in Łomża region, the implementation of such missions exceeded the Germans' expectations. Thus, while the same German units operating in the Łomża region were also active in Belarusian areas, the level of aggression and cruelty in Łomża was much higher than that in Belarusian areas. Was there massive intimidation of the population? Even in the areas of Lithuania, Latvia, and Estonia, where the local population was apparently much more favorable to the Germans than in Łomża, the *Einsatzgruppen* reports mention difficulties in initiating pogroms.[14]

What impact did the German occupation in the *Generalgouvernement* have on the neighboring areas, especially on the Łomża area? How did Germany, perceived as the enemy number one in Poland in the late 1930s, which won the September campaign in 1939, occupying and annexing vast areas of Poland and persecuting and committing crimes against the Polish population, suddenly became the locals' ally in the Łomża region? Did the information about German behavior not reach the Soviet occupation zone? Did the local population suddenly consider the enemy as their friend? Were the locals prepared to murder their neighbors for the Germans? Even if these pro-German views were held only

14 Arad et al. 1989, p. 73.

by a small part of the population, these difficult questions remain valid and are often not addressed.

If no orders were given, as the documents suggest, what inspired these actions? Even if there were undercurrents of anti-Semitism, hate, envy, and other bad feelings among the local population against the Jews, how did the arrival of a few foreign officers lead them to murder their neighbors who had lived next to them for decades and centuries? How could they contemplate murder with primitive weapons? Why were the views of an alien, hostile power stronger than the experience of living together in a relatively intact neighborhood, sometimes even with intimate relations? They knew each other and had close commercial relations, sometimes drank vodka and played music together at rural weddings, and many of them went to school together. So how is it possible that this life together ceased to be important?

What is also remarkable is the fact that the far-reaching collaboration in the persecution of Jews persisted even when it became crystal clear that there would be no independent states of Ukraine, Belarus, Lithuania, Latvia, and Estonia under Germany's aegis. In fact, the Ukrainian nationalists of the OUN-B relatively quickly realized the true intentions of the Germans and went underground as early as the autumn of 1941. While they considered the Germans as enemies against whom they took military action several months later, this did not change their attitude toward the Jews.

Perpetrating pogroms and subsequent cooperation in the extermination of Jews were interconnected. Did this cause a moral revolt among the local population or were the victims soon forgotten? The latter seems to be true. How did the Jews themselves see the events—those who were saved from the catastrophe, but lost everyone and everything, like Baruch Milch who lost a son, wife, dozens of family members of various ages, his house, and everything he owned, and maybe most importantly his faith in people and in God? As Milch wrote when he saw for the last time his hometown and the people living there:

> Although I could not take my eyes off the receding town, deep inside I thought it was a pity that even one stone remained there. It would have been better if Podhajce would have been erased from the face of the earth. The whole town is not worth a penny after the destruction of the Jews, because Germany could not achieve such total destruction without local support. [The] Ukrainians were not ashamed to admit

> [...] that their wish was [that] not a single Jew [would be] left to avenge the blood of his brothers, whose only crime was that they were Jews.[15]

By perpetrating pogroms against the Jews, the local population became collaborators in the Nazi plan to exterminate all Jews. Thus, as already mentioned, the pogroms weakened the Jewish population not only in moral and economic terms but also numerically. These factors were fundamentally important for future developments. The pogroms were not a single wave of violence, but, as it turned out, became one of the elements in a long chain of other events leading to the physical extermination of the Jews. In other areas of Europe, where no pogroms happened, the quasi-total annihilation of the Jews also occurred; the Jews' extermination in the territories formerly occupied by the Soviet Union was initiated by and carried out by the Germans, but often together with locals. With the invading army, the *Einsatzgruppen* engaged in eliminating the Soviet political commissars, members of the party, Soviet leaders, and Jews. The pogroms accelerated the marginalization of the Jews. While most pogroms did not systematically exterminate Jews, according to *Einsatzgruppen* reports from the Baltic countries, the actions of the local population not only simplified but also speeded up the process of the physical elimination of the Jews. Because part of the "work" was carried out by local forces, German troops were free for other duties. So the pogroms and the local collaboration clearly hastened the extermination of the Jews.

Equally important was the local population's acceptance of German law and the ethnic hierarchy defined by the Nazis in the occupied areas. The Nazis needed the approval of their newly introduced legislation outlawing the Jews. Often it is claimed that terror and fear reigned in the German-controlled territories. According to this view, the local population would not hide or help Jews and would denounce them to the German authorities, because they feared for their own and their family's lives. However, numerous examples show that this was not always true. Comparing illegal activities in various areas of German occupation shows significant differences among them. Thus, there were systematic violations of the law of the occupiers in some areas. Illegal activities, including traf-

---

15 Milch, Baruch (2003). *Can Heaven be Void?* Jerusalem, p. 244.

ficking, corruption, misappropriation of German property, theft, sabotaging, supporting, or participating in underground movements, all of which carried severe punishments, such as the death penalty, were indeed widespread throughout the German-controlled territories. However, the prohibitions against aiding or hiding Jews and the obligation to denounce them were much better respected than other German rules and laws. Many people were willing to benefit by appropriating property, which they refused to return when the Jews claimed it back.

Pogroms, had they remained an isolated phenomenon, would have been considered as events separate from the Holocaust. However, the pogroms were, in a climate of violence and lawlessness, an integral part of the Shoah. Through their psychological impact on relations between the Jews and non-Jews and their relevance in the overall convergence of factors leading to the extermination of the Jews, the pogroms became a significant element of the Holocaust, not only in terms of direct action but also in a broader sense. Pogroms had a substantial impact on the chain of subsequent events and on the attitudes toward the persecuted, including the lack of action in their favor. This negative approach toward the Jews persisted in the postwar era. In this sequence of events, the final sin is to forget the pogroms. However, in defiance of the perpetrators', collaborators' and bystanders' wishes and will, the Holocaust and the pogroms as an integral part of it will not be forgotten.

Sarah Rosen

The Djurin Ghetto in Transnistria through the Lens of Kunstadt's Diary

Prologue

In the three days between October 12 and 14, 1941, the last days of the holiday of Sukkot, the Jews of Rădăuţi were deported to Transnistria,[1] crowded in stifling cattle wagons of freight trains. Although the deportees knew they were being taken to Transnistria, they had no idea what the final destination was and what fate awaited them there. Among the Jews deported on the third day, October 14, 1941, were Lipman Kunstadt and eleven of his relatives. The long train took them to their first stop in Ataki. Having stopped in Ataki for several days, the deportees boarded rafts and crossed the Dniester River (Nistru in Romanian) toward Mogilev. On October 29, 1941, Kunstadt and his family, among a larger group of deportees, were taken in a truck rented by the Germans to the Djurin ghetto in Transnistria.

1 Transnistria is a region in the southwestern part of Ukraine between the Dniester River on the west and the Bug river on the east. Transnistria was taken by the Germans and Romanians during Operation Barbarossa in the summer of 1941. Transnistria ("beyond the Dniester"—as it was named by Hitler) was an artificial geographical unit created in the Second World War comprising the part of the Ukraine given by Hitler to Romania in return for the latter's participation in the war against the USSR. For more on this subject, see Ancel, Jean (2002). *History of the Holocaust (Romania). Vol.* 2. Jerusalem; Ioanid, Radu (2002). The Holocaust, in *The History of the Jews in Romania. Vol. 4* (The Goldstein-Goren Diaspora Research Center, Tel Aviv University, published in association with the United States Holocaust Memorial Museum); Ofer Dalia (1996). Life in the Ghettos of Transnistria, *Yad Vashem Studies* 25: 175–207; Rosen, Sarah (2012). The Personal, Family and Community. A Case Study of Survival in Murafa Ghetto, *Moreshet* 92/93: 214–233; Dallin, Alexander (1998). *Odessa, 1941–1944: A Case Study of Soviet Territory under Foreign Rule*. Iași; Fisher, Julius S. (1969). *Transnistria: The Forgotten Cemetery*. South Brunswick.

Who was Lipman Kunstadt?

Eliezer Lipman Kunstadt, born on July 22, 1901, in the town of Rădăuţi in the Romanian district of southern Bukovina, was the son of a prominent Rădăuţi rabbi, Yzhak Kunstadt, himself a well-known public figure. His son Lipman, a highly educated person and a journalist by profession, served prior to the deportation as general secretary of the Jewish community in Rădăuţi. He had also translated books from nine languages and published articles in both German and Romanian in the Rădăuţi press.

Upon his arrival in the Djurin ghetto, Kunstadt was appointed secretary of the ghetto committee, and as he says in his diary:

> I used to be the General Secretary of the great Rădăuţi community, and with a little bit of ancestral merit was fortunate enough to find employment as the committee's registrar, with my fee paid in this world, rather than the next: a loaf of bread every morning. It is this employment that saves us from starvation, and besides, for the time being I am spared from falling [*sic*] to a German labor camp.[2]

This entry indicates that Kunstadt owed his employment as secretary of the Djurin committee to his pre-deportation activity in the Rădăuţi community and to his connections with Siegfried Jagendorf, the head of the Mogilev ghetto committee and a central, influential figure among the Transnistria deportees to whom he was related.[3]

Kunstadt filled five notebooks, handwritten in Yiddish in the first-person singular. He wrote every day, often two or three times a day. Kunstadt observed the Djurin environment and life as a journalist and described them both in the light of daily events and occurrences and through his own engagement and involvement in these events, an involvement made possible by his daily work in the committee's offices. Through his association with committee members and community leaders, he witnessed the challenges faced by the Jews in the ghetto and their requests for help from the committee, which he described in his diary.

---

2 Entry dated April 11, 1942, 3 PM.

3 Siegfried Jagendorf was an electrical engineer employed by the German Siemens company. In view of rising anti-Semitism in Austria, where he resided at the time, he returned in 1938 to Romania, to Rădăuţi in Southern Bukovina. He was deported to Transnistria in the fall of 1941. Jagendorf was the manager of the Turnatoria (foundry) in Mogilev and served as head of the Mogilev ghetto committee.

The tone of his diary, which he also used to pour out his feelings and document personal experiences, conveys to his reader his compassion to the suffering of the poor and destitute. This strong empathy and affinity with them probably stemmed from both his sensitivity to his fellow man and his own difficulties in providing for his family—his mother, sister, wife, and two children. The entries are couched in rich, figurative language. Daily events are described sometimes humorously, often caustically, whereas in some cases the reality of the ghetto life draws from him anger and fury. The members of the ghetto committee—both together and individually—and their actions are described in sharp, acerbic terms, especially when they are faced with crucial challenges and decisions. Thus Kunstadt allows us, his readers, to experience his own agitation and turmoil and to understand, however partially, the reality of daily life in the ghetto and the challenges faced by the Jewish committees.

Here I would like to briefly refer to the nature of the genre we generally term "diaries." In his foreword to the diary kept in the Warsaw ghetto by teacher and educator Chaim Aron Kaplan,[4] Polish-Jewish historian Ber Mark referred to the genre's unique nature, especially when compared to memoirs: "A diary is, first and foremost, what was written at the actual time of the events[,] a piece of living reality, since not only its material, but the author's perspective is a distinct document of the time." Mark further emphasizes this uniqueness by distinguishing between a chronicle and a diary:

> The distinct mark of the borderline separating the diary from a chronicle is the personal moment. The chronicle documents events and occurrences every day, at a specific moment in time. The chronicle contains facts, sometimes even accompanied by the author's commentary. It is sometimes written wisely and well [...] but may sometimes be dry and merely informative.

The diary, on the other hand, Mark claims, "ought to have in it the personal, the emotional, the more or less intimate. The diary is where the author pours out his soul."

Amos Goldberg, who has refined the definition even further, claims that the diary is "a text of a narrative nature, capable of organizing the

4 Kaplan, Chaim A. (1965). *Scroll of Agony: The Warsaw Diary of Chaim A. Kaplan.* New York.

writer's human identity as a narrative one."[5] This power of the diary may partially explain the prevalence of the first-person singular in the writings of Jews during the Holocaust. In such a turbulent era, when the components of the identity are so fundamentally undermined, an era where yesterday's concepts cannot explain what is happening today, nor give hope for tomorrow, a person finds it hard to understand himself or the world, impose order on or find meaning in it. It is in such an era that keeping a diary can help the writer preserve a trace of his identity and the coherence of the world into which he had been thrown. The diary spins the thinnest of narrative threads connecting the molecules of the protagonist's crumbling world.[6]

Alexandra Gabarini further asserts that diaries, indeed, cannot convey all experiences of all Jews during the war in their entirety, nor can they convey all experiences of the diarists themselves.[7] However, they can and do shed light on the writers' attempts to imbue their wartime experiences with meaning and understand them. In this context, the value of Transnistria diaries is in conveying the authors' feelings and experiences during their deportation and incarceration in the ghettos, while incidentally shedding light on occurrences in their vicinity, as documentation from the smaller ghettos (minutes of meetings, correspondence etc.) and the committees' offices is sadly sparse.

All the above raises the question of the purpose for which this particular diary was written. The foreword, written after the events described, not long before the diary's publication, indicates that Kunstadt was motivated by two main objectives: the need to document events for posterity, motivated by his profession as a journalist, and an attempt to find solace and some relief from the harsh ghetto life:

> I think the yellowing, faded pages from the Transnistria hell have been given a new life, and their voice will be heard wherever Jews still live, so that the memory of suffering and pain, fear of death and hope, the nothingness and infinite oblivion and the

---

5 Goldberg, Amos (2012). *Trauma in the First Person: Diary Writing During the Holocaust.* Kineret-Zmora Bitan Dvir [Hebrew].

6 Cited from Dr. Leah Prais' lecture on the diary of Feivl Winer during a day symposium on "Jewish Identity and Soviet Identity" held in Jerusalem at Yad Vashem in October 2015.

7 Gabarini, Alexandra (2006). *Numbered Days: Diaries and the Holocaust.* New Haven/London, p. xiii.

> paltry dreams reflected and set down in these five notebooks will have been preserved, if only on paper.[8]

The same sentiment is expressed in the diary itself, as Kunstadt writes on April 7, 1943, eighteen months after his arrival in the ghetto: "While writing about a year's worth of Transnistria memories [...] the written pages testify to one truth that does not lie: death. What I have written of my mother's death imparts real content, and even today I would not have written it any other way."[9]

Although he feels a need to write daily, many days pass without a single entry. This is how he explains this:

> As we know, 12 days have passed since I wrote the previous lines. It is not because events ceased to happen, Heaven forbid, that my pen has taken such a long respite. On the contrary, in the pain-fraught tumult known as the Transnistria exile, each moment is wrapped in news and all kinds of troubles that shock the soul and take one's breath away. The reason for this pause was totally different. The burning fire that had driven me while writing the first pages has been replaced with a deep pessimism, closer to black despair. This started exhausting my brain with silly questions (*kloz kashes*): what for and for what purpose? And if I do succeed in editing the outlines of the Djurin camp chronicles and, in doing so, in setting my feelings in watery ink on a half-penny worth of paper, what then? Will I then live to read, at other times, the reminiscences from the Transnistria hell? Will I be reminded of the suffering? Will at least some of my nearest and dearest live to do so? This is all so unnecessary, so ineffectual. And nevertheless I sat down today, the pen in my hand, because of some news that has shocked me so deeply that I must calm my bedraggled nerves with an ink injection.[10]

Elsewhere he writes:

> I am overwhelmed with grief at the news of the horrific fate of the relatives I grew up and matured with until the deportation. I will never see them again, nor will they see me again. Therefore I seek solace in the mute pages of this notebook, into which I pour out my bleeding heart. They, the listening sheets of paper, hear me without falling into the trap of talk.[11]

Here Kunstadt sets down his second purpose in writing his diary—finding solace and comfort for the suffering in the Djurin ghetto. A diary touches

8 Prologue in the diary, p. 3.
9 Entry dated April 7, 1943, p. 262.
10 Entry dated April 23, 1942, p. 8.
11 Entry later on April 23, 1942, p. 9.

upon many aspects of its author's life, as does Kunstadt's, addressing subjects such as the deportation and the shock experienced by the displaced Jews; the town of Djurin as seen through the deportee's eyes; the encounter with local Jews and the relationships formed with them; the newly created demographic fabric and the ensuing social stratification in the ghetto; the Jewish committee in the ghetto, its members, and their characteristics; daily life in the ghetto; descriptions of Kunstadt's family in daily life circumstances; the Romanian authorities; the environment outside the ghetto and relations with local Ukrainians; references to other ghettos in the Mogilev district, such as Mogilev, Shargorod, Kopaigorod etc.

Of the plethora of themes, the present chapter will address the new reality imposed upon the deported Jews in the Djurin ghetto as reflected in Kunstadt's diary, the relations between the deportees and the local Jews and finally the non-Jewish external environment and Jews' relations with it.

The town of Djurin is located some 45 kilometers northeast of Mogilev and some 25 kilometers south of Shargorod and was built on the slopes of two hills separated by a stream.[12] Jews lived on the eastern slope, later to serve as the ghetto, while local Ukrainians lived on the western slope, across the stream.[13] Before the outbreak of the Second World War, the town's Jewish population numbered some 2,000, all residing in a separate quarter up the hill. The Jewish community was poor, and most Jews barely made a living working in the local sugar factory[14] or the Jewish agricultural cooperative.[15] The town of Djurin had a synagogue, a religious school, and a small Jewish cemetery. The community

---

12 Rosen, Sarah (2013). *The Collective and the Individual: Organization and Family. The Internal Life of the Jews in North Transnistria's Ghettos (Moghilev, Şargorod, Djurin, Murafa and Berşad), 1941–1944*. Jerusalem (PhD thesis, Hebrew University in Jerusalem).

13 Yad Vashem Archives (YVA), Miriam Savion, vt 11435; Shlomo Steinmitz, interview conducted on January 17, 2010, at his home in Ramat Gan; Jehudith Nir, interview conducted on February 15, 2011, at her home in Ramat Gan; YVA, Menachem Bernstein, vt 8819/03.

14 Rosen 2013, pp. 36–38.

15 The agricultural cooperative was a common collective entity created in the USSR during the 1920s and the 1930s, based on collective labor and sharing of profits among the workers.

was led by Rabbi Hershel Karalnik, who was respected by everyone.[16] The local town committee, the *obscina*, was responsible for burials and *kashruth* (Jewish dietary laws) and acted as an intermediary between the Jews and the Soviet authorities.[17]

With the outbreak of the war, all fit Jewish males were conscripted to the Red Army, leaving only the elderly, the sick, women, and children—numbering about 1,000—in the town. The sugar factory, the town's main source of employment, was bombed, partially destroyed, and ceased operations, leaving the Jews with no source of income.

On July 22, 1941, Djurin was occupied by German and Romanian troops, aided by Ukrainian militias. As soon as the Romanian authorities took over the town, in the fall of 1941, the Jews were required to wear the Yellow Star and their freedom of movement was curtailed. Throughout the war, the Jews of Djurin remained in their quarter, which had become the ghetto.

Shared plight—
manifestations of solidarity with deported Jews

The first deportees to arrive in Djurin in September 1941 were Jews from Hotin (Khotyn) in Bessarabia. Nearly naked, barefoot, and ill, having wandered for weeks from one camp to another, they were housed in the synagogue where most died shortly afterward. From late October 1941 until January 1942 Djurin was flooded by hundreds of deportees who had formerly stayed in Mogilev. Most were deported from Bukovina, some from northern Moldova (Dorohoi) and Bessarabia. In total, 3,500 deportees reached Djurin—2,000 from Rădăuţi, 400 from Vijniţa, 300 from Suceava, and 200 from Hotin. The remainder came from Gura Humorului and Câmpulung, Vatra Dornei, Siret, Cernăuţi, and Dorohoi. The single trait common to all deportees was this forced concentration in a single locality, whereas interactions between them were the result of circumstances and the hardships of extreme conditions.

16 Lavi, T. (1970). *The Community Registry Romania, Vol. 1*. Jerusalem, pp. 421–425; see also Rosen 2013, pp. 36–38.

17 YVA, vt 10547, group testimony: ghettos of Mogilev, Shargorod, and Dzhurin.

Inspired by Rabbi Karalnik, local Jews welcomed the deportees with open arms. They managed to accommodate some two-thirds of the deportees in their own homes, crowded eight to ten people per room, and even provided them with blankets and house wares. Some 1,000 whom the local Jews were unable to house in their homes were given shelter in cow byres and storerooms.[18]

All of the above raises the question of the nature of the relationships between the various groups in the crowded ghetto. As we have seen, the locals, themselves abjectly poor, welcomed the deportees and made room for them in their crowded homes, albeit for a small fee. Indeed, during the deportees' first months in the ghettos (the winter of 1941–42), the common daily hardship generated codependence and reciprocal relations between locals and newcomers: the meager rent paid by the deportees was an additional income that slightly improved the locals' bleak economic plight. Moreover, the deportees brought with them from Romania goods rarely seen in Ukraine at the time (fine textiles, shoes, tablecloths, housewares, clothing etc.).

In his diary, Kunstadt describes both their welcome into Djurin and the local Jews' poverty and wretchedness:

> The local Jews, who have never known exile and have spent their lives crowded in tiny rooms, are even more downtrodden than us, who have been uprooted from our places of residence and nearly forgotten that we, too, once had homes of our own [...]. Some of the Djurin inhabitants make a living selling houseware, others live only on the rent they receive for letting a corridor or a cot, and the rest go begging and hold out a bowl for a portion of warm soup in the local soup-kitchen or half a loaf of bread from the local charity.[19]

Complementary evidence indicates that the deportees, fluent in Romanian and German, became intermediaries between the local Jews and the Romanian and German authorities. The local Jews, on the other hand, speaking the native tongue and well acquainted with the local Ukrainian way of life and culture, mediated between the deportees and their new,

---

18 Rosen 2013, pp. 36–38.

19 Entry dated July 17, 1942, 2 PM, p. 93.

alien environment.[20] The common tongue in which all Jews communicated with each other was Yiddish. Within a short while, the local Jews had become a minority in their own town, outnumbered by the deportees.

The coalescent human and demographic fabric conjoined people from different cultural backgrounds and possessing different mentalities and financial means. The practical consequences of this change caused ups and downs in relations between the local Jews and the deportees thrust upon them, creating a need to bridge the gaps between the various groups, and challenging all.

In his diary, Kunstadt often refers to the cultural gap and the differences of mentality separating the various groups and, in particular, to the classes formed in the ghetto. These differences that affected each of the groups and the relations between them will be discussed below.

The new demographics in the ghettos

As we have seen above, the destinations the deportees found themselves in left a harsh impression on them—both due to the living conditions, so different to those they had been accustomed to, and the enormous cultural differences between themselves and the local Jews (whose culture, notably, was profoundly influenced by that of their equally poor non-Jewish peasant neighbors). The Bukovina deportees were shocked by the dilapidated appearance of the Djurin ghetto and the wretchedness of the entire area as well as the local Jews' poverty. Both infrastructure and houses were crumbling, and the inhabitants lived in deplorable, or in the deportees' words, "primitive" conditions.

The collectivization programs enforced by the Soviet authorities prior to the Romanian-German occupation led to a chronic shortage of basic foods among both Ukrainians and Jews. With the arrival of the deportees, the Jews had to crowd without even basic amenities in houses that were mostly dilapidated clay or wooden huts with beaten earth floors.

To illustrate the shock of the first encounter with local conditions and the dilapidated infrastructure, Kunstadt describes the all-pervading mud in the Djurin ghetto:

---

20 YVA, Yehuda Tenenhaus, vt 7748; Kurt Schternshus, vt 937; see also group testimony, Murafa and Barsad ghettos, vt 10552; group testimony, Dzhurin, Shargorod, and Mogilev ghettos, vt 10547.

> The Djurin mud is an agonizing, tormenting plague, a sticky addition to the black suffering. As soon as the gates of the Djurin paradise opened before me, on 29 October 1941, at ten at night, this mire clung to me in all its grace. We have only just climbed down from the German truck that had dragged us to this corner, and already I was introduced to the mud. It was a dark, wet evening, and I slid and found myself lying face down in a revolting, thick, ice-cold mess[,] my sole consolation was not being alone in this, as I was not the only one sporting this fine appearance. The stubborn mud kept swelling to this very day, in May, so much that I had no choice but to surrender to it.[21]

Local Jews' references to the deportees' complaints highlight the profound cultural chasm separating the two groups, as Kunstadt writes in his diary:

> The local Jews were quite used to the mud clinging to everything and were unable to comprehend why the Bukovina refugees kept complaining and resenting it. How come? For they themselves, their fathers and grandfathers all lived out their lives in this very mud, married, fathered children, attended celebrations and funerals with the mud sticking to the soles of their shoes.[22]

Another phenomenon the deportees were unaccustomed to was the total absence of toilets in Djurin. In his observations, Kunstadt humorously describes the phenomenon of people relieving themselves in the streets or at entryways and the ensuing scandal. This phenomenon, common to all the Transnistria ghettos, attests to local Ukrainian customs and culture:

> Incidentally, there are other reasons to learn things anew in Djurin [...]. Here, for instance, is a question every Bukovina refugee asks himself at least once a day if his bowels are in good shape: Why doesn't anyone in Djurin know of that secret place which even the Emperor goes to alone? Should we ask whether the Jews of Djurin are angels, having no need for such a place? No, they are as much flesh and blood as those strange Bukovina Jews, but have been peculiar creatures for generations and find an answer wherever and whenever they can, as long as, God forbid, no one—and in particular, no policeman—sees them in the act [...]. Oh well. So fines are paid and voices are raised to the heavens—screams of home owners suspecting someone to have done the foul deed on their doorstep and even the harsh tongue of passersby showing the finger. Indeed, every morning the entire ghetto seethes for a while, policemen drag offenders to the committee, women screech, do-gooders rush

21 Entry dated May 6, 1942, p. 31.

22 Ibid.

> to beg for clemency from committee members, until the turmoil quietens down, and the next morning the sequence starts all over again.[23]

With deep puzzlement and in a cynical tone, Kunstadt introduces the explanation for the lack of toilets:

> Today, Djurin residents claim, they can do nothing, as doing something requires food—materials currently unavailable, such as oranges, pepper, or [...] paper. But it is a cheap excuse. Not too long ago food was plentiful, war did not rage yet and no one lifted a finger to furnish the apartment with that hidden place. One sees the same customs not only in Djurin, but in all localities between the Dniester and the Bug.[24]

Yet another unhappy phenomenon Kunstadt describes in his diary is the absence of water wells in the Djurin ghetto:

> Thus, for example, the woeful trouble of water. The town of Djurin and its 8,000 inhabitants—two thirds Jews in the ghetto uphill and one third Ukrainians in town, in the sugar factory quarter (where a large sugar factory operated until the war). There people are literally dying for a sip of water. The place has a single water well, an ancient facility, which can be reached with difficulty equal to the parting of the Red Sea. During mud season one drowns, and in the winter one drags oneself at great peril up the mountain—over a kilometer on flooded, slippery soil. People armed with cans, jugs and pails stand in a long line by the pump and wait, sometimes for hours, until they can get a little water. There are always fights, with people often coming to blows over who gets a pail of water sooner, and who sacrifices their health to gain a little rusty water as old as Methuselah. When, as happens at least once a week, God intervenes and the pump is out of order, the entire town remains without a sip of water [...]. The inhabitants of Djurin never saw fit to dig a few more wells. Yet if you talk to them, you will hear the claim that they alone are truly civilized, while the newcomers from Bukovina have never had even a taste of civilization.[25]

Kunstadt also sadly describes in his diary the housing shortage and the intolerable conditions in the apartments, entries that offer a glimpse into locals' living conditions: "Near us lived Dr. Gabor and his family. His apartment was no more luxurious than mine: a dilapidated roofless ruin, without doors and real walls. The cold rain fell hard on the poor walls as well as the humans and the various covers."[26]

---

23 Entry dated May 6, 1942, p. 32.

24 Ibid.

25 Ibid.

26 Entry dated April 4, 1942, p. 10.

In the same context of the harsh living conditions, Kunstadt describes his and his family's lodgings:

> We—myself, Daza [Kunstadt's wife] and the children—are living in a dark little room, two meters long and three meters wide, with not enough room to drop a pin. In this hovel we eat, cook, sleep and write literature for posterity! I do not know what to advise myself under such pressure.[27]

Similar descriptions can be found in other diaries (e.g., by Miriam Korber, Cerna Bercovici, and Mordechai Kupstein),[28] testimonies, and memoires. These attested to the huge chasm separating what the deportees had left behind and the local Jews and their culture, a chasm that resulted in considerable condescension toward the locals.

By April 1942, a ghetto committee was established, comprised of deportees from Southern Bukovina. The newcomers, now the "new masters," started dictating how the ghetto should be run. The Ukrainian Jews, now the ghetto's weakest and most vulnerable group, were the first to be put on the lists of those selected to do forced labor outside the ghetto and the last to receive relief sent from Romania.

Although himself one of the deportees, Kunstadt harshly criticizes this phenomenon:

> According to the list the shipment contains a few shoes, about twenty suits [...]. In Djurin there's need for shoes with heavy, double soles, suitable for walking in marshes and snows [...]. Since the items were sent specifically for the deportees from Romania, the committee would certainly give a little to the Ukrainian Jews, and

---

27 Entry dated October 19, 1942, p. 180.

28 Korber Bercovici, Miriam (1995). *Jurnal din Ghettou—Djurin Transnistria, 1941–1943*. Bucharest. Miriam (Mimi) Korber was seventeen-and-a-half years old when she was deported with her family from Rădăuţi in Southern Bukovina. Her family arrived at the Mogilev ghetto, and after a few days was taken by trucks to Djurin. Miriam survived, returned to Romania, studied medicine, and worked as a pediatrician in Bucharest.—Cerna Bercovici, in Avni, S. (2003). *Kimpulung-Bukowina. A Memorial of the Jewish Community in Kimpulung and Surroundings. Vol. 1* (published by the community of former residents of Câmpulung-Bukovina and surroundings), p. 220f. Twelve-year-old Cerna Bercovici was deported with her family from Câmpulung in Southern Bukovina and had to march by foot from Mogilev to the Shargorod ghetto.—Mordechai Kupstein, in Avni 2003, pp. 228–258. Mordechai Kupstein was deported with his family from Câmpulung in Southern Bukovina and ultimately arrived at the Shargorod ghetto. Having survived the war, he emigrated to then-Palestine, joined the IDF and was killed during the 1948 war in the battle for Jerusalem.

> it is precisely the escapees from the camps by the Bug, almost all Ukrainian Jews, who are dressed in rags, not a shirt on their back, their feet wrapped in rags. Putting the local Jews and us, esteemed Romanians, in the same group would be unacceptable. At first the locals welcomed us as important guests, but in time the tables have turned, and perhaps both sides are to blame. *In their own eyes, the Djurin old-timers regard themselves as important descendants of Jewish royalty, although they owe their survival to the uninvited guests.* Throughout Transnistria, the Romanian occupation authorities have deported all Ukrainian Jews from any localities where no Romanian refugees were present and have sent them to camps near the Bug where most of them have perished.[29]

The above quote highlights the fact that in the eyes of both the German and Romanian occupying forces, the local Jews were regarded as first candidates to be sent outside the ghettos to the German-controlled camps across the Bug. Kunstadt describes the injustice done to the local Jews with much bitterness and anger.

Within the ghetto population, classes and a social hierarchy soon emerged: at the center of power were members of the local leadership and their cronies from Southern Bukovina as well as deportees who had managed to bring with them (at great risk) money and valuables. In his rich, vivid language, Kunstadt compassionately describes the ghetto's most vulnerable inhabitants, those destitute, hungry Jews, among them the deportees from Bessarabia and Northern Bukovina as well as the local Ukrainian Jews. He calls them, half sarcastically, half angrily, *treif* (*treif* is non-kosher food, a Yiddish derogatory) and '*kaparot* sacrifice,' the butcher's knife raised above their heads. His diary indicates that the local Ukrainian Jews were the first ones to be sent away from the ghettos:

> The Romanian overlords in Shargorod [the Shargorod ghetto] explained to him [Dr. Rosenstrauch, head of the ghetto] that Djurin is too full of Yids and that overcrowding may damage their health. So indeed, in view of this justifiable claim officials in charge have arrived at the conclusion that the Jewish collective should be left in place and part of it should be transferred to the camps near the Bug, across the river, to the Germans. The head of the camp was given no inkling over whom the threat hangs and who is to decide who would be selected to leave. It is thought that the Ukrainian Jews as well as the Bessarabians and the "treif" Northern Bukovinians would be the sacrificial roosters for Kaparoth.[30]

29 Entry dated February 7, 1943, 8 PM, p. 247.

30 Entry dated January 4, 1943, 7 AM, p. 220.

And there was one more, even lower class, namely the Ukrainian Jews who had escaped from the camps across the Bug and sought refuge in the ghetto. These Kunstadt dubs "*treif* of *treif*," which in his cynical imagery tells the reader even more emphatically that they had no right to exist: "Some of those in hiding are '*treif* of *treif*,' not even Romanian, the scant remainder of the Jewish communities in Ukraine where German and Romanian murderers have slaughtered nearly all Jews."[31]

Kunstadt's diary further indicates an inner division into two additional subgroups: those privileged enough to have some chance of being repatriated to Romania, "kosher" Jews deported from northern Romania (from Dorohoi) and Southern Bukovina and therefore not suspect of Communist leanings, on the one hand, and, on the other, Jews from Bessarabia, Northern Bukovina, and local Djurin Jews who had all lived under Soviet rule and were consequently suspected to have Communist sympathies.

He writes thus in his diary:

> True, on some blessed days a thin ray of light breaks through the black clouds. Then the air is filled with rumors that salvation is nigh and the deportees are soon to be repatriated, if not all, then at least the more privileged ones, those from southern Bukovina and northern Moldova. For they have never had a taste of the *treif* Red regime under Soviet occupation and are therefore regarded by the Romanian authorities as more "kosher," than the Northern Bukovinian or Bessarabian Jews whose souls have been drugged.[32]

The external environment and the ghetto's relations with it

Relationships with the local Ukrainian population were complex, affected by different, contradictory factors. On the one hand, the anti-Semitism prevalent among both rural and urban Ukrainians was a given with a profound negative impact on these relationships. On the other, local Ukrainian peasants, who suffered as much as the Jews under the Romanian occupiers, could feel a measure of sympathy toward the Jews.

31 Ibid.

32 Entry dated May 7, 1942. The term "northern Moldova" refers to deportees from Dorohoi in northern Romania. The Jews of Southern Bukovina as well as the Jews from Dorohoi had never lived under Soviet occupation and were thus not suspect of having Communist sympathies.

Although official policy under the Soviet rule expressly prohibited any anti-Semitic activities, Ukrainian nationalists commonly assumed the Jews to be avid supporters of the Soviet regime and hence deserving of an especially hostile treatment. Anti-Jewish policies during the Romanian-German occupation lent these anti-Semitic sentiments legitimacy and enabled the Ukrainian residents to join in on the slaughter of Jews by the Romanian army and gendarmerie and to benefit from the looting of the property of the deported and the dead.

This collaboration between Ukrainian nationalist groups (who opposed the Soviet authorities) and the Germans and Romanians in persecuting the Jews is a well-known phenomenon, in particular during the first stage of the ghettos' establishment and up to the formation of a Jewish police.

In his diary, Kunstadt refers to two groups of Ukrainians—Ukrainian nationalists and rural peasants. The former included members of Ukrainian militias who collaborated with the occupying forces. He describes how Ukrainian militiamen helped gendarmes drag Jews out of their homes for forced labor. Complementary evidence indicates that these militia men also served as guards in the forced labor camps where their treatment of the Jewish inmates was cruel and brutal: "We have been informed that 30 slave laborers escaped the peat mines[33] in Tulcin, and there is reason to assume all were killed by Ukrainian policemen or gendarmes."[34]

In full collaboration with the Romanian gendarmes, Ukrainian militias prevented Ukrainian peasants from bringing their produce to the markets. In other instances, they would descend on the markets; riot; indiscriminately beat anyone they encountered, whether Jew or peasant; and together with the gendarmes would upturn the peasants' stands and trample their goods. This is how Kunstadt describes it in his diary:

> The peasants were prohibited in advance from bringing not only flour, potatoes and bread to market [...] but also beans, chickpeas, barley and livestock [...]. This morning, peasants unaware of the order brought plentiful goods. The market was as full as any rich market befitting the rich Ukrainian soil [...]. This entire splendor did not

33 Turf deposits mined for peat (called *torf* in Romanian and Yiddish) located near Tulcin.

34 Entry dated August 17, 1943, 9 PM, p. 300.

> last for more than a quarter of an hour, when suddenly Ukrainian militiamen and gendarmes armed with whips wildly attacked and destroyed all that goodness, even kosher goods such as butter and eggs.[35]

The second group mentioned often in Kunstadt's diary is that of the rural peasants, simple, downtrodden people who barely eked out a living working the land. They, too, were affected by the German occupiers and later the Romanian authorities, who treated them brutally. This treatment generated a deep hatred of the occupiers and in some a measure of empathy to the Jews and their plight. The Romanian authorities demanded that the peasants continue to work the land, only to be robbed of their crops by the same authorities. Kunstadt describes it thus:

> There were two obvious reasons for the scarcity of goods in the market. First of all, the Romanian occupying forces rob the peasants of their wheat, livestock, dairy products and all kinds of foods, leaving the farmers barely enough to live on, unless they hide, risking their lives, some of the crops [...]. By order of the governor of Transnistria, General Alexianu, local peasants are prohibited from not working the land on weekdays to prevent any loss of taxes collected by the state.[36]

Another factor affecting relations between the Ukrainians outside the ghetto and the Jews incarcerated within were economic interests that were also the main drivers behind the food trade and Ukrainian peasants' willingness to take the risk of employing Jews and giving them lodging. Complementing testimonies to Kunstadt's diary indicate that the peasants mercilessly exploited the starving Jews' hunger, in order to acquire items they never had before. Indeed, with the arrival of the deportees, there was a significant increase in the variety of goods sold in the markets of the kolkhozes and towns. Many peasants, who coveted the valuables brought by the Jews from Romania (fine suits, furs, bed linen, jewelry, and gold watches), could now get them for a meager meal or a few pounds of potatoes:

> The local peasants have heard that veritable treasures can now be found in the streets of Djurin, and hordes of Goyim [gentiles] from the vicinity climb up the hill to grab Jewish possessions for next to nothing. Clothes, shoes, bed linens, tables, chairs and housewares are thrown outside [...]. The cunning peasants see at first glance how desperate the Jews are for cash and haggle much harder before they

---

35 Entry dated July 5, 1942, p. 91.

36 Entry dated January 8, 1943, 9 PM, p. 41.

> show even a single mark, sucking blood to the last drop. Jews peel the tin roofs from over their houses and scrape the walls for pennies, drag out the last bunk bed, part with the last Shabbat suit and their sole remaining pair of galoshes, women remove their wedding rings and their gold earrings.[37]

Unlike the Ukrainian nationalists who often displayed a rabid anti-Semitism, some peasants showed empathy, which found its expression in acts of mercy and compassion, to the Jews' suffering. This is seen in Kunstadt's account of how differently the Ukrainians treated refugees who had managed to escape the camps of Pechora or Vapniarka and tried to find shelter in the homes of local Ukrainians:

> Very often the gentile woman, out of pity, gives the vagabond a slice of bread, while her husband sneaks out and hands the "criminal" over to the gendarmes. In some cases, however, Ukrainians show kindness, provide food and clothing and some even shelter [the escapees] in their attic for a while.[38]

In another instance, Kunstadt recounts how Jews escaping from labor camps were fed by Ukrainian peasants:

> Here's a Djurin miracle for you: the Jews of the Kryzhopil forest all returned home, but in such a state! Exhausted, in rags [...]. Their escort beat them mercilessly with their rifle butts and tortured them ceaselessly. They would have collapsed of hunger were it not for Ukrainian peasants in some villages who pitied them and gave them food.[39]

Complementary testimonies indicate that peasants willingly accepted the services of Jewish artisans and craftsmen—carpenters, builders, painters, leather workers, tanners, and tailors, whose wages they paid in food and firewood. Many Jews took seasonal work in return for food and lodging.[40] In the winter of 1942–43, for instance, a quota of knitted garments for the German army was imposed on peasant wives, who in turn hired Jewish girls to knit for them. This is also documented in Kunstadt's diary:

---

37 Entry dated July 17, 1942, 2 PM, p. 94.

38 Entry dated October 10, 1942, p. 182.

39 Entry dated October 17, 1942, 2 PM, p. 175.

40 YVA, Bat Sheva Akerman, vt 11356; Kalman Schechter, vt 8797.

> During the summer there was another source of livelihood with a respectable income of three marks a day [...]. It is a way of making a living during the summer months, just like the income made by quite a few girls and women who used to sneak out of the camp and work for local farmers.[41]

Sometimes the peasant women grew to love the young girls so much that they were willing to keep and adopt them.[42] All the above evidence indicates how humanitarian, religious, and economic motives intertwined and worked together to generate acts of compassion and kindness. In other cases, the local peasants cooperated with the ghetto residents in passing on information to the "sealed in" ghettos, a phenomenon also described by Kunstadt: "A few days ago all the Jews in Ierusinca, in the Mogilev district, were deported to Pechora. The peasants tell us that Jews were deported from other places, too."[43]

Kunstadt noted in his diary that it was from peasants that the ghetto residents learned of the murder of the Jews of Vinnytsia over death pits during an *Aktion* conducted by SS men:

> Peasants arriving at Djurin brought with them the bitter news and said that for several days afterwards the earth above the graves was still moving. News spread quickly through the camp, creating panic. Some thought: "In what way is Djurin any better than Vinnytsia?"[44]

In conclusion, the arrival of large groups of deportees and the rapid increase in the number of the Jews incarcerated in the ghetto resulted in a significant rise in population density, accompanied by severe absorption and demographic problems. The circumstances of the deportations generated a new human and demographic fabric in the ghettos, the population of which consisted of Romanian deportees and Jews native to the region. The deportees' arrival to the Djurin ghetto brought together Jews from different cultural backgrounds with very different mentalities and economic capacities.

---

41 Entry dated March 25, 1942, 9 PM, p. 255.

42 Meller (Faust), Hanna (1985). *Beyond the River*. Beit Lohamei Haghetaot [Ghetto Fighters House], p. 145; YVA, Hanna (Faust) Meller, interview conducted on March 12, 2010, at her home in Haifa; Miriam Savion, vt 11435.

43 Entry dated February 16, 1943, 9 PM, p. 244.

44 Entry dated April 28, 1942, 6 AM, p. 16.

The arrival of the deportees turned the locals into a minority in their own hometown, outnumbered by the newly arrived Romanians. Moreover, the Jewish leadership in the ghetto evolved from among the Bukovina deportees and maintained this role until the end of the war. Consequently, the deportees became the "new masters" in Djurin, imposing their own agenda. In practical terms, this change resulted in ups and downs in the local Jews' relations with the deportees who were forced upon them. Coping with the new circumstances presented a challenge to all the groups in the Djurin ghetto population.

Despite the differences, these groups also had quite a few things in common. The deportation and displacement as such and the betrayal by their homeland and by "good" neighbors were shared by all and left all deportees feeling affront and anger.[45] The difference between these two groups stemmed from two main factors—their culture and the ensuing mentality, linked to their places of origin, and the circumstances, and mode of their deportation. These two factors find expression in Kunstadt's above-discussed highly cynical and caustic writing.

The relationships formed with the Ukrainian non-Jewish population outside the ghetto show how varied relations between Jews and Ukrainians were: Where the Ukrainian peasants had common interests with the Jews, humanitarian and religious motives could come to the fore and drive them to help the Jews fit more easily in their environment. On the other hand, the benefits the peasants gained from Jews working in their homes and farms were yet another incentive to help the latter. [46]

Hence, as Kunstadt's diary shows, relations between Jews and the Ukrainian population outside the ghettos were based on both parties' similar reality of life under the occupation, the famine, the emergence of a barter system, the availability of a cheap Jewish labor force, and the peasants' humane sentiments. In other cases, these sentiments had to be awakened through bribes, while at times the bribes elicited manifestations of humane sentiments in people otherwise devoid of them.

---

45 Yeri (Joseph) Rom, a Suceava deportee, expressed these sentiments of affront and betrayal in a poem he composed. See: Fuchs, Benzion (ed.) (2007). *The Book of the Jews from Suceava (Shutz) and the Surrounding Community*: www.jewishgen.org/yizkor/Suceava/Suceava.html (accessed on April 22, 2016).

46 Ofer 1995, p. 198.

Epilogue

Kunstadt survived the deportation along with most of his family, except his mother and his brother-in-law. During the 1950s, he and his family emigrated to Israel; in the 1960s they moved to the United States where they lived in the Bronx, New York. In the United States, too, Kunstadt kept writing, mainly in Yiddish, and publishing in the Jewish press. Even in the United States, where he spent his last years, he published articles in Hebrew and English. His feuilletons, with his trademark gentle humor, became quite popular among his readers.

He died in 1978, aged 78, and in 1982 his relatives typed the original manuscript of the diary on a typewriter and added annotations. The final text of the typed diary comprises 340 10-inch pages. The diary was printed in a limited edition of a few copies, some are kept by descendants and others are preserved in several libraries in Israel.

Gali Tibon

Two-Front Battle: Opposition in the Ghettos of the Mogilev District in Transnistria 1941–44

An "alternative leadership" is a leadership that challenges the existing order and the acting leadership, or according to Israel Gutman: "Two leadership groups: the first group is the existing one, and the second group seeks to replace it."[1] Was there an alternative leadership to the Jewish committees in the ghettos of the Mogilev district in Transnistria? What were the reasons for the emergence of an opposition and what were the issues, differences of opinion, and the fierce arguments in these ghettos? How did the Romanian government react to the opposition and the criticism against the acting Jewish committees?

The main topics to be discussed here are:

1) Arguments, criticism, and opposition to the monopoly of the Jewish committee in economic, labor, and commercial affairs in the ghettos of the Mogilev district, including opposition to the monopoly of the Jewish committee concerning kosher slaughter.
2) The rivalry between Michael Danilov and his group from the Dorohoi district, Romania, and Siegfried Jagendorf, head of the Jewish committee in the Mogilev ghetto.
3) The position of Zechariah Pitaru versus Meir Teich, head of the Jewish committee in the Shargorod ghetto.
4) The status and role of the Zionist youth movements versus the older leadership in the district's ghettos.

The subject offers an in-depth look into the social and economic gaps, which are reflected in the fierce arguments about the right way to lead the Jews in the ghetto. It also presents the modes of action vis-à-vis the

1 Gutman, Israel (ed.) (2008). *Issues in the Research of the Holocaust: Criticism and Contribution.* Jerusalem, p. 150; Trunk, Yeshayahu (1979). The Typology of the Jewish Councils, in Gutman, Israel and Rachel Manbar (eds.). *Patterns of Jewish Leadership in Nazi Europe, 1933–1945.* Jerusalem [Hebrew].

Romanian authorities, the struggle over the limited resources and the disputes relating to economic issues and among opponents who criticized the morals of the committees' members in the district's ghettos.

The controversies in the ghettos of the Mogilev district during the Holocaust reflect the hardships of the opposition groups conducting a two-fold battle: against the acting leadership and against the Romanian authorities of Transnistria.

Arguments, criticism, and resistance to the Jewish committee monopoly in the fields of labor, commerce, and economy

The Jewish committees sought to organize and take charge of the district's labor resources, work arrangements of the ghetto's Jews, and the economic initiatives in the ghettos. The Jews had to pay taxes to the committee and receive a license in order to engage in commerce or provide services in the ghetto. More than one conflict erupted over the private initiatives of Jews and the committee's wish to be the decisive economic agency. The Jewish committee also battled against soaring prices of merchants and against profiteering, alongside the Romanian authorities.[2]

In order to closely supervise the economic life in the Mogilev ghetto, the Jewish committee, headed by Jagendorf, objected to private economic initiatives. It dismantled the independent labor groups and placed the Jewish labor arrangements around town in the hands of the labor-coordination department of the Jewish committee.[3] For example, work and residence permits on behalf of the civil administration, which had been obtained by engineer Galber as a private entrepreneur who managed an employment agency, were revoked. The Jews whose permits expired upon the committee's decision had to request new permits from

---

2 Yad Vashem Archive (YVA), Jagendorf Collection, P9, file 6 [Romanian]; YVA O-3/1237, Max Anzer [Hebrew].

3 Jagendorf, Sigfried (1991). *Jagendorf's Foundry. Memoir of the Romanian Holocaust 1941–1944* (edited with commentary by Aron Hirt-Manheimer). New York, p. 114.

the committee or move on to another destination in Transnistria.[4] Jagendorf insisted that all the bakeries in Mogilev would be under the patronage of the committee, including the monopoly over *matzah* baking on Passover.[5] The committee directed the Jewish workers to the workplace, managed the bakeries and public kitchens and the few stores and factories in the ghettos. In order to strengthen its exclusive holding on the economy of the ghettos, the committee sought the help of the Romanian prefect who refused independent commerce and economic initiatives.[6]

The committee acted as a monopoly also in the field of meat slaughter (*shchita*): the only people allowed to engage in kosher slaughtering in the ghettos of Mogilev were authorized slaughterers of the Jewish committee who paid a tax into the community's coffers on their income. They barely had any work as there were only few people who could afford to buy meat;[7] even the improvement in their situation in 1943, when the Russian front moved to the west, did not change the reality in which groceries in general and meat specifically were scarce.

The Romanian government strictly prohibited cows' slaughter as cows were meant to provide milk to the population and the military forces of the entire district.[8] The little beef that was available was the source of dispute between the non-authorized slaughterers in the ghetto and the Jewish committees. There was a fierce controversy regarding the taxes of kosher slaughter. The Jewish committees, which insisted on their right to hold the monopoly over kosher slaughtering, faced slaughterers who fought for their livelihood—and for their lives. Hannah Meir's father and uncle battled against the slaughter monopoly of the Jewish committee in Mogilev; her parents were arrested by the Jewish police and would not

---

4 Strochlitz Archive, Haifa University R3H22, Hilda Kostin; YVA O-3/123, Yitzhak Yalon, Yad [Hebrew]; Consiliul Național pentru Studierea Arhivelor Securității (CNSAS), P - 8279, vol. 1 [Romanian].

5 Korber, Mirjam (1993). *Deportiert: Jüdische Uberlebensschicksale, 1941–1944. Ein Tagebuch*. Konstanz, p. 87.

6 Jagendorf Collection, P-9 file 7, document of Nasturas, December 17, 1942; P-9 file 6, letter from Jagendorf [Romanian].

7 Kunstadt, Lipman (1980). *Traybt men yidn ibern deniester: togbukh funem transnistrishn gehe* [Persecuting Jews across the Dniester: A Diary from the Hell of Transnistria]. Haifa, p. 42 [Yiddish].

8 Deletant, Dennis (2010). Transnistria and the Romanian Solution to the Jewish Problem, in Brandon, Ray and Wendy Lower (eds.). *The Shoah in Ukraine: History, Testimony, Memorialization*. Bloomington/Indianapolis, pp. 156–189, here p. 178.

cooperate.[9] In Shargorod, "[the slaughterer] Elharnd bought and slaughtered veal from a Ukrainian farmer (without a license), and the pretor Dindelgan executed him."[10]

It is not clear who informed the Romanian government about the non-authorized slaughtering: it might have been one of the authorized slaughterers in the ghetto who worked against an opponent who slaughtered without paying a tax and therefore lowered the price of the meat. It is also possible that the ghetto's administrators approached the pretor, wishing to warn other Jews from slaughtering without a license and without paying taxes to the committee. There were no independent stores or merchants in Shargorod, but rather a supervised commerce, which could only take place through the Jewish committee's cooperative store. The strictness of the committee regarding economic control in the ghetto was in line with the battle of the Romanian government against slaughter, the black market, and prices rising in the district.[11]

In the Dzhurin ghetto, the local butcher who had lost his livelihood and customers upon the Romanian conquest refused to allocate some of his profits to the Jewish committee. Another slaughterer who worked without the committee's license but had a permit from Dzhurin's Rabbi Herschel Karalnik was summoned to a serious investigation.[12] This story reflects a complex struggle for authority in the ghetto. In prewar Dzhurin, Rabbi Herschel Karalnik had enjoyed a strong position. He was popular among the Jews in the town as well as among the Ukrainian residents and the local authorities with whom he negotiated when it was necessary. The arrival of thousands of Romanian Jews changed the demographics as well as his position. Karalnik was no longer an authoritative, senior rabbi, but one of several, maybe the least of them all. He was replaced by Rabbi Baruch Hager from Siret. Karalnik accepted Hager's authority

---

9 YVA O-3/11832, Chana Meir [Hebrew].

10 Arni Seppter's testimony, in Avni, Shamaya (ed.) (2003). *A Memorial of the Jewish Community in Kimpolung and the Surroundings*. Tel-Aviv, p. 313 [Hebrew]; Carp, Matatias (1947). *Cartea Neagră*. Bucharest, p. 271.

11 Ancel, Jean (2002). *The History of the Holocaust, Romania. Vol 2*. Jerusalem, p. 795 [Hebrew].

12 Artzi, Yitzhak et al. (2003). *Our Siret: The Story of a Jewish Town*, p. 190 [Hebrew]; Kunstadt 1980, pp. 42–45.

and leadership, but insisted on providing his own permits and authorizations to the slaughterers.[13]

For the Jewish-Ukrainian population in the ghettos, it was not clear whether the kosher slaughtering tax served as a means for the Jewish committee to control the economic resources in the ghetto or whether it was indeed a tax for the benefit of the community, since the local Jewish communities were the last in line to enjoy any benefit and the first to be sent to the forced labor camps and to the starvation camps such as Scazineti/Skazintsy and Pechora. It should also be noted that the wealthy Jews in the ghettos were mostly from Southern Bukovina, and they often rented homes in the Ukrainian neighborhoods. Therefore, they were not obliged to pay direct taxes to the Jewish committee, while the local Ukrainian Jews who lived in the ghetto itself were obliged to pay taxes to the committee, which was perceived as the Jewish committee "from Romania" and not as their representative. Refusing to pay the slaughtering tax was a way to object to the slaughtering monopoly and to undermine the committee's authority and the exclusivity it claimed to have on community services.[14]

The rivalry between Dorohoi and Southern Bukovina residents in the district's ghettos

Two groups of Dorohoi residents, one headed by Zechariah Pitaru at the Shargorod ghetto and the other headed by Michail Danilov at Mogilev, quickly discovered that they were the minority in the Mogilev district. They both challenged the leadership of the Jewish committees, which was exclusively dominated by the Jews from Southern Bukovina. Dorohoi's Jews saw themselves as Romanians for all intent and purposes since the district had belonged to the Romanian Regat since long ago. They spoke Romanian for generations and believed that their transfer to Transnistria was a bureaucratic mistake that would be corrected soon.[15]

---

13 Rabbi of Nadvorna Dov Yissachar Rosenboim, personal interview, Bnei Brak, summer 2010.

14 There were frequent battles over kosher slaughtering licenses and objections to the heavy taxation also in the communities of Southern Bokuvina before the war. See the slaughterers' dispute in prewar Siret: Artzi et al. 2003, p. 27.

15 CNSAS, file P-45109.

The rivalry between Michael Danilov and his group from Dorohoi and Siegfried Jagendorf, head of the Mogilev Jewish committee

As opposed to chairmen like Teich in Shargorod and Jagendorf in Mogilev who left transcripts in which they presented their version and points of view on the events and on their conduct as leaders, Danilov did not leave any documents, aside from his declaration in his trial after the war.

Danilov served in the Romanian military until 1932. He was one of the supporters of Iuliu Maniu and a member of the Romanian Peasants' Party. He was a lawyer and, shortly before the war, served as the head of the Darabani Jewish community in the district of Dorohoi. In 1940, like all the Jewish lawyers in Romania, he was expelled from the bar association, and in 1941, he was jailed in the Targu Jiu camp for allegedly betraying the regime[16] and was released only to be deported with his young family and his community to Transnistria. It seems as though he is the most tragic character among the Jewish leaders in the Mogilev district. Danilov felt at home within the Romanian culture. He strongly wished to identify with Romania's goals in the war and wanted to continue to serve his homeland, sending Jews to forced labor that was required for the military effort. In 1943, he was sentenced in Transnistria for attempting to bribe a clerk of the Romanian Ministry of Industry. In a further trial, he was sentenced and convicted in July 1945 in Romania as a "war criminal who cooperated with Hitler and Antonescu's government and conspired against his own people to make profits at their expense."[17]

The conflict in Mogilev between Jagendorf and his supporters, who came from Southern Bukovina, and the Danilov group from Dorohoi erupted already on December 29, 1941, due to the labor duties in Mogilev: Jagendorf claimed that Danilov's group consisted of 178 families, totaling 641 people, based on which they received bread, but contrary to the agreement between them, the group did not place the right number of workers.

Jagendorf demanded that all the men in the group, including Danilov himself and his deputy Yanko Malkesh, be assigned to work.[18] Danilov on his part claimed that the public kitchen served boiling water instead of

16 Shlomo, David (ed.) (1992). *Dorohoi: Generations of Judaism and Zionism. Vol. 4.* Kiryat Bialik, p. 174 [Hebrew].

17 CNSAS, file P-7795, vol. 4, Jagendorf Collection, P-9, file10 .

18 Jagendorf Collection, P-9 file 6.

soup, that the food portions were too small, and that Jagendorf and the committee's members took care of the Southern Bukovina Jews at the expense of the Dorohoi Jews. Jagendorf saw Danilov and his group as a threat to his leadership, and the rivalry between them also affected the portrayal of Danilov's character in the history of the Romanian Holocaust.[19]

The heart of the conflict between them was the transfer to the Scazineti/Skazintsy camp. The initiative was the idea of Prefect Baleanu in February 1942. Jagendorf was then the head of the Jewish committee and believed that a transfer of hundreds of Jews from the ghetto to Scazineti/Skazintsy could benefit the ghetto. He expected an agricultural village where they would be able to make a living, and he prepared a plan for their settlement in the place. Instead, they arrived at an abandoned, uninhabitable Soviet army base. The prefect insisted on executing the plan and his replacement, Constantin Nasturas, gave the decisive order on May 29, 1942. The main question that arose was who decided on the list of the Jews to be sent to Scazineti/Skazintsy. Dumitrie Stefanescu and Romeo Orasanu (commander of the legion of the gendarmerie) claimed in their trial after the war that they made the list together with Jagendorf.[20] Jagendorf claimed that the list did not specify who would go to Scazineti/Skazintsy, but rather who was worthy and deserved to stay in Mogilev, that he determined the criteria, and that the Jewish committee approved that "the selection of the Jews who would remain in Mogilev was based on the following objective criteria: necessity, productivity, discipline, labor and honor."[21]

The decisions of the Jewish committee and the Romanian government were executed by the Jewish police, supervised by Danilov. Nasturas and Orasanu required that Danilov pledge his life and the life of

19 Danilov's appeal request dated August 20, 1946, in CNSAS, file P-7795, vol. 4. See also: Rosen, Sarah (2013). *The Collective and the Individual: Organization and Family. The Internal Life of the Jews in North Transnistria's Ghettos (Moghilev, Şargorod, Djurin, Murafa and Berşad), 1941–1944*. Jerusalem (PhD thesis, Hebrew University in Jerusalem).

20 Stefanescu's statement in his retrial, in CNSAS, file P-8279, vol. 1.

21 Samuel Kaufman's testimony, in Jagendorf Collection P-9 file; CNSAS, P-7795, vol. 1.

the Jewish committee members that no Jew who had been sent to Scazineti would escape back to Mogilev.[22] Two weeks after the transport, on June 14, Jagendorf resigned. Danilov replaced him from June 16, 1942, and stayed on until August 1, 1942.

The argument regarding the responsibility and the blame for sending 3,000 Jews from Mogilev to Scazineti/Skazintsy was not over even after the war.[23] During Danilov's tenure as temporary chairman, from June 16, 1942, until August 1, 1942, no transports took place from the ghetto to the starvation camps, and during his second tenure, from November 1, 1942, to December 15, 1942, a second transport took place, including a few dozens of Jews to the Pechora camp. The large transport to Pechora in October 1942 was executed by Chairman Yosef Shauer, Jagendorf's confidant, who also resigned immediately afterward.

From the collective recollection of survivors, as it is reflected in many testimonies, Danilov was responsible for the two transports to the starvation camps in Scazineti/Skazintsy and Pechora for two reasons:

1) During this time, Danilov served as the head of the "Jewish guard" at the Mogilev ghetto, including its two departments, the labor coordination department and the Jewish police department. These institutions were the operating entities of the Romanian government and the Jewish committee, and Danilov oversaw all activities in general and the transport of Jews to slave labor in the German camps in the Bug area in particular. Danilov came in direct contact with the Jewish population of the ghetto in its toughest moments. Therefore, his character was perceived as a more central and influential one in these life-and-death situations compared to the committee chairmen at Mogilev who were more distant, less accessible, and less exposed to criticism. His overall role and especially the second transport to the Pechora camp

---

22 Lavi, Theodor and Jean Ancel (1970). *Encyclopedia of Jewish Communities in Romania. Vol. 2*. Jerusalem, p. 465 [Hebrew].

23 CNSAS, P-7795, vol. 4. See the Jagendorf Collection for details on the Scazineti/Skazintsy plan and the transport estimates. YVA, P-9, File 6, Jagendorf Collection. Documents dated March 28, 1942, April 3, 1942, April 8, 1942; Jagendorf 1991, p. 117f.

provoked the people's rage against him and highlighted the controversy around the role of the Jewish committee.[24]

2) Danilov did not have an economic powerbase within the ghetto. While Jagendorf enjoyed his powerful standing among both the Jewish population and the Romanian government due to his role as the manager of an essential plant, the foundry (*turnatoria*), Danilov tried, together with Donenfeld, to set up a compound of stores that would have served the population in the ghetto. This attempt failed due to the objection of Moshe Katz, who asked to manage the stores by himself,[25] and Jagendorf, who managed commerce and labor compound in the foundry.[26]

Some of the survivors claimed that Danilov used to settle "personal disputes" through his position and role at the committee. For instance, Kalmanovich claimed that Danilov had sent him to the Pechora camp due to a dispute that erupted between them,[27] and others said Danilov used to steal items from packages that were received from the Jewish aid in Romania and that they were afraid of him.[28] On the other hand, some survivors, mostly from Dorohoi, spoke in his favor.[29] These testimonies strengthen the assumption that some of the public criticism toward him and the rivalry with Jagendorf stemmed from the fact that each of them represented a different hometown in the ghetto and fought to receive resources for his community.[30]

Danilov and his confidants felt that they had been pushed away from the Jewish leadership in Mogilev and demanded that a representative on their behalf be included in the committee. Jagendorf, on his part, did the best he could to not include Danilov in the Jewish committee and dealt

---

24 YVA O-3/1525, Israel Halfan; YVA O-3/1238, Yitzhak Yalon; YVA O-3/11150, Hannah Hazenfratz [Hebrew].

25 Member of the Mogilev committee and chairman of the committee of the Mogilev ghetto since May 1943.

26 David Marcus' testimony, CNSAS, P-7795, vol. 1 [Romanian].

27 YVA O-3/1104, Baruch Kalmenovich.

28 YVA O-3/1232, Pesach Rosenberg; YVA O-3/1525, Israel Halfan; Rabinovitch, Naphtali (1965). *Me and my Hometown*. Tel Aviv, p. 364f., p. 388 [Yiddish]; CNSAS, P-7795, vol. 4.

29 YVA O-3/13014, Freiling-Avivi; YVA O-3/7578215, Yehoshua Atias Kushmaro; Avni 2003, p. 31; Botoroaga file and others, CNSAS, vol. 1 P-7795, vol. 4.

30 CNSAS, P-7795, vol. 4.

with many pressures from both the prefecture and the legion of the gendarmerie in Mogilev, since Danilov, like Jagendorf, enjoyed the support of some Romanian government officials in the district, headed by commander Danulescu.

In December 1942, Jagendorf launched an investigation on behalf of the audit committee, headed by Emanuel Fandrich and Joseph Lauper, against the labor coordination committee, headed by Danilov, on the allocation of spaces to private stores. The report's conclusions indicated that Danilov was personally responsible.[31] In January 1943, another report stated that Danilov "provided tax reliefs to his confidants and to himself."[32]

Despite the fierce disputes between them, there were also friendly gestures: Danilov sent a support letter to Jagendorf after the latter had been beaten by the gendarmerie in January 1942,[33] and Jagendorf made efforts to release Danilov from the Vapniarka camp in the fall of 1943.[34]

The character of Michael Danilov as it is portrayed by the Jagendorf collection, the testimonies in the archives in Israel and in the United States, and in the memorial books is highly negative. He is portrayed as a traitor and as a willing collaborator in war crimes committed by the Romanians. In documents of Romania's secret service archive, the CNSAS, however, he is portrayed as a more complex person. Witnesses in his trial claimed: "We, the people of Dorohoi, had nothing in Transnistria but Adv. Danilov, who acted with devotion to protect our interests and ease our suffering."[35] The opening line—"We, the people of Dorohoi" —is the heart of the matter. Danilov's insistence on the place and the rights of the Jews of Dorohoi in the Mogilev ghetto created a collision course between himself and Jagendorf, whose main priority was the communities from Southern Bukovina. While the connections groomed by Jagendorf with Prefect Baleanu and those of Moshe Katz with the inspector of the legion of gendarmerie, Botoroaga, were perceived as legitimate and as part of the wish to save the community, Danilov's connections with the Romanian gendarmerie were criticized. He was perceived as the one who

31 The Jagendorf Collection, P-9, file 7.

32 Jagendorf 1991, p. 139; YVA O-3/1232, Moshe Rabinovich.

33 The Jagendorf Collection, P-9, file 13.

34 Jagendorf 1991, pp. 144–147.

35 CNSAS, file 1 P-7795, vol. 1.

came in contact with the government to join his friends in the Romanian military from before the war, to improve his situation, and to make a fortune. This position contradicts the fact that Danilov came out of the war very poor and in the worst economic standing of all the leaders of the Jewish committees in the Mogilev district.[36]

The position of Zechariah Pitaru against Teich in the Shargorod ghetto

The Jews of the Dorohoi district arrived at Shargorod in an extremely difficult situation. After most of the family men were sent to forced labor, the remaining Jews, including women and children, the sick and the elderly, were deported to Transnistria.

A procession of 900 Jews from Dorohoi arrived at the Shargorod ghetto in the terrible cold of November 1941, and the Romanian pretor demanded the procession to leave immediately. The attempt of the Jewish committee to convince the pretor to allow the Jews of Dorohoi to stay for a few days failed, and only the intervention of Ukrainian peasants prevented them from being sent away.[37] Teich summarizes the story, quoting the pretor: "Storing the masses shall bring upon us their illnesses and we shall die too." And in his own words: "Unfortunately, he was right."[38] Zechariah Pitaru from Dorohoi thought otherwise. He assessed that there was no shortage in living space since most of the original Jewish population of Shargorod had escaped with the retreating Soviet forces and that it was possible to squeeze in the Jews from Dorohoi into the existing apartments and accommodations. But the Jews who had arrived from Southern Bukovina with "money and jewelry," he said, "were much better settled in Shargorod and not interested in more very poor Jews arriving."[39]

Pitaru further claimed that the committee favored the Jews of Southern Bukovina over others and sent only non-Bukovina Jews to forced labor missions.[40] The son of Pitaru and his friend were among those who

36 CNSAS, file P-7795, vol. 4

37 Carp 1947, p. 88.

38 Teich, Meir (1958). Ha-minhal ha-yehudi ha-otonomi be-geto shargorod (Transnistria), *Collection of Studies on Chapters of the Holocaust and Heroism* II: 214–215.

39 YVA O-3/2469, Zechariah Pitaru. See also: Carp 1947, p. 210f.

40 YVA O-3/6591420, Leah Schulz; Strochlitz Archive, R3H22, Emma Lustig.

were sent to forced labor. The son escaped from the road-construction works and told the father about the horrible working conditions in the woods of Capusterna (Kopystyrin). Pitaru approached the civil administration at Shargorod, asking to transfer his son from that camp. He received a negative answer and went to Mogilev, by foot, without a traffic permit, to talk directly to major Orasanu.[41] Surprisingly, Orasanu listened to his complaint carefully and took him in his car to Shargorod, where he held an investigation. Orasanu gave an order to transfer the Jews from the woods where they were held in under terrible conditions to the village of Capusterna itself. This decision must be understood in light of the fact that the labor camps in Capusterna were anyway shut down as the Jewish labor force was needed elsewhere. Pitaru, of course, was not aware of the circumstances and associated the transfer order with Orasanu's positive attitude.[42]

Pitaru's approach to the Romanian government was perceived as negative by the Jews who referred to him as an "informer" who violated the common ethical code that no one approaches the government in order to solve internal disputes within the Jewish population.[43] Most of the Jews did not have access, as individuals or in groups, to the representatives of the Romanian government in the ghetto, certainly not to the senior ones.[44] This explains how brave and extreme Pitaru's action was from the start to the end without sharing it with the Jewish committee at Shargorod and against Teich's position as well as against the position of Shauer, the head of the Jewish committee in Mogilev. Even Danilov was afraid to get involved in the incident, which led to a dispute between Dorohoi and Southern Bukovina Jews.

---

41 YVA O-3/2469, Zechariah Pitaru.

42 YVA O-3/2469, Zechariah Pitaru. On the change in the Romanian policy regarding the labor camps in the forest, see: Lavi/Ancel 1970, p. 3.

43 Miller, Menashe (1993). *Be'emek habacha*. Haifa: Mekor Habracha Institute; *Diary of Baruch Hager*, dated September 18, 1942, p. 227.

44 Gutman, Israel (1991). The Judenrat as Leadership, in Malkin, Irad and Zeev Zachor (eds.). *Leaders and Leadership*. Jerusalem, pp. 265–286, here p. 273. YVA O-3/12184, Tony Dramer Rosenberg; YVA O-3-2515, Israel Halfon; Butnaru, I. C. (1992). *The Silent Holocaust: Romania and its Jews*. New York, p. 134; Ancel, Jean (2003). *Transnistria 1941–1942: The Romanian Mass Murder Campaigns, History and Document Summaries*. Tel Aviv, p. 1295; USHMM, RG-31.011M, reel 9; Jagendorf Collection, P-9, file 6 and file 13.

Pitaru's action indeed led to a major improvement for his son and his group in Capusterna, but he also paid a heavy price for standing against the Jewish committee in Shargorod and against the representatives of the Romanian government of the district. He was severely beaten by the gendarmerie of Shargorod because he went against Teich and because the gendarmes were reprimanded by Orasanu.[45] The dispute between the two Jewish groups in the Shargorod ghetto became a dispute between the two gendarmerie divisions of the district, the one in Mogilev and the one in Shargorod.

The Romanian government and the opposition to the Jewish committees in the ghettos of the Mogilev district

The Romanian government was inconsistent in its attitude toward the sources of opposition to the Jewish committees. On the one hand, they were interested in maintaining the position of the Jewish leadership and supported the oppression of competing groups, which sought to contact the representatives of the government in Transnistria independently and to offer services, and on the other, they tried to weaken the acting Jewish leadership, while strengthening the dependency of the Jewish committee on the Romanian government and using internal disputes within the Jewish population to establish their control. Position holders in the Romanian government, military and civil administration had contacts with Jews who represented the committee's competing groups, such as the Jews of Dorohoi who offered benefits and large amounts of money to officers and civil position holders in the region.[46]

Despite the inconsistent behavior, the Romanian government preferred to manage the ghetto through one clear and influential Jewish leadership and therefore chose to stand by the acting leadership in almost all the disagreements that took place in the ghettos. The strength of the Jewish committees in the ghettos stemmed also from the support of the Romanian government almost against any opposition in the ghetto,

45 YVA O-3/2469, Zechariah Pitaru.

46 According to Stafensco, more than 7 million Lei were collected from Jews (CNSAS, P-8279).

and in certain cases the Jewish committee even asked them to repress the objections to its actions. For example, in the Mogilev ghetto, the committee delivered some information to the Romanian gendarmerie about the trader Pistiner for charging high prices, and the Romanians imprisoned him and beat him.[47] On November 5, 1942, in the Dzhurin ghetto, the Romanian government's representative, Pretor Dindelgan, acted on behalf of the Jewish committee to violently repress the opposition in the ghetto and harshly slapped Jews who avoided forced labor.[48] The pretor did the same thing when he was called by the Dzhurin Jewish committee to handle David Wasserman who, despite being a familiar public figure at Rădăuți before the war, lost his public position in the Dzhurin ghetto.[49] In the case of the dentist Leon Hirschhorn, Prefect Login himself ordered his expulsion from the ghetto due to his criticism of the Jewish committee. The strong reaction of the committee against Hirschhorn and the involvement of the Romanian government in the incident brought an end to the open criticism against Dzhurin's Jewish committee: "Hirschhorn, who dared complaining, was taken away at night with his family, he was beaten and sent to a camp by the Bug. Since then, there is no more opposition."[50]

In these cases, the pretor was the operating branch of the Jewish committee. It seemed that the pretor acted accordingly not only because he was bribed by the committee but also because he thought it was important to repress the objection to the acting committee. The Romanian government supported the Jewish committee's exclusive control over the population in the ghetto, as long as the committee followed its demands. The Romanian security forces preferred to work with a central and exclusive authority in each ghetto, thus ensuring that the committee's heads and their friends were personally responsible for following their orders. The groups that had no access to resources and bore the heaviest brunt of forced labor and from which Jews were sent to Scazineti/Skazintsy and Pechora could not establish a leadership of their

47 YVA O-3/1237, Max Ancer.

48 Ibid.; YVA O-3/1526, Zeev Shar; Kunstadt diary, p. 193; Rosenstock, Wolf (1989). Die Chronik von Dschurin, *Dachauer Hefte*, p. 60.

49 Ibid., p. 60.

50 Ibid., p. 73.

own and could not express their objections because they realized that the Romanian security forces stood by the acting leadership.[51]

The position and role of the Zionist youth movements versus the committees' leadership in the district's ghettos

The Order no. 1, dated September 1941, banned any kind of political organization.[52] Nevertheless, youth groups in the ghettos of the Mogilev district came together and organized some activities. Most of these activities were focused on discussions, sing-alongs, and networking among the members as well as on the attempt to contact their friends in other ghettos. The largest and most significant movement was *hanoa'rhatzioni* whose members maintained the connections that were formed in the various groups before the war.[53]

A significant group of the Bnei Akiva movement was also active in the Shargorod ghetto.[54] The Zionist activity of the youth movement started in the Mogilev district ghettos in the winter of 1942, when the members of the Zionist group of Vatra-Dornei became organized and other members from Bukovina groups joined them. The activity included helping friends in other towns[55] and was focused on maintaining high morale and proving practical support for the members.[56] It was not an easy task to plan their future in the reality of Transnistria. They felt isolated, worried about their lives, their families, and their future. This pessimism is reflected in the *Courier* journals, issued by the Zionist youth in

51 Litani, Dora (1981). *Transnistria*. Tel Aviv, p. 56; Kunstadt diary, p. 61.

52 Ancel 2003, p. 549.

53 Ben-Zion, Shmuel (1986). *The Circumstances which Led to the Setting Up of the Training Groups at the Dzhurin Ghetto in Transnistria* (Dapim Studies on the Holocaust). Haifa, p. 225f. [Hebrew]; Shani, Haim and Moshe Sharf (1976). The Zionist Youth in Transnistria—in the Dzhurin and Shargorod Ghettos, *Massuah—Annual Collection for the Memory and Awareness of the Holocaust in Israel* 4: 209–214 [Hebrew]; YVA O-3/6350723, Mendel Fox.

54 Knoller, Rivka (1989). *The Activities of Religious Zionist Youth Groups in Europe During the Holocaust 1939–1945*. Ramat-Gan, p. 59f. [Hebrew].

55 YVA O-3/1238, Yitzhak Yalon.

56 Same as youth movements in the Polish ghettos, see: Gutman 2008, p. 164.

the Dzhurin ghetto, portraying a picture of isolation: the feeling that everyone needs to care for his own, that a society makes no more sense when it is unable to interconnect, and that this strengthened the rules of nature where each person becomes stronger at the expense of another. The gatherings, lectures, and discussions were meant to fight these feelings of pessimism, which threatened to isolate each of the youngsters within their families, and to build a supporting social system that would give them hope and encouragement. The movement filled the social and morale needs, which helped the youth to maintain a proper humane picture in a socially twisted reality.[57]

In Shargorod, an underground organization of Jewish-Ukrainian youngsters was set up: "The resistance included activities such as burying and hiding crops and other products in the kolkhoz so they would not give them away to the Romanian military."[58] This underground coming-together was known to the Jewish committee of Shargorod, which covered up for the Jewish partisans from the area who hid in the ghetto.

The Jewish population in the Mogilev district ghettos, youngsters and adults alike, distrusted the Romanian government. On the other hand, there were fewer public displays of distrust on the part of the youth movements under the older Jewish leadership. The movement's leaflets included some criticism, mostly expressed indirectly, which rarely referred to certain individuals or particular groups.[59] The *Courier* journal was published against the position of the Dzhurin ghetto's Jewish committee. The members of the youth movement leveled criticism at the older leadership of the various ghettos and disagreed with the way the aid funds from Romania were allocated. Nevertheless, the content itself did not include any calls for rebellion against the Romanian government or against the Jewish leadership in the ghetto. The poems and the plays that were published in it did not include direct and open personal criticism, and they

---

57 YVA O-3/1526, Zeev Sharf. See also: Shani/Sharf 1976, p. 213. Ben-Zion 1986, p. 228f.; Yalon, R. et al. (eds.) (2001). *Sefer ha-zikaron shel yehudei vatra dornei veha-seviva* [Memorial book of the Jewish Community in Vatra Dornei and surroundings]. Tel Aviv: p. 331; YVA O-3/8819, Menachem Bernstein [Hebrew].

58 YVA O-3/963, N. Cohen; YVA O-33/973, Clara Muscal; Yalon et al. 2001, p. 329f.

59 Bauer, Judea (1989). *The Reactions of Jewish Groups*. Tel-Aviv, p. 127 [Hebrew]; Shani/Sharf 1976, p. 210.

did not express any reservations regarding the legitimacy of the leadership.[60] Some cynical and implicit criticism can be found in the plays that were published in the newspaper, such as the end of the scene of a play where Jewish policemen are picking up Jews for forced labor and looking for some who were hiding: "The work of the Jewish policemen is tiring, therefore, we have to praise them for the courage and patience they show while on duty in favor of our colony."[61]

Despite the underground nature of the Zionist activity, it was not an alternative leadership. The youth movements in Mogilev did not challenge the leadership and did not want to take part in it, but rather to set up a support system for their members. The gatherings included Zionist contents, and although they went against government orders, the Romanians did not act against them because they presented no practical risk to the authorities. The Jewish committees in Mogilev, Shargorod, and Dzhurin knew about these activities as well, as some of the meetings took place at the house of one of the policemen of the Jewish ghetto police,[62] but since the movement acted alongside the local leadership and did not present itself as an alternative, unlike other movements in occupied Poland, they did not see it as a threat.[63]

Most of the members of the youth movements in Mogilev came from Southern Bukovina hometowns, and their family members worked in the foundry or under the Jewish committee.[64] Most policemen of the Shargorod ghetto police belonged to the Zionist youth movements.[65] Some of the aid funds that arrived from Romania were especially allocated to members of the youth movements.[66] There were also movement members who were sent to risky forced labor, but most of them felt that it was

---

60 The Mogilev youth movement wrote in the underground newspaper *Ghetto—Ganduri din Exil*, in The Labor Archive. The Pinhas Lavon Institute for Labor Research [Romanian].

60 Shani/Sharf 1976, p. 163.

61 *Courier*, issue 12, in The Labor Archive. The Pinhas Lavon Institute for Labor Research.

62 Shani/Sharf 1976, p. 210, p. 162.

63 "Courier, an underground newspaper in Transnistria," *Yediot Yad Vashem* 31 (1963), pp. 40–43.

64 YVA O-3/1238, Yitzhak Yalon.

65 Teich 1958, p. 214.

66 Shani/Sharf 1976, p. 162.

less risky to follow the committee's leadership, and they avoided direct confrontation.

Conclusion

No actual alternative leadership was developed in the ghettos of the Mogilev district in Transnistria, and there was no call for rebellion or any attempt to establish an alternative administrative structure, although the existing Jewish public institutions seemed arbitrary and unjust. The fundamental perceptions of the leadership regarding the way to act were accepted most of the time, and the critics and opposition acted in the same way as the leadership when they had the opportunity to hold a public position in the ghetto, since they assumed that these were the proper actions to take under the circumstances. Pitaru, for example, the fierce opponent of Teich in Shargorod, established with his friends a Jewish committee and a Jewish police in Capusterna, similar to the structure of the committee and the Jewish police in Shargorod. Equally, the Jewish committee and police in Capusterna created working relations with the Romanian forces in the area, exactly as the Shargorod committee did.[67]

There was also Rabbi Baruch Hager who criticized the Dzhurin Jewish committee for bribing the Romanian authorities and creating a constant demand for more bribes, and then he himself was forced to bribe the Romanian command of the district.[68] The rivalry between Danilov and Jagendorf was partly personal, partly motivated by the competition over the allocation of resources between the Southern Bukovina Jews and the Dorohoi Jews in Mogilev. Danilov did not object to the preference of one hometown to the other but complained about the exclusion of his group from any access to resources. Likewise, the Jews of Cernăuţi complained that they were not represented in the leadership and that their representation was rejected under the false claim that the Romanian authorities objected to it.[69]

Those who held positions in the Jewish committees were aware of the criticism against them. Teich wrote an essay after the war claiming that there was no other way and that fighting would have led to the mass

67 YVA O-3/2469, Zechariah Pitaru.

68 YVA O-3/2472, Baruch Hager; Miller 1993, p. 236.

69 The Carp Collection, O-11, file A-8-99.

murder of the Jewish people, which would have been left without any organization. The entire document is of a pure apologetic nature, and it seems that he not only delivered a historical testimony but also defended his conduct and decisions in the darkest hours.[70]

Jagendorf was also aware of the possible public criticism against his actions. He made sure to write orderly reports to the Jewish leadership in Romania and to other entities and made efforts to ensure proper documentation and order. The descriptions of his personality and appearance leave no doubt that order and preciseness were indeed part of who he was, however, his insistence to keep each receipt and each list shows that he was thinking about the public perceptibility of the committee's conduct and of the foundry he restored in Mogilev. In his letter to the *Centrala* in Bucharest, dated September 1942, which was written following an argument about the extent of the aid that was sent to Transnistria, he wrote: "One day, both you and I, will be held accountable for our actions and for our oversights."[71]

The opposition to the Jewish leadership in the ghettos of the district adopted two primary modes of actions:

1) Grudge and resentment against the acting Jewish committees, including feelings of jealousy, anger, helplessness, and even hatred, which stemmed from the inability to protest against it freely. This resentment was bluntly expressed in Pitaru's behavior in the dispute with Teich and in Hirschhorn's conduct against the committee in Dzhurin.
2) Moral and social criticism against the leadership's conduct and the positioning of a different ethical model. This criticism was expressed in the press of the youth movements, by Hager in Dzhurin and in the writings of Kunstadt, which were not published during the war.[72]

Despite the condemnations and the criticism, the discussed groups or individuals did not suggest a different model for action concerning the

70 Teich 1958, pp. 233–235. Kessler suggested forced resistance, but his suggestion was rejected. See: Avni 2003, p. 32.

71 The Jagendorf Collection, P-9, file 7; YVA O-3/13097, Menachem Rash.

72 The Jagendorf Collection, P-9, file 10, letter of Max Heisman to Jagendorf regarding the criticism against him, dated May 29, 1949.

Romanian rule in the district's ghettos, but rather a different dosage of actions to be taken by the Jewish committees: fewer bribes, a more efficient organization of aid allocation, a more just allocation of labor etc. As long as there was a feeling of immediate risk in the ghettos, it was unified in its support of the central leadership, and the critical voices were softer. Only at a later stage, in the fall of 1943, and after they had established connections with the Jewish community in Romania and received aid, and after the Romanian government's attitude toward the Jews had become more moderate, a louder and clearer public criticism was leveled against members and heads of the Jewish committees and against the preservation of power by the acting leadership.

Diana Dumitru

Challenging Stalinist Justice: A Review of Holocaust Crimes after 1953

Over 320,000 Soviet citizens were arrested after the Second World War as a result of the Soviet state's effort to punish "collaborators" with the Axis powers within the former occupied territories.[1] The investigation and trial materials of these cases have been inaccessible to scholars for decades. Fortunately, a part of the files were copied and made available by the United States Holocaust Memorial Museum in Washington (USHMM) and by the Yad Vashem Archive. These unique historical documents provide a wealth of information on the participation of the local population in the Holocaust in Eastern Europe, stimulating important research.[2]

Among numerous topics for analysis, the study of postwar trial materials offers the possibility to grasp the impact of de-Stalinization on the Soviet legal system, including the significance of this transformation for Holocaust-related cases. In general, experts of Soviet history understand under the term "de-Stalinization" a broad and complex transformation of Soviet society after Stalin's death.[3] Amid various aspects of societal change, de-Stalinization included a renewed scrutiny of previous condemnations, acknowledging the abusive nature of "Stalinist justice." This contribution illuminates the impact of the post-Stalinist review on the cases of "collaborators" condemned for anti-Jewish violence. In the fol-

1 See the following article: Penter, Tanja (2005). Collaboration on Trial: New Source Material on Soviet Postwar Trials against Collaborators, *Slavic Review* 64(4): 782–790. Penter (p. 783) cites the data of the Russian Federal Security Service which announced that during the years 1943–1953 more than 320,000 Soviet citizens were arrested for collaboration with the Nazis.

2 See the following excellent survey of debates on the collaboration in Eastern Europe: Dean, Martin (2004). Local Collaboration in the Holocaust in Eastern Europe, in Stone, Dan (ed.). *The Historiography of the Holocaust*. Houndmills, pp. 120–140.

3 Jones, Polly (ed.) (2006). *The Dilemmas of De-Stalinization: Negotiating Cultural and Social Change in the Khrushchev Era*. New York.

lowing, I will focus on dossiers referring to crimes committed on the territories under Romanian administration, namely Bessarabia and Bukovina.

The majority of defendants from the analyzed cases were convicted in accordance with article 54-1 "A" of the Penal Code of the Ukrainian SSR (adopted in 1927) for felonies defined by Soviet legislators as "counterrevolutionary crimes" that included "treason of the Motherland." On paper, "treason of the Motherland" covered actions intended to hurt the military potential of the Soviet Union, the country's independence or territorial sovereignty, espionage, betrayal of military secrets, and desertion.[4] In reality, a much wider range of activities fell under this category. The defendants who lived in the "occupied territory" during the Second World War were accused of a variety of illicit acts, including violence against local Jews, Soviet activists, and partisans as well as different kinds of "assistance" to Romanian or German personnel and authorities.

At this point, an attentive reader may be tempted to deduce that the convictions imposed under article 54-1 were not legitimate and may assume that trumped up charges were an essential part of the Stalinist legal system. Accounts of torture of suspected citizens accused of various "anti-Soviet" activities during the Stalin era are widespread. The memories of contemporaries corroborate these facts. Bronislava Voițițkaia, a resident of the village of Cereș (Bukovina), remembered that after the war her father was denounced by a villager for "demolishing the bust of Stalin." The man was severely beaten both during his arrest in front of his entire family and while in police custody. Bronislava recalled her father returning home completely bald and frail after several years of incarceration.[5] This and other sources reinforce the assumption of the prevalent use of massive coercion by Stalin's police. Still, when dealing with files of perpetrators of anti-Jewish violence during the war, there is convincing evidence that while the investigation process may have been marred by abuse, its findings were credible.[6] This contribution aims to

4 Уголовный кодекс РСФСР. С изменениями на 1 июля 1938 г. (М.: Юридическое издательство НКЮ СССР, 1938), pp. 27–32.

5 Interview with Bronislava Voițițkaia, Cereș, Storozhynets district (Ukraine), April 2011.

6 Dumitru, Diana (2014). An Analysis of Soviet Postwar Investigation and Trial Documents and Their Relevance for Holocaust Studies, in David-Fox, Michael et al. (eds.). *The Holocaust in the East: Local Perpetrators and Soviet Responses*. Pittsburgh, pp. 142–157.

enrich our knowledge about the Soviet postwar trials and further nuance our understanding of the Soviet investigations of Holocaust-related crimes by exploring the effects of post-Stalinist inquiry on the latter cases.

As mentioned above, there were far-reaching changes in the Soviet Union in the aftermath of Stalin's death. In 1953, a multifaceted process of reforms was started by the country's leaders, aiming at removing the elements that helped to keep Stalin's grip on power. This process included political rehabilitation of thousands of victims who were repressed without due legal basis during Stalin's rule. The leadership of the Soviet state admitted that "Stalinist justice" had threatened everybody, including closest loyalists, with arbitrary executions and that many people had received undeserved punishments before 1953.

After receiving signs of political relaxation from the Kremlin, numerous prisoners sought to revoke their "Stalinist convictions" by vigorously claiming their innocence, accusing witnesses of slanderous depositions in court or stressing the use of coercion during the course of investigation in order to force defendants into self-incrimination. Still, the systematic review of the archived cases was not necessarily due to individual pleas, but due to the official decision of the Soviet state to scrutinize "Stalinist convictions." On May 4, 1954, the decision of the Presidium of the Central Committee of the Communist Party of the USSR regarding the reappraisal of all files of people condemned for "counterrevolutionary activities" was put into action. This order installed one central committee and a number of regional committees across the country and staffed them with representatives of the Prosecutors' Office, the KGB, the Ministry of Internal Affairs (MVD), and the Ministry of Justice. The central and local committees functioned from May 1954 until March 1956 and managed to review the files of 337,183 people. In the case of 153,502 people, decisions were taken to terminate or reduce their sentences, to release them from exile, or to grant them amnesty. As a result of this effort, 14,338 persons (4.2 percent of the cases) were rehabilitated, while the sentences of the 183,681 of people were recognized as correct.[7]

The analysis of the review process undertaken by the authorities in 1954–55 allows us to transform the numbers presented above into actual

7 Petrov, A. G. (2005). *Reabilitatsia zhertv politicheskikh repressii: opyt istoricheskogo analiza. Vol. 2*. Moscow, p. 71.

stories and to illustrate how the process evolved and ended. The research highlights a number of irregularities in the investigation processes during the Stalin era as well as the social relations in place a decade after the Holocaust. At the same time, the questioning of witnesses and convicts about cases that occurred a decade earlier prompt us to reflect on the issues of human memory, the relationship between ordinary people and the authorities, and the connection between social context and justice. Below, I use material from a number of Soviet postwar trials in order to exemplify the various routes and outcomes of the reevaluation of the "54-1" files.

The group case of Grigory Vizir, Samson Guchok, Nikolai Maksimov, Stepan Oleniuk, Matvei Hodan, and Nikolai Haren provide eloquent illustration of the passions and calculations involved in the process of reevaluation. In 1948, the men were condemned for the killing of a Jewish family in the village of Stanivtsy-Dol'shni/Ştăneştii de Jos (Northern Bukovina). One year after Stalin's death, in March 1954, Samson Guchok wrote a letter of appeal in which he vigorously denied his guilt in the aforementioned crime and asserted that he had incriminated himself during the investigation and in court because of the physical abuse he was subjected to (presumably while in police custody). Eight months later, Grigory Vizir, another convict from the same case, sent an official letter asking for a review of his conviction as well. Vizir also denied his guilt and claimed that his condemnation was based on "slanderous testimonies of the witness Levariuk" and on self-incrimination, and that he was beaten during preliminary investigation and forced to sign a false testimony.[8]

In March 1955, the Prosecutor's Office started an investigation of Vizir's letter of complaint, specifically asking for the following actions and clarifications: (1) to question the main witnesses of the case in order to learn more about the relationship with the convict; (2) to find out if the witnesses of the case would reaffirm, correct, or reject their old statements, 3) to "demand explanations from the persons who investigated the condemned Vizir" and, in particular, to find out "if somebody beat the detainee Vizir during the preliminary investigation."[9]

8 Yad Vashem Archives (YVA), TR 18, File 4, Arkhiv Sluzhby Bezopasnosti Ukrainy, Chernovtsy, p. 259.

9 Ibid.

In his renewed interrogation, the witness Mikhail Levariuk offered an unchanged account of the events he claimed to have witnessed in the summer of 1941: immediately after the withdrawal of the Soviet army, a group of villagers assembled with the goal of killing local Jews. Among these villagers was Grigory Vizir who killed Ida Zitsman with a wooden pale.[10] Another witness also firmly reconfirmed his early statement and stressed that he "will never be able to forget the terrible picture" of witnessing Grigory Vizir killing Ida Zitsman who at the moment was pregnant. Nevertheless, at least one discrepancy was revealed when hearing the testimony of Fevronia Pochadiuk, another witness to the case. As in her previous testimony, the woman had attested that in the summer of 1941, before the Romanian army entered their village, Vizir together with "other traitors" took part in the pogrom against her Jewish neighbors and in the killing of Ida Zitsman. However, if in her first deposition Fevronia affirmed that she *herself* saw how Vizir hit Ida, in 1955 she denied it. She mentioned seeing Vizir and another villager both armed with wooden pales, approaching Ida, but after that Fevronia ran inside her house. When questioned about the inconsistency between her old and new testimonies, Fevronia replied that, in her opinion, she told the same in court (that she did not see the killing), but that her statement "was written like this because Vizir confessed himself." Despite her absence at the moment of killing, Fevronia insisted in 1955 that it must have been that the two villagers killed the Jewish woman because no other people approached Ida during the same time. In sum, the 1955 testimonies sealed for the second time the condemnation of Grigory Vizir and that of the other convicts from this case.

Another similar case of Grigory Yalovski suggests that convicts' vigorous complaints transformed the reviews of their cases in something more substantial than mere formality. In 1945 Yalovski was sentenced to twenty years of prison and confiscation of his property after being found guilty of crimes committed in the town of Edineţ in July 1941. Specifically, he was proven guilty of taking part, together with Romanian soldiers, in pogroms and shootings of the local Jewish population as well as being part of a committee that decided who from the local Jews was to be killed immediately and who was to be sent to camps.[11] Of central importance

10 Ibid., p. 263.

11 USHMM, case of Yalovski Grigory, file nr. 1381, p. 84.

for Yalovski's conviction was the accusation, confirmed by several witnesses, of the murder of Iosif Meiler. Importantly, during his trial, Yalovski refused to admit any guilt, denied having taken part in pogroms or having been a member of the selection committee and insisted that the witnesses' testimonies were false, especially the deposition of a witness named Boguch. He accused the latter of holding a personal grudge because Yalovski was earlier engaged to Boguch's sister but refused to marry her.

Starting the scheduled review of Yalovski's case in May 1955, a military prosecutor asked to invite Grigory Meiler, the grandson of Iosif Meiler and one of the main witnesses in the case, to the KGB office for renewed interrogations. Yet, at the time of this request, the officials could not locate Grigory Meiler, since he was no longer living in Edineț.[12] By the end of May, Captain Molyakov, the person entrusted with the review of Yalovski's case, formulated his conclusion on the file. In Molyakov's opinion, there was convincing evidence of Yalovski's crime, and therefore he recommended maintaining the 1945 court's decision.[13] On July 6, 1955, the republican committee of the Moldovan Soviet Socialist Republic (MSSR) agreed with the suggestion and officially formalized the decision. However, the story did not end there, and in March 1956 a new investigation followed, most probably prompted by Yalovski's complaint sent to the general prosecutor of the Soviet Union.[14]

The indication of additional investigation was issued from the military prosecutor's office of the Odessa Military District (OdVO), signed on March 10, 1956. The three-page document had the signature of the military prosecutor, Major-General A. Popov, and was addressed to both the head of the KGB of the MSSR, A. Prokopenko, and the deputy of the military prosecutor of the OdVO. The document reveals the meticulous eye of its author. First of all, it indicates that "as visible from the materials of the case, the testimonies of the witnesses are contradictory, and therefore extremely suspicious." To illustrate the point, Popov specifies that

12 USHMM, case of Yalovski Grigory, file nr. 1381, p. 79f.

13 Ibid., p. 87.

14 The letter itself was not included in the dossier, but one document makes reference to such a letter being sent by Yalovski. In the letter Yalovski asserted that he was convicted based of the false testimonies of Boguch and Misevski and asked to be freed from prison. USHMM, case of Yalovski Grigory, file nr. 1381, p. 202

during the court hearings, Grigory Meiler stated that the killing of Iosif Meiler occurred in the house of the Katz family, however, during the same hearings, when answering additional questions, he changed his deposition and responded that his grandfather was killed in their own house, but in front of the Katz sisters.[15] Second, Popov pointed out that during the case's investigation, Grigory Meiler declared that Yalovski broke his rib with his rifle butts and stabbed his neck with the bayonet, but no medical expertise verified the allegation. Third, Popov highlighted that there were other puzzling irregularities: the biography of the witness Nudelman indicated that he was illiterate, yet under his deposition there was a signature. Fourth, the document highlighted that during preliminary investigations, a witness named M.F. Fuks stated that S. Stelman told him that she personally saw Fuks' son being killed by Yalovski during a mass execution, for which Stelman was selected as well. Popov could not understand how it was possible for Stelman to survive, if she was targeted for execution, and why she was not interrogated during the preliminary investigation.

Popov included a list of specific actions to be undertaken before June 1, 1956, in order to clarify all the aforementioned aspects. The list demanded the re-interrogation of key witnesses; the medical expertise of Grigory Meiler; to find and interrogate the Katz sisters; to find and question Stelman about the execution and check if she would be able to confirm Yalovski's murder of Fuks' son. On June 11 the head of the investigative department of the KGB of the MSSR wrote back to announce that they were unable to meet Popov's deadline, since six of the witnesses had changed their residency, and it was necessary to find their new locations before they could be interrogated.[16]

The first re-interrogation took place on July 18, 1955, and the examined witness was Grigory Meiler. The details of his questioning differed significantly from the testimonies provided a decade earlier. The accusation of inflicted bodily harm started to fall apart—this time Meiler denied any broken rib and claimed that Yalovski hit him in the chest with his rifle butts and "lightly cut the skin" on his neck when pointing the rifle to his neck.[17] A disconcerted interrogator challenged Meiler to explain how

15 Ibid., p. 91.
16 Ibid., p. 94.
17 Ibid., p. 100.

"truthful" in general his depositions in 1944 and 1945 were when testifying against Yalovski, and why earlier Meiler had stated that he saw Yalovski kill his grandfather, while in 1955 he denied seeing the killing himself. Grigory Meiler insisted his current (1955) deposition was truthful, but he "could not explain" why the minutes of the 1944 interrogation included conflicting information.[18] To many other questions, Meiler responded with "I don't remember," including to the question about the Katz sisters, whom he earlier identified as eyewitnesses of the killing of his grandfather.

Was Meiler consciously doctoring his responses in 1955 or did he simply not remember the incident that had taken place a decade earlier? In the described context, it can be assumed that Meiler, with or without the interrogator's encouragement, exaggerated certain facts when testifying in 1944–45, driven by the desire to ensure that his grandfather's killer would meet a deserved punishment. At the same time, minor incidences of contradictions could have indeed been involuntary.[19] Still, we cannot exclude that other factors could have been at play during the review of Yalovski's case.

In a puzzling manner, most witnesses asked to testify in 1955 on Yalovski's case stated that they did not know anything about the convict's criminal activity during the occupation, nor did they see him with a rifle, nor did they know about his participation in the selection committee.[20] Importantly, no direct incriminating testimonies were produced by Jewish witnesses. Only the testimony of Isak Davidovich Kirzhner, who was not a resident of Edineț in 1941 (he was arrested in Cernăuți and brought to Edineț camp), mentioned that while in the Edineț camp, he heard discussions about Yalovski's participation in the killings of Jews (*raspravy*).[21] The other testimonies of Jewish residents of Edineț led to dead ends. For example, S. Vasserman (born in 1897, interviewed in Yiddish through a

18 Ibid., pp. 106–112.

19 Meiler may have not possessed the best memory as an individual or maybe was not the most curious mind. In 1955, during the interrogation, he could not remember the patronymic of his grandfather. At the same time, we are aware that numerous individuals do not know the names of their great-grandfathers.

20 USHMM, case of Yalovski Grigory, file nr. 1381, p. 137, p. 146, p. 147, p. 155, p. 157, p. 161, p. 165, p. 177.

21 Ibid. p. 171. Vasserman, similarly to Kirzhner, was interned in the Edineț camp before being deported to Vinnitsa.

translator) mentioned that he did not know Yalovski and could not say anything about him.[22] To the interrogators' question who exactly took part in the shootings of Soviet citizens, he responded briskly: "I don't know about this."[23] As it happens, Vasserman seemed informed about Jewish deaths, but could not say anything about the perpetrators. Thus, he acknowledged that he knew that Meiler was killed during the first days of the occupation, but he "did not know about the circumstances." He admitted knowing about the killing of Moishe Fuks, but did not know about "the details" of the crime.[24]

Liubovi Zitser (born in 1923, maiden name Stelman) was interrogated in 1955 for the first time in relation to Yalovski's case. She told the story of her miraculous survival of the mass execution carried out by Romanian soldiers and local collaborators: after being hit by a bullet, Liubovi fell down and woke up later in a pile of corpses. During the night, she escaped from the execution site. Indeed, Zitser confirmed that there was a selection committee in 1941 in Edineț and that this committee sentenced her to death. According to Zitser, the committee was made up of Romanians and local inhabitants whose names she claimed not to know.

Following another line of inquiry, a host of inaccuracies transpired during Zitser's interrogation. The young woman confirmed that Ksil Fuks, the son of Moishe Fuks, was in the group of executed people in Edineț, yet when asked to name the person who killed Ksil, Liubovi's response was: "I don't know." Liubovi confirmed the information from the preliminary investigation materials that after her survival she talked to Ksil's father about the execution, however, she denied naming Ksil's murderer. Apparently frustrated with the outcome of the questioning, an obstinate interrogator asked Zitser bluntly if she ever named Yalovski as Ksil's killer. The woman responded that she did not know Yalovski. The interrogator insisted on the information that on October 1, 1944, Moishe Fuks had testified that he had learned from Sluva Stelman that his son was killed by Yalovski. Zitser was immovable: indeed, she was Sluva Stelman since she was both called Liuba (short form of Liubovi) and Sluva, but she denied that she named Yalovski.[25] Unfortunately, Moishe Fuks died in 1948

22 Ibid., p. 182.
23 Ibid., p. 184.
24 Ibid., p. 185f.
25 Ibid., p. 193.

and could not be called for interrogation. All in all, Zitser mentioned only one gentile name, Tatarinikov, during her entire interrogation. Tatarinikov had come to arrest her together with a Romanian soldier.[26]

The person who remained most faithful to his earlier depositions was the witness Ilia Misevski, a Russian born in Edineț in 1909, who had worked as a blacksmith during the war. Unlike the other witnesses to the case, Misevski was found and interrogated by the representatives of the Ministry of Internal Affairs on May 18, 1956, approximately 3,000 kilometers away from his native town, in the region of Kurgan. In his 1956 deposition, Misevski asserted that Yalovski served for the Romanian administration in Edineț and said that he saw him in 1941 "riding on a horse through the streets of Edineț with a tricolor [the Romanian flag] band over his shoulders and with a rifle in his hands." Misevski did not see Yalovski killing anybody or robbing Jews, however, he stated that "during the first days of the occupation Yalovski armed with a rifle rode a horse and was shouting that 'now there is the Romanian power, we won, we have to beat Jews [*nado bit' evreev*]'."[27] Misevskii also mentioned that he knew from the residents of Edineț that after the first Romanians had entered the town, a group of volunteers "robbed and killed Soviet citizens" and that Yalovski was one of them.

Still, one inaccuracy surfaced during this interrogation as well. The interrogator asked Misevski if indeed in March 1944 Yalovski personally told him about the killing of Iosif Meiler. The former confirmed the discussion, but corrected that it occurred in the summer of 1941 and not in 1944. Misevski named two other gentiles who were in his smithy during that particular conversation with Yalovski, but those witnesses died later during the war. Popov's sharpness was proven when he assumed that the signature was not by Misevski who was illiterate. Misevski reaffirmed that in 1944 he was not able to write a single letter; therefore he did not sign the testimony and did not know who signed for him. He only remembered that during his interrogation, Grigory Meiler had been in the same room and could have signed for him.[28]

26 Ibid., p. 189.
27 Ibid., p. 120.
28 Ibid., p. 123f.

Finally, in December 1956, the review of Yalovski's case officially came to a close. Compared to the trial indictment, the review's conclusion was more modest when listing the evidence. Nevertheless, it still asserted that the materials of the review contain sufficient evidence of Yalovski's guilt and recommended to reject the convict's appeal.[29] However, since Yalovski was characterized positively by the administration of the camp where he was serving the sentence, a decision was taken to reduce his sentence from twenty to fifteen years in prison.

Again, how do we explain the multiple discrepancies in Yalovski's case? Clearly, the materials from Yalovski's file indicate that some of the officials who investigated crimes of "collaboration" during and immediately after the war were ready to cut corners in their investigations. The mysterious signatures under the testimonies of illiterate witnesses or the reference to the presence of two witnesses in the same room during an interrogation are signs of wrongdoings. At the same time, additional considerations might have been at play as well. Conceivably, both Jews' and gentiles' "forgetfulness" were techniques to deal with a troubling past and complex present. A decade after the Holocaust, when many of the old wounds started to heal, even the Jews who suffered at the hands of locals may have been less willing to stir up old passions and to face the resulting antagonism, choosing instead to live tranquil lives in their ethnically mixed communities. On the other side, the rise of official anti-Semitism in the Soviet Union during the late 1940s and early 1950s may have resulted in Soviet Jews feeling particularly vulnerable. In the situation when the state withdrew its political support for Jewry and anti-Semitism became more widespread in various circles, some Jews may have concluded that testifying about the crimes committed by gentile neighbors would not have been the wisest thing to do.

As mentioned above, starting with 1954 and continuing for two subsequent years, the employees of the KGB and the Ministry of Internal Affairs scrutinized their archives and numerous files, submitting the relevant ones to inspection by official committees. In this context, it is important to make clear that the cases selected for further investigation

---

29 Ibid., pp. 262–264.

were representing a minority, while the majority of dossiers were considered to contain sufficient evidence of the convicts' guilt and were therefore in no need for additional inspection.

A good example is the case of Sergei Gîncota and Ivan Petrachi. In 1945 these two residents of the village of Costești were each sentenced to twenty years in prison for serving in the Romanian police during the war. The linchpin of the accusation referred to the murder of a Jewish woman, Fekla Gitman, and her three children in the summer of 1941. According to the material in the file, Gîncota and Petrachi together with Romanian gendarmes arrested the Gitman family, marched them to the outskirts of the village, and killed them there. The accusation was primarily built on the defendants' confessions and on the testimony of Gitman's landlord, Ivan Sergeev. During the preliminary investigations, Sergeev testified that during one night in August 1941, Gîncota and Mereacri came to his house and took away Gitman with her children. After some time, Sergeev heard six shots. On the next day, Sergeev went to the police office to ask about Gitman's whereabouts and was told by Gîncota that the Jewish family had been shot and their bodies had been thrown into a local ravine. Sergeev declared that he later found the naked body of Gitman and the bodies of her three children in the ravine; he buried them all.[30] This disturbing testimony, together with the confessions of Gîncota and Petrachi, appear to have sealed the case. A more mindful prosecutor would have paid attention to the limited number of witnesses and to the fact that the witnesses were not called to testify in court; the court's decision was based exclusively on preliminary investigation material. Most probably, the decision in this case was influenced by the defendants' confessions and the credible testimony of a key witness.

The trajectories of the post-Stalinist reviews suggest that the presence or the lack of confessions of defendants was not of primary importance for the final decision in a case. There is sufficient evidence that the prosecutors ruled out additional investigations even if the culprit never admitted his guilt. This happened in the case of Anufrii Sapozhnik, sentenced in 1945 to fifteen years in prison for physically abusing and robbing Jewish individuals in the town of Kamenka.[31] During his investigation and trial, Sapozhnik never admitted any wrongdoing and claimed

30 USHMM, file 1335, p. 72.
31 USHMM, file 1275, case of Sapozhnik Anufrii Fedoseevici.

he did not know the witnesses. Despite Sapozhnik's earlier position, Prosecutor Sokolov, assigned to review the case, was convinced he had all the needed evidence in the archived dossier and stopped short of asking for clarifications. In this particular context, the depositions of five eyewitnesses—all Jews—presumably outweighed Sapozhnik's resolved denial. Witnesses' credibility most likely was fortified by the fact that all of them were part of a group of Jews herded in downtown Kamenka by Romanians in 1941. The witnesses saw Sapozhnik, as part of that group, hitting the Jews assembled in the center with a stick, including striking a Jewish woman named Shapir multiple times. Shapir later died on the same spot.[32]

Sokolov recommended keeping the condemnation of Sapozhnik, and on May 7, 1955, the committee of the MSSR confirmed this recommendation. One year later, yet another committee dealing with the cases of the persons serving their sentences for political and economic crimes in the Karaganda camp (where Sapozhnik was imprisoned) took note of the positive behavior of Sapozhnik in the camp and of the fact that he was an invalid. Twelve years spent by Sapozhnik in prison were judged sufficient. An order to release him was issued.[33]

If anything at all, the reviews of Stalinist convictions highlight how difficult it was to overturn previous sentences even in cases where the evidence was deemed relatively "thin." This was the case of five peasants from Costești who were accused in 1946 of forming a "kulak group" involved in "anti-Soviet treacherous behavior" during the war, which contributed to the betrayal of Soviet activists and "the consolidation of occupants' power."[34] The case was heard twice in court. Initially, in February 1946, the Military Tribunal of the NKVD acquitted the defendants "in absence of corpus delicti." However, after the prosecutor's protest and the resulting additional investigation, the defendants were found guilty and sentenced to ten years in prison and the confiscation of property.

The dossier of the defendants from Costești exposes the intricacy of what appears to be—from a legal point of view—a "shallow" case. The investigation and court materials show signs of insufficient evidence of

32 Ibid., pp. 60–65.

33 Ibid, p. 66.

34 The Archives of the Security and Intelligence Service of the Republic of Moldova (SIS), Nr. 0758, File of Bîrsan Anton, Bocancea Mihail and others.

the defendants' "treacherous activity," noticeable even to a non-specialist in law. The materials indicate that in 1942 the defendants testified in a Romanian court in the case of three Soviet activists (later imprisoned and deprived of civil rights), but the witnesses were not able to demonstrate that the defendants made any incriminating affirmations against the mentioned activists. The accusation of organizing a "kulak group" was also not supported by convincing evidence, and all defendants firmly denied the allegation.

It is interesting to note that one charge surfaced during the investigation of the peasants from Costești, but did not make it to the final list of accusations, namely the pillage of the Jewish property. Thus, the defendant Mihail Bocancea was incriminated by the statement of Zelda Gruman whose property was robbed in July 1941. Zelda identified Bocancea among the robbers and refuted the defendant's explanation that the property of Jews, which he was seen carrying home by many other villagers, was bought.[35] Four additional witnesses testified to the pillage of Jewish property in the village of Costești, including a villager named Iosif Tendler. The latter emphasized that after the war, Zelda Gruman asked Tendler to accompany her to Bocancea's house in order to request the stolen property. However, only after Bocancea was arrested his wife returned part of this property to the legal owners at the request of the local Soviet council. During the interrogation, Bocancea's wife claimed that this property was taken in order "to preserve it [*na khranenie*]."[36] There is no indication of other anti-Jewish activities by Bocancea except that several statements mention his membership in the anti-Semitic Cuzist Party in interwar Romania.[37] Two other defendants from the same case, Gheorghii Lungu and Grigorii Cenușa, were accused of stealing hundreds of kilograms of corn from the Jewish families Rozenberg and Gruman.[38]

During the session of June 13, 1955, the Committee of the Moldovan SSR, entitled with the review of criminal cases of the persons condemned for "counterrevolutionary activity," stressed the insufficiency of the collected evidence in the cases of the convicts from Costești and

35 Ibid., pp. 317–319.
36 Ibid., p. 318.
37 Ibid., p. 340.
38 Ibid., p. 336f.

recommended to submit a protest to the Military Tribunal of the OdVO. All five convicts were released. The document indicates that the former convicts benefitted from the amnesty of September 17, 1955, which also officially removed their previous conviction. This amnesty pardoned "Soviet citizens who collaborated with occupants during the period of Great Patriotic War of 1941–1945" and removed their convictions. The Military Tribunal of the OdVO still managed to produce a confusing document, highlighting that "the criminal activity of the convicts is confirmed by the testimonies of the witnesses in court as well as by the statements during the preliminary investigation, which were not taken into the account by the [review] committee" and therefore there were "no grounds for the full rehabilitation of any of the convicts."[39]

The arrests and trials of perpetrators of the Holocaust continued long after Stalin's death. For alleged perpetrators arrested after 1953, it was more difficult to invoke "abuses" when they demanded a reevaluation of their cases. In the more liberal political context, legal technicalities became more important. The example of the case of Victor Dascal, a Bessarabian arrested in November 1955 in Bucharest, after being uncovered hiding with a fake identity, is interesting against this background. Dascal was accused and sentenced in February 1956 to twenty-five years of prison for his participation in the summer of 1941 in the murder of fifteen Jewish inhabitants of the village of Ghincăuți (Bessarabia). In the summer of 1944, Dascal was briefly arrested, but managed to escape and hide in Romania where he lived quietly for eleven years. In 1961 the Council of Ministers of the MSSR received an appeal from Dascal demanding a review of his case. In his appeal, Dascal argued that the Soviet court was not authorized to adjudicate his case since he was, according to the law from June 1948, a Romanian citizen. Dascal was asking to "clarify his statute as a Romanian citizen and send him to spend the rest of his sentence to Romania, as it was done in the case of many other prisoners from Romania."[40] The vice-prosecutor of the MSSR found Dascal's argument "unfounded" and highlighted that from 1940 on, Dascal had indeed been a citizen of the Soviet Union, and in 1941, while

39 Ibid., p. 402.

40 Ministry of Internal Affairs of the MSSR, case of Dascal Victor, p. 449.

living in the occupied territory, "took direct part in the shooting of Soviet citizens."[41] Dascal's request was rejected.

The next round of reassessment of postwar cases took place during the *perestroika* and was further continued after the collapse of the Soviet Union. The renewed official criticism of Stalinism—supplemented by emerging nationalism—was the driving force behind the new round of political rehabilitation of "Stalin's victims." Officially, the need to bring justice to innocent people was at the forefront of these campaigns, yet if we take a closer look at the Holocaust-related files, we do not see any signs of fresh efforts to untie the multiple interwoven strands of earlier investigations. There were also objective reasons hindering a reevaluation of many cases as most of the protagonists of those investigations had passed away by the late 1980s.

The review materials added by the Moldovan prosecutors during the late 1980s and in the 1990s appear as repetitions of earlier findings. In this sense, the details assembled by their colleagues during the 1955–56 reviews stand out as examples of genuine inquiry. In most of the cases referring to the killing and abuse of Jews, the Moldovan prosecutors copied *ad verbatim* the earlier conclusions by their Soviet predecessors. The only novelty was the fact that the decisions were written in Romanian and in some cases were now referring to the crimes as "policies of genocide against the Jewish population."[42]

Occasionally, full rehabilitation was applied to former convicts involved in less bloody affairs. For example, the case of our five protagonists mentioned in the dossier from Costești came under review in May 1989, when the deputy prosecutor of the MSSR put forward an appeal. More than fifty years after the events, at least one of the condemned, Gheorghii Lungu, was still alive in the town of Glodeni. Apparently, Lungu's complaint activated the prosecutor's appeal. The decision followed quickly: by November 1989 the Presidium of the Supreme Court of the MSSR annulled the 1946 conviction and offered a full rehabilitation to the convicts. Ironically, the summary of the evidence of the case by the deputy prosecutor of the MSSR, Demidenko, duplicated the 1946 trial resolution, but reached an opposite conclusion: Demidenko recommended the rejection of conviction and the closing of the case of Bîrsan,

41 Ibid.

42 USHMM, file nr. 1276, the case of Sapozhnik Timofei Mikhalilovici.

Bocancea, Cenușa, and others because of the lack of corpus delicti.[43] One month later Gheorghii Lungu received by mail the document that confirmed his legal rehabilitation. He was informed that he was allowed to demand the reimbursement of his confiscated property, the restoration of his work experience (length of service at work) for the years spent in prison, and the allocation of his pension.[44]

While many applauded the rehabilitation process and the "historical justice" that presumably was taking place, not everybody was prepared to celebrate. The least prepared to cheer post-Stalinist amnesties and the *perestroika* rehabilitations were the former victims. In 1991 the official newspaper *Sovetskaia Moldavia* published an article entitled "The Tragedy of Pepeni." The author S. Pavlevici carefully depicted the killing of over 200 Jews in Pepeni, including men, women, and children. The author described the massacre as primarily a "Romanian gendarmes' affair," avoiding to overemphasize the (crucial) role of villagers in this killing.[45] Without any doubt, Pavlevici knew well the full story of what had happened in Pepeni. In July 1941, scared by rumors about the Soviet army's return and a potential liberation of the Jews who had initially been locked in Pepeni's town hall, the chief of the gendarmes, together with two gendarmes and two dozens of villagers, slaughtered all the Jews during one night. Initially, the Romanians threw a grenade into the town hall, after which they began shooting through the windows. Meanwhile the locals used bats, shovels, and other tools to kill those who tried to escape. The NKVD depositions of one of the defendants present a chilling description of the Pepeni mass murder:

> After the shooting stopped outside and while the moans of people who were not dead yet could be heard, I entered the building with a bat in my hands and saw a nasty image. The people who were alive were hiding behind the dead ones, hoping to save their lives. But they did not manage to do this. I personally killed 15 people inside the house with my bat. I beat them so much that the bat was dripping with blood. Afterwards I turned over the dead, searching for the living among them.[46]

43 Ibid., p. 406.

44 Ibid., p. 415.

45 Pavlevici, S. (1991). Pepenskaya tragedia, *Sovetskaia Moldavia* (July 12).

46 USHMM, RG-54.003*40, Record of the case of Sadovei Ivan, p. 16.

The defendant named numerous Moldovans from Pepeni, describing their participation in the massacre:

> We were all armed with strong bats with which you could easily kill a person. Equally, each of us took part in trying to make it impossible for the Jews to escape the building. While the shooting was going on, we used bats to kill anyone who was trying to avoid death [by escaping] through the window. [...] There were times when the defenseless victims, rushing from one side to the other, headed toward the window hoping to be saved, but after seeing us they jumped back. However, if they succeeded, then our blows simply made them crush back into the room, where they were finished off.[47]

All gruesome details of the killing contained in the minutes of the interrogations of defendants may have been unknown to some villagers of Pepeni, yet they could not escape noticing the arrests and trials of the villagers involved in this crime. By the end of his article, Pavlevici briefly raised the issue of gentiles' participation in the murder of the Pepeni Jews, noting that after 1944, "most of the participants in the killings of Jews were prosecuted for the committed crime." Yet the author could not suppress himself adding the following comment: "I do not want to particularly dwell on this, but will say this: some persons after the death of Stalin were granted amnesty, and they returned to our land."[48]

The review of Holocaust-related cases after Stalin's death did not result in spectacular conclusions or massive amounts of overturned convictions. The few cases of reduced prison terms were rather outcomes of broad political amnesties, individual decisions based on humanitarian considerations, such as a prisoners' deteriorating health, or exemplary behavior in jail. Still, it is important to observe that the material gathered during the review highlighted that Soviet investigations after the war had been prone to cutting corners in order to produce solid cases in court. Sensing the ethos of the era, some witnesses in these cases, especially when simultaneously appearing in the role of victims, may have been inclined to use a less nuanced language in their depositions and to bend their own narratives to ensure a conviction and punishment.

A decade later, when the review was undertaken, the political atmosphere was different. Both investigators and the interviewed witnesses understood that this time the primary goal of the questioning was the

---

47 Ibid.

48 Pavlevici 1991.

search for possible judiciary mistakes. As a result, more careful and accurate, which also meant less accusatory, depositions surfaced. A frequent answer given to many of the interrogators' renewed questions was now the response, "I don't know". We can assume that in this changed political environment, both Jews and gentiles (although for different reasons) were not willing to ignite old tensions. Nonetheless, even the most prudent depositions provided abundant evidence of horrendous crimes committed by gentiles in 1941. Ultimately, even if clearly aware of various legal faults of previous investigations, the Soviet prosecutors had little or no reason at all to assume that convicted criminals were innocent people. The prosecutors acted accordingly.

Tuvia Friling

The International Commission on the Holocaust in Romania: A Personal "Behind the Scenes" Perspective

Many have perceived the International Commission on the Holocaust in Romania as an expression of realpolitik, a *sine qua non* for Romania, a strategy for salvaging Romanian president Ion Iliescu from the hole he had dug himself by making the ludicrous proclamation that there had never been a Holocaust in Romania. Additionally, many believed its foremost objective was to cleanse Romania of the stains blackening its past, as a prerequisite to its potential acceptance into the European Union.

Others saw the Commission as Romania's honest attempt to confront its past, an attempt that drew upon deep social, moral, theological, and political undercurrents running through the various European nations in the aftermath of the Holocaust, and a form of response to the fundamental questions the Holocaust evokes as a universalistic event that transformed national perceptions and identities.

When I was offered the opportunity to participate in the Commission, while serving as the state archivist of Israel, the Prime Minister's Office, and as professor at Ben-Gurion University of the Negev, I stood with those who viewed the initiative as a synthesis of the above motivations, and in either event, as one that was essentially—and at least in its significant aspects—*la longue durée* process.[1]

Thus, my opinion, which I believe to have shared with most of the Commission members, is that its ultimate purpose was to neither prepare nor submit a report, but to realize an important opportunity stemming from the aforementioned event and its political implications, in order to

1 On the three types of processes (the "courte durée," "temps intermédiaire," and "longue durée") as conceived by Fernand Braudel, see, for instance, "Braudel on the Longue Durée: Problems of Conceptual Translation," *Immanuel Wallerstein Review (Fernand Braudel Center)* 32(2); 2009: 155–170.

contribute somewhat to a complex and multifaceted shift that would connect to the social undercurrents fomented by the Holocaust—*including in Romania*. A shift in perception, identity, and mentality all of which, as we have learned from Fernand Braudel, are thorough, *longue durée* processes, whose results would only be revealed, if at all, in generations to come.

The International Commission included upwards of thirty members from five different countries—Romania, the United States, Germany, France, and Israel: a promising combination of intellectuals, historians, and public figures, so diverse that plainly no type of subdivision be it national, religious, professional, or ideological could transform into homogenous opinion or interest groups.[2]

Furthermore, each respective group included figures from a variety of backgrounds, which, from the outset, placed them in assorted positions within their "natural" groups. The Romanian group included dissidents alongside with affiliates of the Romanian regime. Likewise, the Jewish group included Israelis, Romanians, and Americans, and each was carrying his own load.

The first—and perhaps most fundamental—question had already been resolved by virtue of Elie Wiesel and the other Commission cofounders' decision on what the Commission would *not* address. Both Elie Wiesel and others ruled out discussions on "whether or not there had been a Holocaust in Romania," determining that the primary question should address "the origins and expressions of the Holocaust in Romania." Through this prism, the very fact of the Commission became a kind of victory for those who demanded that Romania commence its introspection by *recognizing that the Holocaust had indeed occurred within its borders*.

Naturally, announcing the Commission was preceded by multifaceted and complex preparation. Figures and organizations key to this process included Elie Wiesel, the appointed Commission chairman, with all that this role entailed; Avner Shalev, chairman of the Yad Vashem Directorate; Irena Steinfeldt, then head of Avner Shalev's bureau, and additional representatives from Yad Vashem; Dr. Radu Ioanid, director of the United States Holocaust Memorial Museum (USHMM) in Washington

---

2 For a list of names, see: International Commission of the Holocaust in Romania (ed.) (2005). *Final Report*. Iași, p. 4.

D.C., a native Romanian and current American citizen, whose father was involved in government factions and who had his own diverse ties in Romania; Professor Mihail E. Ionescu, then head of the Institute for Political Defense and Military History, a general and historian, who was also associated with various Romanian government factions. Ioanid, Ionescu, and I also served as the three co-vice chairs of the Commission.

The American group included Jewish American members of the B'nai B'rith organization and the American Jewish Committee. Furthermore, there were various Romanian, American, and Israeli Foreign Office and embassy officials in Israel, Romania, and the United States who laid the groundwork for the Commission to assemble.

On October 22, 2003, the Commission became a known fact, with emphasis on its independent and unaffiliated status. The Romanian government delineated the structure and budget for the Commission over the course of two deliberations, the first on February 20, 2004, and the second on May 5, 2004.[3] The primary task of the above-mentioned entities, once they had agreed on the actual Commission and defined its structure, was drafting its written mandate. In the discussions, various ideas, intentions, and personal wishes crystallized into several core tasks.[4]

The first was, as mentioned previously, of a historical research orientation: assembling updated research data on the origins, expression, and implications of the Holocaust in Romania. This included the relevant territorial issues regarding regions outside of Romanian rule during the years in question. Members of the Commission also concluded that in the short period of designated time, during which they were also to submit a report before the end of Iliescu's presidential term, and considering discrepancies in existing research on the matter at hand, they could not conduct the research themselves, but rather try to professionally and pragmatically base themselves on the most updated research available. Naturally, this research was based on the documentation available at this point in time. The documentation comprised only a portion of what researchers should have been able to access, and *this lack* produced one of the Commission's objectives, namely to ensure that Romania would,

3 Final Report 2005, p. 7.

4 Ibid., pp. 381–390.

from here on out, open its various archives to local and foreign researchers, as would any democratic country that respects the right of the public to information and freedom of research.

The second task was of a public, educational, and heritage-driven political and judicial orientation, and if the first task required Commission members to *face the past*—the second demanded they turn *toward the future*. Among the objectives were the following: (1) a commitment by the Romanian government to include Holocaust studies in general, and the study of its origins and expression in Romania specifically in elementary and secondary school curricula; (2) a commitment by the Romanian government to open its various archives to local and foreign researchers on any subject related to the Holocaust in Romania as a way to encourage and expand scholarly study of the subject in its universities and research institutes, as well as the establishment of a research and educational institute dedicated to the Holocaust in Romania; (3) the adoption of accepted international frameworks of Holocaust commemoration, including the proclamation of a national Holocaust commemoration day, which was first implemented in Romania *one year following submission of the final report.*[5] We hoped this was a signal of how the Commission and its future findings on Romanian authority and perhaps the Romanian nation would be received.

Additional initiatives in the commemoration domain were: (a) the establishment of a commemoration site at a central Bucharest location; (b) the rehabilitation of Jewish sites destroyed or damaged during the Holocaust, including locating and rehabilitating neglected, abandoned, or destroyed Jewish graveyards. A further issue was the phenomenon of Holocaust denial, its analysis, and the trials of war criminals in post-Holocaust Romania and the Communist era.[6] The burdensome and loaded matter of Jewish property in Romania and personal reparations for Romanian Jews had already begun penetrating the discussion as well for the entire complex and varied significance it carried and continues to carry.

---

5 Holocaust Memorial Day was first observed in Romania on October 9, 2005, during a special parliament meeting attended by President Traian Băsescu. The following day, he launched the program for Holocaust studies in elementary schools and for anti-Semitism awareness.

6 Final Report 2005, p. 390.

In order to illuminate the different spheres in which—despite the vitriolic and loathsome acts, murders, and massacres—the grace of humanity was exhibited in Romania—members of the Commission deemed it necessary to discuss the "righteous among the nations" in Romania—and so it was.

The Commission operated in several frameworks concurrently: the Commission as a plenum; the Commission as topic-specific subcommittees; the Commission chairmanship vis-à-vis and within the Commission plenum; the Commission chairmanship vis-à-vis and with the subcommittees; the Commission chairmanship vis-à-vis ad hoc political and professional bodies; and, of course, the Commission chairmanship in itself.

The Commission convened for three plenary sessions. The first was held at the USHMM in Washington D.C. (May 16–22, 2004), the second at Yad Vashem in Jerusalem (September 6–9, 2004), and the third in Bucharest (November 8–13, 2004) on the eve of the final report's submission to President Iliescu on November 11, 2004. A final session, which was also a last-minute attempt to settle all unresolved issues, finalized the wording of the report in the two official languages of submission, Romanian and English, and evaluated the translations and their accuracy.

Along with the plenary sessions, Commission members participated in various subcommittees by topic, usually headed by one or two facilitators who oversaw the discussions and ensured that deadlines were met and tasks were performed within the delineated time frame. Heads of the committees and co-vice chairs remained in ongoing contact in order to address unexpected challenges, respond to questions, consult one another, and establish courses of action. One can hardly overstress the gravity, diligence, responsibility, and dedication exhibited by participants of each committee, both members and facilitators.

The Commission was faced with a variety of obstacles throughout. I will name but a few: The Romanian delegation was extremely stratified and diverse. In addition, it was perhaps the most complex and most interesting. It included historians, activists, heads of the small Jewish community in the country from the past and present. The delegation included both members who identified as affiliates of the old Communist regime and its longtime opponents, and it was no challenge to detect the great tension between them. The Romanian Jewish group was also heterogeneous, and distinctions were easy to detect not only in members' approaches, but also in their accounts of the past as well as their perception of the task at hand and their role in the Commission.

One of the tensest moments of confrontation within the Romanian group transpired on the first plenary session in Washington. During those hours of preliminary discussion, when it appeared, at least to the Commission chairmanship, that it was possible the sessions would implode at their very outset, a dispute developed between members of the Romanian delegation, which reflected the gulf between the "conservative" camp and what might be considered the "dissident" camp. The absence of one of the heads of the Romanian delegation—who was strongly associated with the Romanian "institution"—was interpreted to be a "political" declaration driven by his perception of the Commission as "surrender" on Romania's part, and his unwillingness to be affiliated with it. Another conservative figure who, at the opening of the session, announced his take on the best way to address the conflict aroused a heated exchange, with some delegation members demanding he confront the fact that Romania had changed and continued to change, and refrain from disgracing the delegation with these types of statements. In response, he sat in loaded silence throughout the duration of the Commission sessions.

In order to address such issues, the Commission chairmanship assembled prior to each plenary session, during the weeks of daily plenary sessions and, on occasion, several times in one day. The intention was to try to anticipate parts of the agenda that might derail the discussion from a professional and pragmatic trajectory. It was abundantly clear that nearly every Commission member had a personal stake in the matter and at times an unsettled "account" or a heavy burden. We therefore tried to establish agendas that did not congest one session with too many controversial subjects and design them in such a way that made the emotional burden of painful and agonizing matters bearable to most members. This entailed the thoughtful assignment of chairpersons to each day and discussion and the preparation of possible responses for moments of crisis.

An additional example of such moments occurred during the assembly at Yad Vashem in Jerusalem. It was clear to the Commission chairmanship that assembling at this location would expose the plenum to the various expectations, requests, and wishes of organizations representing Romanian Jewish immigrants in Israel and those of Romanian activists and civilians who would seek to address the Commission. We assumed that many would not be satisfied with knowing that the Commission included the leading researchers of the Romanian Holocaust who had written most studies on the subject, and, naturally, would still wish to address the Commission and express their torment, pain, and personal or communal story.

We knew that some were also against the Commission in principle and believed that its conception, birth, existence, and future were a sin. We assumed that they too would not spare Commission members their opinion, particularly the Romanians among them, and particularly those who had joined believing that Romania must confront its past and begin the long, complex, and agonizing process of potential rehabilitation, for this was a significant mission for Romanians and Romania and not exclusively for the Jews who had lived or remained there. We were concerned—and for good reason—that Israeli organizations which objected to the Commission would target their wrath primarily at the Romanian delegates who believed this journey was a national obligation and should have begun much earlier.

We were also aware that the Romanian community in Israel is represented by many different organizations which did not agree as to their ultimate representative or chairman. Therefore, we would be asked to allow numerous "chairmen" to make an appearance which was simply *not possible* considering the tight, busy schedule of the Commission.

The decision that the "chairman of all chairmen"—at least whomever most agreed upon—addressed the Commission produced moments of extreme tension at the aforementioned assembly during which he announced his opinion of the Commission, Romania, and its delegates. This was one of the most difficult, embarrassing, and tense moments endured throughout the Commission sessions.

An additional question that arose as early as during preliminary discussions on establishing the Commission was how its report should address the matter of the Gypsy (Roma) people. Along with the decision and understanding that it was important to integrate this issue into the discussions, the framework of such discourse had to be determined as well as who would represent the Romani people. This question was also met with more than one answer…[7]

Another decisive question and complex moment concerned our dear colleague at Yad Vashem, the late Jean Ancel. My opinion, which I shared with a journalist following Ancel's passing, is that Jean Ancel was the authority of the Commission, although this by no means detracts from the significance and contribution of all Commission members, experts, and researchers.

My belief, which I shared with Jean Ancel in difficult and tense moments when he would write me a note saying, "Tuvia, I cannot bear these statements," is that the Commission itself was a type of victory in his years-long struggle for Holocaust research in Romania and for public awareness on the subject. Jean found it challenging to sit through some of the discussions. Already at the Washington plenary session, I asked if he would be so kind as to sit by me.

I wished to consult him on every piece of data, any nuance of evaluation that came up on which I was unsure in terms of accuracy and substantiality, but I also sought his proximity because I was aware of Ancel's profound sensitivity. I asked that whenever he felt the discussion was developing in a way he could not bear, he would write me a note, or signal me, so that I as co-vice chair may try to enable him, and perhaps others who shared his sentiment, to take a breath, relax, and return to the discussion as contributing participants after some time.

It was not only the Romanian delegation and some of its members' statements that often troubled Jean, but also his complex relationship—one of mutual respect, but also professional rivalry and discord—with Radu Ioanid, who, as mentioned earlier, also served as co-vice chair. Just as Jean Ancel was crucial to the Commission for all that he embodied, Radu Ioanid was equally significant for all the relative advantages he offered to the process. These tensions were palpable and sometimes even put the Commission's progress at risk.

One of the primary disagreements between Jean Ancel and Radu Ioanid concerned the number of Holocaust victims in Romania and the territories under its authority. Ancel referenced his own data while Ioanid and others named a lower figure. Both sides held their ground from the

---

7 Ibid., pp. 232–254.

outset of discussions and almost to the final moment in which the report was signed. Each cited his resources and insisted on his professional tactics and approach. The main concern was that any version that included only one of the numbers—determined by one side—would spur the objection of the other camp, to the point of withdrawing from the Commission on the eve of its conclusion.

Another concern stemmed from the possibility that a respectable, professional Commission, whose findings would undoubtedly be subject to scrupulous examination, would be caught in an error or exhibit bias on such a crucial matter. In order to bypass this obstacle, and with the assumption that the researchers' data was not sufficiently decisive for a "final" determination to be made, it was suggested that the issue be postponed until researchers gain access to a more rich and diverse body of documentation than was available at the time. Thus, instead of naming one number that was not unanimously agreed upon anyhow, citing a *range of the number of victims* based on the available research was proposed, along with a diligent and accurate account of the respective numerical resources and evaluations. This proposal was accepted by the members of the Commission and eventually used in the final report.[8]

Discussions on this issue continued almost until the final moment of the Commission sessions. Likewise, debates and inquiries on the translation of the report from English to Romanian proved to be quite tense. Here too, the concern was that certain sentences and phrases written by the Commission in English were being translated into Romanian in a soft, delicate, "minimizing" tone, if at all. Throughout the final Commission session—which was a particularly tense and overloaded day—at least in discussions between the three co-vice chairs and Elie Wiesel, it was intermittently suggested that submitting the final report to the president would be forgone should the Israeli delegation disapprove of the Romanian translation.

The report, which was later published in English and Romanian, was 400 pages and 17 chapters long and included opening remarks by two

---

8 Ibid., p. 380f. The Commission concludes that between 280,000 and 380,000 Romanian and Ukrainian Jews were murdered or died during the Holocaust in Romania and the territories under its control. An additional 135,000 Romanian Jews living under Hungarian control in Northern Transylvania also perished in the Holocaust as did some 5,000 Romanian Jews in other countries.

Romanian presidents, Iliescu (upon preparation and submission) and Băsescu (upon publishing), Elie Wiesel's address at the submission ceremony,[9] conclusions, and indices. The later published volume of photographs and documents in their original language, edited by Commission member Lya Benjamin, was another product of the Commission's activity.[10]

The final pages of the report included central findings and recommendations concerning both the historical component and practical and applicable conclusions. Recommendations were offered regarding the public, formal, and national announcement of the report's submission, its publishing, and its distribution.[11] Needless to say, we worried that the president or his successors would "bury" the report after utilizing it politically—an inclination that is not exclusively relevant to Romanian politicians. The chapter on education in Romania included an assessment and reevaluation of all books on the Holocaust and discussed the production of new textbooks for elementary schools, as well as teacher training and the establishment of a proper educational resource-base on the subject.

The commemoration section of the report stated that Romania must announce a Holocaust memorial day and determine its ceremonial and symbolic components; additional vehicles of commemoration were also suggested, such as museums and guaranteed access to archives and the diverse documentation they contained.[12]

Commission members also noted a series of topics they did not have the time to discuss fully and recommended that a continued effort be made to address them: a reinvestigation of war criminals who were acquitted on various occasions, the location and trial of collaborators and war criminals, and Holocaust denial and deniers. Commission members also recommended that the Romanian government establish an agency to ensure the fulfillment of its recommendations.[13]

On the eve of November 11, 2004, the final day of the Commission's activity, the report was submitted to President Iliescu at the Cotroceni

---

9 Final Report 2005, pp. 9–13, p. 17f.

10 Benjamin, Lya (ed.) (2005). *Documente*. Iași, p. 622.

11 Final Report 2005, pp. 381–390.

12 Ibid.

13 Ibid.

Palace in Bucharest. This draft was produced at the very last minute in office printers and bound in giant, adorned leather bindings. The ambiance in the ornate room in which the ceremony was held combined every tone befitting of such an event: anticipation and tension, sadness, pain and courage, and the feeling of witnessing a historical moment.

Upon submitting the report, the Commission's duty had been fulfilled and its appointment concluded. During these moments in the presidential palace, I saw, to no surprise, the image of my father and mother before my eyes, former Romanian citizens. Although they and the rest of my family had been relatively fortunate, the stories they had told me as a child about their homeland, Romania, echoed through me. An image flashed before me, which I had time and again imagined throughout my life: my father standing in a leaky tent during the harsh winter of 1951, at a transit camp in Be'er Sheva, Israel, playing Bach on a violin he had packed in the single suitcase he was permitted to bring, a suitcase whose shell also contained the circumference of his identity. He played his music, or so I believe, to digest the displacement and expulsion, the lot of most Romanian immigrants in the *Aliyah* wave of those years.

As I witnessed the President of Romania receive the report and make his address, the heads of the Romanian government listening, at this singular moment, which belonged to the president, their president, the president of their nation Romania, but also to me, as a Jew, an Israeli, and a Zionist—I stood with my parents, Ida and Aaron, may they rest in peace. In this sense, my participation in the Commission, a Commission whose members told them, the Romanians, how their nation had slaughtered our nation, a Commission whose members called upon them to courageously face their past, was a form of closure. Personal closure.

Along with the symbolic and ceremonial value of this event, a report was submitted that delineated the spheres, expressions, and phases of the Holocaust in Romania and the territories under its authority. The report illuminated the roots of the Holocaust and of anti-Semitism in Romania and the courses of action Romania was expected to take in all fields included in the Commission mandate.

The address made by the Romanian president as well as the speeches by Elie Wiesel and the three co-vice chairs elucidated that the Commission had not assembled for the purposes of a report. It was established, rather, to stimulate processes of reform, to underscore and activate deep undercurrents within Romanian society, and to channel them into an operational process within which Romania addresses its past—in the fields of research and education, heritage, commemoration, and the memory of the Holocaust that took place within its borders. The above-described processes are each slow and fragile, convoluted and demanding; and only time will tell whether the aforementioned objectives have been successfully implemented.

Michael Shafir

Public Discourse and Remembrance: Official and Unofficial Narratives

The late chairman of the Federation of Jewish Communities in Romania (FCER) Nicolae Cajal (1919–2004) claimed at one point that in Romania there might be anti-Semites, but there is no anti-Semitism. The subtle distinction was referring to public discourse, in which no trace of anti-Semitism can be found in the current millennium on one hand and the overt or covert anti-Semitic discourse not rarely encountered either among politicians or among leading intellectual public figures on the other hand.

In this chapter, I distinguish between *official* versus *unofficial* memory of the Holocaust and its remembrance to drive home the point that there is an official and an unofficial narrative. The latter narrative continues to rely on powerful cultural resources and, as Rafał Pankowski demonstrated in the case of Poland, such resources and their net of links to both real and imagined history determine outcomes at the end of the day.[1]

Walking the post-Communist memory lane

Right after the change of regime, the figure of Marshal Ion Antonescu, Romania's wartime military leader responsible for the extermination of at least 280,000 Romanian and Ukrainian Jews and some 25,000 Roma, executed by the Communists in 1946, was transformed into a "hero" figure and became the object of a semiofficial cult. On the eve of the anniversary marking his execution in 1991, parliamentary deputies rose in a minute of silence in his memory. The initiative belonged to Petre Țurlea, a deputy representing the then ruling Party of Social Democracy in Romania, a social-democratic formation that would eventually become today's Social Democratic Party (PSD). Although mainly promoted by the

1 Pankowski, Rafał (2010). *The Populist Radical Right in Poland. The Patriots*. London/New York, p. 6, pp. 95–104.

anti-Semitic, Hungarophobic, and anti-Roma Greater Romania Party (PRM), the Antonescu cult crossed party boundaries and included members of the "democratic opposition," such as the National Peasant Party Christian Democratic (PNȚCD) and the National Liberal Party (PNL).[2] A documentary film and a motion picture depicting Antonescu in this light were made, and attempts to force his judicial rehabilitation failed at the last moment.[3] By the time the ending of the cult was imposed by a Governmental Ordinance in 2002 (see below), between six and eight statues had been erected in memory of Antonescu, 25 streets and squares had been renamed after him, and in Iași even the "Heroes" military cemetery carried the dictator's name.[4]

Although Ion Iliescu is credited (under circumstances yet to be discussed) with being the first Romanian head of state to have officially acknowledged his country's responsibility for the Holocaust perpetrated against its Jewish citizens, this is not accurate. President Emil Constantinescu, who served one term (1996–2000) between two Iliescu presidencies, preceded him. It is true, on the other hand, that Constantinescu's formulations were historically inaccurate, illustrating at the same time an attempt (conscious or unconscious) to deflect the main responsibility to the Germans. In a message addressed to the FCER, marking international Holocaust Memorial Day on May 4, 1997, Constantinescu wrote that while the Holocaust had not been "planned by Romanians" and while some Romanians had risked their lives to save Jews,

2 For details, see: Shafir, Michael (1994). Marshal Antonescu's Postcommunist Rehabilitation: *Qui Bono*, in Braham, Randolph L. (ed.). *The Tragedy of Romanian Jewry.* New York/Boulder, pp. 349–410, here p. 360f.; Shafir, Michael (2011). Romania's Tortous Road to Facing Collaboration, in Stauber, Roni (ed.). *Collaboration with the Nazis. Public Discourse after the Holocaust.* New York, pp. 245–297, here p. 255f.

3 Shafir 1994, pp. 351–361; Shafir 2011, pp. 256–260.

4 Currently, and in defiance of the legislation discussed below, one street continues to be named after the wartime leader in the town of Beiuș, Bihor County, and the local council of Târgovişte, Dâmboviţa County, obstinately refuses to annul his honorary citizenship of the locality. See Florian, Alexandru (2016). Memoria publică a Holocaustului în postcomunism, *Polis* 4(1). There is also a bust of the marshal in the regional museum of Argeș County in the town of Pitești. While the law allows this for didactic purposes, it certainly does not allow the eulogies that surround the bust. There is also a monument for Antonescu at Movila lui Burcel (Vaslui County), depicting him as giving the order to Romanian soldiers to "cross the river Prut" and liberate Bessarabia in 1941. I owe the latter information to historian Adrian Cioflâncă.

> [w]e are also aware that other Romanians, blinded by criminal furor, participated in this horrible crime, in implementing the Nazi project of the Final Solution. On more than one occasion Romania's wartime authorities attempted to oppose the Nazi demand for the full liquidation of the Jewish population, organized the immigration of groups of Jews to Palestine, and even openly protected some individuals of the Jewish community in Romania. But the same authorities organized deportations and promoted racial legislation. Today we accept responsibility for this dramatic inconsistency. The sacrifice of hundreds of thousands of Jews from all over Romania is a burden on our heart, on the heart of all Romanians.[5]

It should be noted that although Iliescu on several occasions earlier had condemned the atrocities committed by the Iron Guard (the Legion of the Archangel Michael) and the anti-Semitic policies of the Antonescu regime, he never spoke of Romanian involvement in the implementation of the Final Solution. On this occasion, Constantinescu admitted for the first time that the individual guilt of leaders and their followers could translate into the collective responsibility of future generations. During a visit to the United States Holocaust Memorial Museum (USHMM) in Washington on July 18, 1998, Constantinescu once again spoke first of saving the Jews rather than the persecution that preceded it. At the same time, the president remarked, "despite these [commendable acts] no one has the right to ignore [Romanian] responsibility for those Romanian citizens who were persecuted rather than protected by the Romanian state, [a fact that] cannot and must not be eluded."[6]

Following Constantinescu's letter to the FCER acknowledging Romania's collective responsibility for the Holocaust, historian Floricel Marinescu published an angry article in the mainstream *România liberă*'s weekly supplement *Aldine*. He argued that "from a strictly quantitative perspective, the number of crimes perpetrated in the name of Communist ideology is much larger than that of those perpetrated in the name of Nazi or similar ideologically-minded regimes." Marinescu added that unlike Constantinescu, no prominent Jewish Romanian personality had apologized for the role some Jews had "played in undermining Romanian statehood, in the country's bolshevization, in the crimes and atrocities

5 *Realitatea evreiască* (April 16–May 15, 1997).

6 *Realitatea evreiască* (July 1998).

committed [by them]." As for Antonescu, he was "by no means a war criminal, as some Jews depict him."[7]

There is a humorous side to the Marinescu incident, for soon after his attack on Constantinescu, he was appointed a member of the presidential staff. There is a serious aspect as well, for the story is illustrative of the discrepancy between the official and the unofficial memory, including the memory of the former's promoters. More important, however, is to realize that the Marinescu saga illustrates the discourse that would come to dominate much of the post-Communist reaction to the Holocaust, and not only in Romania.

Double Genocide, Holocaust obfuscation, and competitive martyrdom

There are three intertwined aspects to that discourse. The first is the repeated use of the Double Genocide theory. In a nutshell, the Double Genocide theory places the Gulag and its local derivate on par with the Holocaust. In its more benign form, it calls for "symmetry" in condemning the two, equally repulsive in its eyes, atrocities of the last century, and for a similar "symmetry" in applying punishment to those guilty for them. In its (rather common) aggressive form, it insists on the role played by Jews in communization, which should exculpate, in the eyes of the theory's partisans, local collaboration with the Nazis.

The second aspect, "Holocaust obfuscation,"[8] channels the debate precisely on the alleged guilt of the Jews in bringing and installing in power communism, with the purpose of justifying local participation in the perpetration of the Shoah, which is by and large ignored, while autochthonous resistance against communism is grossly exaggerated. With this purpose in mind, no distinction is made between the Nazi genocide and the Stalinist crimes against humanity, in spite of the fact that according to international legislation both are exempt from the status of limitations.

---

7 "Despre 'perplexitate' față de 'revisionismul românesc,'" *România liberă*, supliment *Aldine* 104 (March 7, 1998).

8 The term was first utilized by Dovid Katz in: On Three Definitions: Genocide, Holocaust Denial, Holocaust Obfuscation, in Donskis, Leonidas (ed.) (2009). *A Litmus Test Case of Modernity. Examining Modern Sensibilities and the Public Domain in the Baltic States at the Turn of the Century*. Bern, pp. 259–277.

This prompts the third and last aspect, namely "competitive martyrdom."[9] In search for positive heroes capable of replacing the ousted and artificial Communist symbolism, and against the background of Communist Holocaust neglect and/or distortion, the Double Genocide approach is fast becoming in these countries the master commemorative narrative, one in which the myth of anti-Communist resistance finds both hero-models and exculpation for the past. Within the framework of a century dominated by the Holocaust as a paradigmatic genocide, competitive martyrdom is the synthesis of all these elements. It strives to provide an alternative dominant narrative, not an alternative paradigm, for the paradigm remains genocidal. In the substituted narrative, the collective trauma of denationalization and Sovietization prevails over any attempt to drive attention to the suffering of Jews and Roma during the Holocaust, the more so as Jews continue to be perceived as instruments of communization.

The Double Genocide theory was first ventured in the Baltic States (to be more precise, in Lithuania) soon after the fall of communism. Lithuania was also the first state to grant Double Genocide institutional recognition, by passing legislation that prohibits the denial of both Nazi and Communist "genocides" in 2010.[10] It was followed in the same year by Hungary. The denial of Communist crimes was also introduced in the

---

9 For earlier use of the concept, see: Chaumont, Jean-Michel (1997). *La Concurrence des victimes: génocide, identité, reconnaissance*. Paris; Besançon, Alain (1998). *Le Malheur du siècle. Sur le Communisme, le Nazisme et l'unicité de la Shoah*. Paris, p. 138; Bartov, Omer (2000). *Mirrors of Destruction: War, Genocide and Modern Identity*. Oxford, pp. 71–75; Rosenbaum, Alan S. (2001). Introduction to First Edition, in Rosenbaum, Alan S. (ed.). *Is the Holocaust Unique? Perspectives on Comparative Genocide*. Boulder, pp. 1–9, here p. 2. According to Pankowski (*The Populist Radical Right in Poland*, p. 109), Western-based Polish sociologist Irineusz Krzemiński published in 2002 an article where he proposed "an interpretation of contemporary Polish anti-Semitism without Jews as a result of the competition of two national narratives, both claiming supreme martyrdom, or, in other words, the competition of suffering."

10 In Lithuania, "genocide" has been officially "redefined to include victims of Soviet deportations" and the NKVD (The People's Commissariat for Internal Affairs) and the KGB (Komitet gosudarstvennoy bezopasnosti) were "officially declared to be criminal organizations, thus bringing them in line with the Nürnberg tribunal's definition of the SS." Bartov, Omer (2013). Conclusion, in Himka, John-Paul and Joanna Beata Michlic (eds.). *Bringing the Dark Past to Light. The Reception of the Holocaust in Postcommunist Europe*. Lincoln/London, pp. 663–694, here p. 668.

penal code (albeit in different forms) in Latvia, the Czech Republic, Poland, and Moldova.[11]

Romania has not (yet?) followed suit, although it has been often urged to do so by local pundits and politicians. On the other hand, Bucharest was one of the sponsors of a failed December 2010 initiative that would have made Double Genocide into biding legislation for all European Union (EU) members. The proponents (Lithuania, supported by the foreign ministers of Bulgaria, the Czech Republic, Latvia, Hungary, and Romania) wanted to criminalize the denial of Communist crimes the same way denying the Holocaust is banned in EU countries. The Commission said in its decision that "opinions on the matter are too divided" and "there is no consensus on it." EU justice spokesman Matthew Newman was quoted as saying, "The bottom line is, obviously, what they did was horrendous, but Communist regimes did not target ethnic minorities."[12] Bucharest also supported several European Parliament and Parliamentary Assembly of the Organization for Security and Co-operation in Europe (OSCE) resolutions that transformed the day of August 23 (the date of the signing of the Molotov-Ribbentrop Pact in 1939) into the European Day of Remembrance for Victims of Stalinism and Nazism, thus putting the two regimes and their atrocities on par. These resolutions were generated by the so-called Prague Declaration, initiated in June 2008 by a number of academics and prominent former anti-Communist dissidents, such as the former Czech and Lithuanian presidents Václav Havel and Vytautas Landsbergis.[13]

Memory boulevard and adjacent streets

The change in the official Romanian discourse on the Holocaust was generated by Bucharest's quest to join NATO and the EU. Against the background of protests in the United States and Israel triggered by the

11 Andreescu, Gabriel (2011). Interzicerea Negării Crimelor Comuniste pe Plan European: Norme, Ideologie, Drepturi, *Noua Revistă de drepturile omului* 1: 41–58; Socor, Vladimir (2012). Moldova Condemns Communism at Long Last, *Eurasia Daily Monitor* 9 (July 12, 2012).

12 *The Guardian* (December 21, 2010).

13 See: Shafir, Michael (2012). Istorie, memorie și mit în martirologia competitivă Holocaust-Gulag, in Gherghina, Sergiu and Sergiu Mișcoiu (eds.). *Miturile politice în România contemporană*. Iași, pp. 297–358.

Ion Antonescu cult in Romania, President Iliescu attended in January 2001 a ceremony marking the 1941 Iași pogrom, where he felt compelled to declare: "no matter what *we* may think, international public opinion considers Antonescu to have been a war criminal."[14] This was as honest an admission that Romanian and Western memory on the Second World War did not coincide as Iliescu was capable of.

By early 2002, Romania had been bluntly told by US officials that the conditions for making it into NATO included facing the country's Second World War past, and that an end would have to be put to the Marshal Antonescu cult that had been striving in Romania since 1990. On a visit to Romania in February 2002, Bruce Jackson, chairman of the U.S. NATO Committee did not mince words: "Give me a bulldozer and I shall immediately destroy all Antonescu statues," adding that adherence to democratic values includes facing the historical past and that this adherence is "not negotiable" in the NATO accession process.[15]

The Defense Ministry on March 18, 2002, launched a syllabus on the Holocaust at the National Defense College in Bucharest and in a message to participants then Prime Minister Adrian Năstase said that "the future cannot be built on falsification and mystification" and that the 1941 pogroms in Iași or (the decimation of Jews in) liberated Bessarabia and Bukovina, as well as the later deportation of Jews to Transnistria, had been "in no way different from [...] the Nazi operation known under the name of the Final Solution." In his message, Năstase announced that the government had approved an emergency ordinance prohibiting the display of "racist or fascist symbols," the erection of statues or commemorative plaques for those condemned in Romania or abroad for "crimes against peace" and for "crimes against humanity," as well as the naming of streets and other places after those personalities. Exceptions were to be made only for museums, where such statues could be displayed for the purpose of "scientific activity" carried out outside "public space." Ordinance 31/2002, which was issued on March 13, also outlawed organizations of "fascist, racist and xenophobic character" that promote ideas "on ethnic, racist, or religious grounds" and extended this prohibition to both registered and unregistered foundations and any other form of organization consisting of three persons or more. The ordinance provided

14 *RFE/RL Newsline* (January 22, 2001), emphasis by the author.

15 *România liberă* (February 27, 2002).

penalties ranging from fines to 15 years in prison for those infringing its regulations or denying the Holocaust.[16]

Emergency ordinances become effective upon their issuance, but must eventually be approved by the parliament in order to become laws. Debates in parliamentary commissions had shown that this was by no means to be taken for granted. While the Senate's Human Rights' Commission approved the ordinance's text without amendments on April 9, 2002, in the Defense Commission representatives of the National Liberal Party joined those of the PRM in demanding that the text be amended. It was claimed that the Holocaust was a diffuse concept that needed clarification; and it was also claimed that the article in the ordinance prohibiting Holocaust denial infringed on human rights in general and on the right of freedom of expression in particular.[17] After twice postponing approval, the Judicial Commission agreed on June 5 to an amended text, based on the proposal made by Senator Gheorghe Buzatu (1939–2013), at that time a senator and PRM deputy chairman. Buzatu, who was a historian, proposed that the Holocaust be defined as "the systematic massive extermination of the Jewish population in Europe, organized by the Nazi authorities during the Second World War." In other words, by definition, there had been no Holocaust in Romania, since the extermination of Jews there had not been "organized by the Nazi authorities." The same amendment had been approved on May 29 by the Senate's Culture Commission, which had also heeded Buzatu's argument.[18] The Judicial Commission also reduced the maximum penalty for setting up organizations of a "fascist, racist or xenophobe" character from 15 to 5 years in prison.

The definition was perfectly in line with Buzatu and his associate's peculiar "selective negationism,"[19] which did not deny the Holocaust as having taken place *elsewhere* but excluded any participation of members of one's own nation in its perpetration. The ordinance was finally approved by parliament, but with a delay of four years.[20] The procrastination was obviously intentional. As approved, the new law did not carry

16 *Monitorul oficial al României*, no. 214 (March 28, 2002).

17 *Mediafax* [independent news agency] (April 9, 2002); *Cotidianul* [Bucharest daily] (April 15, 2002).

18 *Mediafax* (July 5, 2002); *Curentul* [Bucharest daily] (May 29, 2002).

19 See: Shafir, Michael (2002). Between Denial and "Comparative Trivialization:" Holocaust Negationism in Post-Communist East Central Europe, *ACTA* 19: 52–59.

20 Law no. 107, in *Monitorul official al României*, no. 377, May 3, 2006.

the Buzatu-proposed amendments. Rather, employing the definition of the Holocaust included in the report issued by the International Commission on the Holocaust in Romania (see below), it defined the Shoah as "the state-sponsored systematic persecution and annihilation of European Jewry by Nazi Germany, *its allies and collaborators* between 1933–1945," adding to it the specification that the country's Roma population had also been subjected to "deportation and annihilation"—a slight departure from the commission's formulation, which also mentioned "people with disabilities, political opponents, homosexuals, and others."[21]

The setting up of the commission has its own peculiar saga. It followed an Iliescu blunder in an interview with a journalist from the Israeli daily *Ha'aretz*.[22] Engaging in "Holocaust trivialization," the former president told the interviewer that the "Holocaust was not unique to the Jewish population in Europe. Many others, including Poles, died in the same way." But only Jews and Gypsies, the interviewer observed in reaction, had been "targeted for genocide" at that time. To which Iliescu responded: "I know. But there were others, who were labeled Communists, and they were similarly victimized. My father was a Communist activist and he was sent to a camp. He died at the age of 44, less than a year after he returned." Although Iliescu admitted that massacres of Jews had been perpetrated on Romania's territory proper and observed that "the leaders of that time are responsible for those events," he insisted, "[i]t is impossible to accuse the Romanian people and the Romanian society of this. When Germany declared [*sic*] the Final Solution—a decision that was obeyed by other countries, including Hungary, Antonescu no longer supported that policy. On the contrary, he took steps to protect the Jews. That, too, is historical truth." He also went on to observe: "Antonescu also had his positive side. In 1944, when Hungary under Horthy was implementing the Final Solution and transported its Jews to death camps, including residents of northern Transylvania, which was then under Hungarian rule, Antonescu was no longer doing that." As to the historians' claim that the shift in policies toward Jews was due to Stalingrad, Iliescu readily acknowledged that this "is correct" but deemed the detail to be "not important." In an attempt to hush the international scandal created by the

21 International Commission on the Holocaust in Romania (ed.) (2005). *Final Report*. Iași, p. 381, emphasis by the author.

22 *Ha'aretz* (English edition, July 25, 2003); see also: *RFE/RL Newsline* (July 28, 2003).

interview, the president proposed the setting up of what became known as the Elie Wiesel Commission, after the name of its chairman.

Established in October 2003 and ending its works one year later, the Commission proved to be a milestone in the Holocaust's official narrative, in the sense that by signing its conclusions, President Iliescu has explicitly endorsed his country's participation in the Holocaust. The unofficial discourse is another matter altogether.

To begin with, the Commission's members (the author of this chapter was one of them) learned from an angry outburst of historian Ioan Scurtu (a nationalist historian and a presidential appointee on the Commission) that no member of the Romanian Academy (the country's most prestigious forum) had agreed to participate on its works.[23] Indeed, the age-dean of historians' members of that forum Dan Berindei had dismissed the issuance of Ordinance 31/2002 from the start. Romania, Berindei said, needs no legislation against Holocaust denial, because "there has been no Holocaust in Romania. There have been some deportation to Transnistria, [Romania] was an anteroom of the Holocaust, but not [the place of the] Holocaust." Or, as he would put it at a debate at the Romanian Academy, the country had only been "a wing of a phenomenon that touched Romania as well."[24]

Historian Florin Constantiniu (at the time a correspondent member of the Academy[25]) proved to be a lot more versatile than Berindei. At a symposium in Bucharest I had the privilege to attend in his company in 2003, Constantiniu did not even come close to Holocaust denial. In his concluding remarks, he said, Antonescu's wartime objective of restoring Romania's 1918 borders were "legitimate" and added that "the marshal remains the only Romanian politician since 1940 who has attempted to restore Greater Romania, the Romanian unitary national state, within its natural borders." For Antonescu to have stopped at Dniester River, he added, was strategically and politically impossible. But he added in what reflected the "symmetric approach" (or Double Genocide theory) more than he might have wished that "Antonescu cannot be reproached for his

23 Historian Andrei Pippidi was a member of the Commission, but would become a "correspondent member" of the Academy only in 2012.

24 Stancu, Oana (2002). Ordonanța împotriva xenofobiei e gândită strâmb, *Jurnalul național* [Bucharest daily] (May 7, 2002).

25 He became a full member in 2006.

alliance with Hitler unless we reproach Churchill and Roosevelt their alliance with Stalin." On the other hand, he said paraphrasing Talleyrand, "Antonescu's policy regarding the Jews was both a crime and a mistake: a crime because it killed thousands of innocent people, and a mistake not only because it opposed national interest, but because it still imposes a heavy burden on the Romanian people."[26]

In the ensuing debates, however, the Romanian historian complained about attempts to impose "political correctness" and dictates from abroad, and wondered why do historians, political scientists, and politicians in general display such "haste" toward Romania's "Antonescu problem," which, he claimed, would find its clarification and solution in due time. While Berindei and Constantiniu shared a common past of informers for the Communist secret police,[27] other historians who stepped in this debate did not do so, but sounded just as strident. In the ensuing debates, former Communist Party (PCR) subservient but nationalist-minded historians would size the occasion to make clear their opposition. This, for example, was the case of university professor Mihail Retegan, who (as if he had ever raised his voice against the PCR under the previous regime) said that he thought the days when the Communist regime was interfering with historical research had been left behind.[28]

There can be little doubt, however, that among historians the most vociferous and prolific opponent of the findings of the International Commission for the Study of the Holocaust in Romania headed by Elie Wiesel was Gheorghe Buzatu. Buzatu is best known as the chief defender of Ion Antonescu, but his prolific publications after 1990 make him stand out in admiration and defense of Romania's interwar radical right as few did overtly, except amateur pseudo-historians and pundits. This includes the Iron Guard and its founder and leader, Corneliu Zelea Codreanu.[29] It also includes constant efforts to depict the Jews in general as subversive

26 Constantiniu, Florin (2003). The Antonescu Regime and the Jews, in *The Holocaust and Romania. History and Contemporary Significance*. Bucharest, pp. 113–121, here p. 120.

27 See: Shafir, Michael (2014). Unacademic Academics: Holocaust Deniers and Trivializers in post-Communist Romania, *Nationalities Papers* 42(6): 942–964.

28 Stancu 2002.

29 See (among others): Introducere, in Treptow, Kurt W. and Gheorghe Buzatu (1994). *"Procesul" lui Corneliu Zelea Codreanu (mai, 1938)*. Iași; Buzatu, Gheorghe et al. (1996). *Radiografia dreptei românești*. Bucharest.

Communist agents.[30] Buzatu was also the first historian in Romania to claim that the only "real" Holocaust has been that perpetrated by Jews against Romanians during the communization of Bessarabia and Bukovina in 1940 and after Romania's own communization after the war. He did so in a brochure printed by a publisher with an unmistakable name: Majadahonda, the place where Legionary (Iron Guard) "martyrs" Ion Moța and Vasile Marin died in January 1937 while fighting on Franco's side in the Spanish Civil War.[31]

The spirit of Holocaust obfuscation was thus fully reproduced by Buzatu: justification of crimes committed against Jews and the rehabilitation of the perpetrators by "demonstrating" that they were acts imposed by Romanian self-defensive postures. One year before his death (2013), Buzatu edited jointly with neo-Legionary activist George Roncea a 27-volume of archival materials by and on the Legion's founder, Codreanu.[32] As it was revealed after his death, Buzatu, writing under the pen name "Koba" (Stalin's underground nickname) to drive home a point, contributed many articles to the blog regularly published by Romania's most vitriolic Holocaust denier and anti-Semite, Ion Coja.[33] It is not, therefore, surprising to find Buzatu referring with disdain to the Final Report published by the Wiesel Commission in a collective history volume published by the Romanian Academy.[34]

Others historians would follow suit, such as Sibiu-based Corvin Lupu. In an article published in the journal *Transilvania* in 2005, Lupu rejected the Commission's Final Report's findings,[35] specifying that "the idea that

---

30 See: Buzatu, Gheorghe (1996). *Românii în arhivele Kremlinului*. Bucharest; Buzatu, Gheorghe and Mircea Chirițoiu (1998). *Agresiunea comunismului în România. Documente din arhivele secrete: 1944–1989*. Bucharest: Editura Paideia, 1998; Buzatu, Gheorghe (2010). *Din istoria secretă a celui de-al doilea război mondial*. Iași.

31 Buzatu, Gheorghe (1995). *Așa a început Holocaustul împotriva poporului român*. Bucharest.

32 *Documente din arhiva Corneliu Zelea Codreanu. Opera Omnia* (Iași, 2012).

33 I "owe" the information to his admirer and collaborator, Victor Roncea. See on his blog (http://roncea.ro) "Ultimul mesaj al Profesorului Gh. Buzatu: A sosit, netăgăduit, momentul Adevărului. Iar acesta se produce pe Internet."

34 See: Buzatu, Gheorghe (2008). Istoriografia și izvoarele, in Giurescu, Dinu C. (ed.). *Istoria Românilor. România în anii 1940–1947*. Bucharest.

35 Lupu, Corvin (2005). Impactul problematicii Holocaustului asupra României contemporane și aspecte ale relațiilor dintre români și evrei, *Transilvania* 3: 26, as quoted in: Florian, Alexandru (2008). Holocaustul ca subiect legislativ, in *Holocaust*

in Romania a genocide (Holocaust) has been perpetrated against the Jewish population cannot be accepted. On the contrary, in my opinion the Jewish people should be grateful to the Romanian people, a fact that has been acknowledged for several decades." He went on to accuse the Jews of "complicity" in having staged a *coup d'état* in December 1989 "against the Romanian national body." One of the components of this "aggression," Lupu added, was "the accusation that Romania carried out genocide against Jews." And he ended by wondering: "Why are they acting with such pettiness? Is money capable of mutilating souls that much?" The Center for Monitoring and Combatting Antisemitism in Romania (MCA, an NGO), the FCER, and even the USHMM demanded that the author be prosecuted in line with the provisions of Ordinance 31/2002, but the Prosecutor General's Office replied that Lupu had not infringed on the legislation's provisions, since he did not deny the Holocaust as such, but only its having taken place on Romanian soil. In other words, the Buzatu "interpretation" of the law carried the day, as it would indeed do in several other cases.

Heartened by his judicial exculpation, in 2013 Corvin Lupu and his son, a junior lecturer at the same Sibiu faculty that his father had for many years headed as dean, published a volume titled *History of International Relations. Europe between 1919–1947*.[36] Not surprisingly, the tome was prefaced by Buzatu, who, among other things, noted that the authors "draw attention to the sometimes overwhelming role played by international Jewry both on world and on Romanian stage" between 1919 and 1947. The infamous *Protocols of the Elder of Zion* might have been defended on the same grounds. According to Buzatu, the authors had the guts to demonstrate that the Jews "made a decisive contribution to setting up and the development of the Bolshevik regime in Russia and the dissemination of Communist ideology in Europe."[37] Indeed, a whole chapter in the volume is titled "The evolution of the world Communist movement. The decisive role of Jews."[38]

Memory and Antisemitism in Central and Eastern Europe. Comparative Aspects. International Conference. Bucharest, p. 209f.

36 Lupu, Corvin and Grațian Lupu (2013). *Istoria relaților internaționale. Europa în perioada anilor 1919–1947*. Bucharest.

37 Ibid., p. 8.

38 Ibid., pp. 77–88.

Were Buzatu and a presumably small and isolated circle of admirers pursuing a quixotic war? Not quite. President Ion Iliescu in December 2004 decorated both Buzatu and his party leader, Corneliu Vadim Tudor, with high state orders, as he was ending his presidential term.[39] Both had been harshly criticized in the Commission's Final Report.[40] In protest, the Commission's chairman, Elie Wiesel, returned to Iliescu the medal conferred on him in July 2002.[41] The inherited narrative[42] had thus prevailed over official memory even for Iliescu, the man who had turned it willy-nilly into official policy.

Nevertheless, the legacy of the Commission is remarkable when it comes to the handling of Holocaust memory. I have in mind in particular three of its recommendations for future action. The first called for "the creation of a national network that would aid on the distribution and sharing of materials and resources for teaching the Holocaust."[43] As a result, the Elie Wiesel National Institute for the Study of the Holocaust in Romania (INSHREW) came into being in 2005. Initially subordinated to the Ministry of Culture, the institute was transferred in August 2012 to the Prime Minister's Office, a step meant to enhance its symbolic status. Although its many critics in Romania depict it as a *Jewish* institution (when not as one of the "international Jewry"), INSHREW is a *Romanian* institution symbolizing state-readiness to confront Romania's "dark past."[44] Or at least it is meant to be so. Its objectives are: (a) identifying, archiving, researching, and publishing documents related to the Holocaust of Romanian Jews, (b) elaborating on and publishing in-depth studies and sur-

39 Tudor was awarded the highest Romanian distinction, "The Star of Romania," while Buzatu was decorated with the order of "Faithful Service" (*Mediafax*, December 13, 2004).

40 See: Final Report 2005, p. 350f., p. 353 for Tudor; p. 321, p. 348, p. 350, pp. 355–359, p. 361, p. 367 for Buzatu.

41 *Adevărul* (December 16, 2004).

42 By "inherited narrative" I mean the combination resulting from several factors: family and peer narratives on one hand, but also the Antonescu-narrative of the Ceaușescu years.

43 Final Report 2005, p. 388.

44 I borrow the syntagma from Himka, John-Paul and Joanna Beata Michlic (2013). Introduction, in Himka, John-Paul and Joanna Beata Michlic (eds.). *Bringing the Dark Past to Light. The Reception of the Holocaust in Postcommunist Europe*. Lincoln/London, pp. 1–14, here p. 1f.

veys on the topic, (c) implementing Holocaust-related educational programs, and (d) promoting representative works on Holocaust history. In fact, INSHREW does a lot more and, above all, it has become the vanguard in the struggle against extremism in general and Holocaust trivialization or obfuscation in particular.

Second, the Commission said "the government of Romania has adopted October 9 [2004] as the official date of Holocaust commemoration." The choice of October 9 followed the suggestion of the Commission, whose works were still ongoing at that time. The day marks the beginning of deportations of Romanian Jews to Transnistria from Bukovina in 1941. Following this decision, Romania became a full member of the Task Force for International Cooperation on Holocaust Education, Remembrance, and Research (ITF), an intergovernmental body whose purpose is to rally political and social leaders' support behind the need for Holocaust education, remembrance, and research both nationally and internationally. One of the conditions for full membership that the ITF (which changed its name into International Holocaust Remembrance Alliance, or IHRA, in January 2013) requires is precisely the marking of such a commemoration day. Government Decision no. 672 of May 5, 2004, established the Holocaust Remembrance Day in Romania. Adopting the decision, the Romanian government declared, in the spirit of ITF's mission, its "commitment to remember the victims who perished, respect the survivors still with us, and reaffirm humanity's common aspiration for mutual understanding and justice."[45] In 2016, Romania is holding the organization's rotating chairmanship.

Finally, the Commission recommended: "A national memorial to the victims of the Holocaust should be erected on public property in Bucharest." After considerable procrastination caused by both ill will and petty business interests (Bucharest's mayor had apparently assigned the location for other purposes[46]), the monument was finally inaugurated on October 8, 2009. Ever since, ceremonies are held on October 9 at the

---

45 https://www.holocaustremembrance.com/member-countries/holocaust-education-remembrance-and-research-romania.

46 Waldman, Felicia and Mihai Chioveanu (2013). Public Perceptions of the Holocaust in Postcommunist Romania, in Himka, John-Paul and Joanna Beata Michlic (eds.). *Bringing the Dark Past to Light. The Reception of the Holocaust in Postcommunist Europe*. Lincoln/London, pp. 451–486, here p. 470.

site, attended either by the head of state or his representatives, governmental officials, and members of the diplomatic corps accredited in Bucharest. The site, however, is not administered by the government, but by INSHREW. More recently, while on a visit to the USHMM in Washington, President Klaus Iohannis said he intends to initiate the construction in Bucharest of a Holocaust museum and a regional center for the study of the Holocaust, side by side with a museum of the prewar Jewish communities in Romania.[47] The latter had been included among the Commission's recommendations and debates on its concept had been ongoing for some time.

From Ordinance 31 to Law 217

Under the heading "Unfinished matters," the International Commission mentioned in the Final Report the need of "Correcting and Enforcing Legislation on Holocaust Denial and Public Veneration of Antonescu." The reference was to Emergency Ordinance 31/2002, which eventually became Law 107/2006. The problems with this law were manifold. The judiciary (prosecutors and tribunals alike) have tended to interpret the legislation forbidding the denial of the Holocaust as if it referred to denial of the genocide having taken place *elsewhere* (although many such cases were also ignored), not in Romania. The presumption remained that in Romania and on territories administered by its army during the Second World War, no Holocaust has been perpetrated, just as suggested by Buzatu and as illustrated by the Lupu case.

Viewed from this angle, the Report had been a total failure, despite its assumption by the authorities. According to official statistics, between 2002 and 2015, only fourteen cases were indicted for infringing the provisions of Ordinance 31/2002. How many were actually convicted is not known. Between 2007 and 2015, out of a total of 294 complaints to the Prosecutor General's Office for infringement of the provisions of Law 107/2006, a procedure was launched in seven cases, involving nine persons. In 2005, a Brașov-based tribunal convicted Iron-Guard apologist

47 See: *Ziare.com* (March 8, 2016); *Adevărul Live* (April 7, 2016).

Gheorghe Oprița to 30 months in prison, but the sentence was quashed on appeal in 2006.[48]

The Oprița's case did not refer to denial but rather to the cult—not of Antonescu, but of the Legionary Movement. Ordinance 31/2002 and Law 107/2006 did not mention the Movement at all. Time and time again, prosecutors rejected complaints initiated by INSHREW, the MCA, and private persons against neo-legionnaries, indeed even against legionnaires without any "neo." For example, a group calling itself the Iron Guard (but not registered as a political party) displays on Bucharest's Diacon Negruzzi street the "grilled cross" of the Iron Guard emblem (representing a fence formed by several crosses), and roadside crucifixes bearing the same sign are spread all over the country. Iron Guard propaganda is available on the Internet and in bookshops. At several monasteries, such as Petru Vodă in Moldavia, monks openly praise the Guard, and one Youtube posting even shows some nuns singing to Father Justin Pârvu (1919–2013) on his 92nd birthday the (in)famous Iron Guard anthem "Holy Legionary Youth."[49] What is more, in one of its decisions rejecting an INSHREW complaint, the Prosecutor General's Office cited the Romanian Academy's opinion that there was disagreement among historians whether the Legionary movement had been "fascist" or not.[50]

Under these circumstances, it became clear that the law has to be amended in both its main *lacunae.* First, the legislation had to make clear that denying the Holocaust referred to Romania and its own contribution to the perpetration of the Shoah; and, second, the interdiction of propaganda and display of symbols in the public space had to specifically refer to the Iron Guard. After significant pressure from abroad and intensive lobbying by the INSHREW, this was achieved with the approval of Law 2017 in July 2015.[51] The amendment was initiated by three parliamen-

48 *Cotidianul* (June 3, 2006); Clej, Petru (2016). Negarea Holocaustului și activități fasciste—16 inculpați în 14 ani, *Radio France Internationale* (Romania) (April 19, 2016).

49 https://www.youtube.com/watch?v=LPjkEtCzp-Y.

50 Shafir 2014.

51 Legea nr. 217/2015 pentru Modificarea şi Completarea Ordonanţei de Urgenţă a Guvernului nr. 31/2002 Privind Interzicerea Organizaţiilor şi Simbolurilor cu Caracter Fascist, Rasist sau Xenofob şi a Promovării Cultului Persoanelor Vinovate de Săvârşirea unor Infracţiuni Contra Păcii şi Omenirii, *Monitorul Oficial al României* (July 15, 2015).

tarians representing the PNL, one of which, Crin Antonescu, had presidential ambitions at the time. According to malicious comments in the media, Antonescu was thereby hoping to enlist US support for his candidacy. True or not, this reflected the famous canard according to which Romania is ruled by the United States and the United States, in turn, is ruled by Jews. Sadly, Crin Antonescu subsequently confirmed the existence of a huge discrepancy between the official and the unofficial narratives.

Whereas Ordinance 31/2002 had prompted many negative reactions denying Romania's role in the Holocaust and Ion Antonescu's role in particular,[52] this time around reactions tended to focus on the Iron Guard, but had ramifications to the more general debates ongoing in East Central Europe around the crimes committed by the two totalitarian regimes of the 20th century—Nazism and communism. Within this framework, the triad of Double Genocide–competitive martyrdom–Holocaust obfuscation came into pronounced evidence.

Expectedly, publications with overt Iron Guardist profile denounced the amendment without mincing words. The Legionary veterans' journal *Permanențe* (*Consistencies*, printed irregularly since 1998) published a special edition entirely dedicated to the new version of the law. The main contribution was a three-page long article titled "The Abuse of the State against the Citizen's Rights—Still Possible in Romania." The article ended with an "appeal" assumed by nearly all organizations, foundations, and Orthodox Church organizations with Legionary sympathies—no less than 15 in total number.[53] The "appeal" had been issued before the approval of Law 217, in the hope of dissuading the legislature from proceeding with the legislation process. Very little that followed (apart from some injurious attacks on INSHREW and its director and some rather melodramatic outbursts) brought new elements to the legionnaires' arguments and that of their sympathizers. It is therefore sufficient to examine this initial reaction.

---

52 See: Totok, William (2005). Receptarea publicistică a raportului final al Comisiei Wiesel în presa românească şi germană, *Studia Hebraica* 5: 186–195; Shafir, Michael (2004). Memory, Memorials and Membership: Romanian Utilitarian Antisemitism and Marshal Antonescu, in Carey, Henry F. (2004). *Romania Since 1989: Politics, Culture and Society*. Lanham, pp. 67–97.

53 *Permanențe*, ediție specială, no date, 2015.

First, it was argued that Law 207/2015 represented an attack on the constitutional provision guaranteeing freedom of expression and of assembly. This was little else than an emblematic illustration of reactions of extremists (Left and Right) whenever their own anti-systemic capability to undermine democracy is circumvented. To "demonstrate" their contention, the article made use of a syllogism: Since all previous post-Communist attempts to outlaw the legionnaires and their offshoots had failed, this was proof that they had always acted strictly within democratic procedure; yet it was never mentioned that the failure was due to a great extent to Ordinance 31/2002 and Law 107/2006 to specifically refer to the Iron Guard.

The article also utilized as argument the hoax that the Nürnberg Tribunal had allegedly exonerated the Iron Guard from any accusation. The hoax is not very original, being also utilized by sympathizers of Monsignor Jozef Tiso in Slovakia.[54] In reality, the tribunal never dealt with any fascist movements anywhere except for Nazi Germany. It was also claimed in the article that the purpose of the amendments included in Law 217 was to introduce a new form of censorship, similar to that introduced by Stalinist rule in the late 1947 and early 1948. This old-new censorship allegedly would outlaw the reading, studying, and dissemination of works by Romanian intellectuals who, at one point or another, had sympathized with the Iron Guard (Mircea Eliade, Emil Cioran, poet Radu Gyr—author of the Iron Guard anthem "Holy Legionary Youth"—and others). In actual fact, the amendment referred to *propaganda* aimed at exonerating Iron Guard ideology; to *organizing* pro-Guard events; to the dissemination of Legionary symbols; and to the cult of personalities sentenced for war crimes after the Second World War utilizing for this purpose public space. The new law never mentioned and never had the intention to prohibit the republication of works of the former Iron Guard sympathizers when it came to their literary, philosophical, or sociological publications, as critics (not only declared Guard sympathizers) had insinuated. Finally, the article gave full vent to the Double Genocide theory and to competitive martyrdom. The Iron Guard, it claimed, had been in the forefront of the struggle against communism and its leaders and sympathizers imprisoned by the Communists were the martyrs of the nation,

54 Shafir 2002, p. 59.

as proved by the numerous priests with Iron Guard sympathies (for some time dubbed as "Prison Saints" or *Sfinții Închisorilor*).

The "Prison Saints" were all, or nearly all, former Iron Guardists, some of which had been imprisoned already by Marshal Antonescu for having participated in the Legionary rebellion against him in January 1941. Their past as members of the Iron Guard is, however, seldom mentioned, and if it is, no mention is made of the Guard's anti-Semitism. There must be dozens of books on the Romanian market by now, and pilgrimages are made to the tomb of Arsenie Boca at the Prislop Monastery, where "wonders" are said to take place. These pilgrimages are apparently very lucrative for those involved in organizing them.[55] His canonization by the Romanian Orthodox Church has started, but this is probably the easiest of all cases, since Boca was not a member of the Iron Guard, but extended help to such members both under Antonescu and under the Communists.[56]

It is not an accident that authors known for their previous attempts to rehabilitate the Iron Guard and its members, including founder Corneliu Zelea Codreanu, edit many of these books. Titles are also worth pondering on. For example, in a volume edited by Răzvan Codrescu (one of the first to attempt Codreanu's rehabilitation), one finds articles by himself, by Sorin Lavric—the author of a eulogy volume on philosopher Constantin Noica and the Iron Guard[57]—but also by Radu Preda, who was appointed director of the Institute for the Investigation of Communist Regime Crimes and the Memory of Romanian Exile (IICCMER) in May 2014. His predecessor, young historian Andrei Muraru, carefully avoided any IICCMER implication into competitive martyrdom and links to Iron Guard promoters. Muraru became a presidential counselor to newly elect President Iohannis Klaus, and his departure radically changed IICCMER's face. Right upon his appointment, Preda, a theologian by training, stated that it was his "obligation" to place "the case of the 'Saints of Prison' on the agenda of the institute."[58] In the aforementioned volume, he authored

55 *Adevărul Financiar* (May 25, 2015).

56 Muttler, Alison (2015). Romanian Church Considers Popular Monk for Sainthood, *Associated Press* (October 1); *Adevărul de Constața* (February 9, 2016; March 16, 2016).

57 Lavric, Sorin (2014). *Constantin Noica și Mișcarea Legionară*. Bucharest.

58 Preda, Radu (2014). Este de datoria mea să pun pe agenda institutului cazurile Sfinților Închisorilor, *Cuvântul Ortodox* (April 26): www.cuvantul-ortodox.ro/recomandari/2014/04/26/radu-preda-iiccmer-sfintii-inchisorilor/.

two articles: one titled "Memory's Mercenaries" and the other "Memory as an Obligation." Lavric's contribution was titled "The Need of Martyrs," while Codrescu himself wrote on "The Martyrology of Communist Jails" and reported on the recently held "First Symposium of Martyrdom."[59] In the former tract he placed side by side anti-Communist militant and Radio Free Europe journalist Monica Lovinescu or PNŢCD leader Corneliu Coposu with Codreanu and Legionary police chief Alexandru Gyka. As Alexandru Climescu formulated it, this was disingenuous "organized confusion."[60]

Apologists of the Guard were also on the vanguard of attacks against the INSHREW and its director, since INSHREW and Florian personally had long pressed lawmakers for the change. Examples abound and can be randomly picked out by any Internet search. Under the auspices of the Professor George Manu Foundation—one of several specializing in Iron Guard cleansing—Cezarina Condurache (a member of *Permaneţe's* editorial board) published a volume in 2015 titled *Faces of Romanian Dignity. Heroes of the Nation and Saints of Prison* and edited another tome titled *The Anticommunist Heroes and Saints of Prison Re-Incriminated by Law 217/2015.*[61]

Lavric's contribution to the latter volume speaks miles about the purpose of this exercise. Titled "Damnatio memoriae" (Latin for "condemnation of memory"), it claims to depict fourteen "traits" of the "persecutor." From the very first "trait" it becomes clear that one is dealing with an anti-Semitic stereotypical endeavor: "The persecutor's first trait is that he descends from the clique [*tagma*] of those who brought communism to Europe. The group of allogeneic conspirators who dreamt of enthroning the Bolshevik revolution in all European countries, those Marxists in whose eyes the proletariat's dictatorship was but an ideological pretext aimed

59 Codrescu, Răzvan (2014). *Cartea mărturisitorilor. Pentru o istorie a învrednicirii româneşti*. Bucharest/Piteşti; Codrescu, Răzvan (2014). *Sfinţii Închisorilor în lumea credinţei. Din rezistenţa României creştine împotriva ateismului communist*. Bucharest.

60 Climescu, Alexandu (2016). IICCMER, centenarul Vintilă Horia şi apologia fascismului. "Diversitate igienică" sau confuzie organizată?, *contributors.ro* (April 8): www.contributors.ro/cultura/iiccmer-centenarul-vintila-horia-şi-apologia-fascismului-"diversitate-igienica"-sau-confuzie-organizata/.

61 Condurache, Cezarina (2015). *Chipuri ale Demintăţii Româneşti. Eroi ai Neamului şi Sfinţi ai Închisorilor*. Bucharest; Condurache, Cezarina (ed.) (2015). *Eroi Anticomunişti şi Sfinţii Închisorilor Reincriminaţi prin Legea 2017/2015*. Bucharest.

at fostering its own hegemony over Europe as a whole, that group represents the grandfathers of those persecuting us today."[62]

The "second trait," according to Lavric, is, in fact, a metaphor borrowed from the history of the Roman Empire where the name of those fallen from grace was banished from even mention, so that "two generations on, nobody knew anymore who that or that person had been." Similarly, "after having physically exterminated his enemies in the Communist prisons, the persecutor seeks to kill them for a second time, destroying their posthumous effigy. The destruction goes from symbolic diabolization to elimination from the annals of collective memory."[63] According to Lavric, this is precisely what the partisans of Law 217 seek to do.

According to the "third trait" attributed by Lavric to the "persecutor," he always poses in representative of the law. The author then spends over half-a-page in clarifying to his readers the distinction between legality and legitimacy, without even once mentioning the name of Max Weber, the real author of the distinction. But when he comes to the fourth "trait," he duly mentions the Nazi constitutional and international relations theoretician Carl Schmitt, citing as illustration Schmitt's diary, written between 1947 and 1951, when he was prohibited from publishing. According to Lavric, this illustrates the "humiliating posture of him whose right to reply has been taken away."[64]

One need not peruse all fourteen traits, for they are actually all summarized in the thirteenth, where Lavric unwittingly confirms the counter-narrative nature of competitive martyrdom:

> The thirteenth trait is that the persecutor atavistically hates those dignified examples that might belittle his acquisitive influence. This is precisely why the persecutor is seized with defiling frenzy [*frenezie profanatoare*] when he hears about heroes (partisans) martyrs (victims of Communist prisons) or saints (clerical figures with power of attraction over the masses). These figures are the totemic capital whose symbol upsets him beyond measure. Why? Because he intuits the field of symbolic force, primordially religious, emanating from such figures. A people that maintain the cult of its dignity examples has immunity that gives a lot of trouble to the persecutors. This

62 Lavric, Sorin (2015). Damnatio memoriae, in Condurache, Cezarina (ed.). *Eroi Anticomuniști și Sfinții Închisorilor Reincriminați prin Legea 2017/2015*. Bucharest, pp. 3–8, here p. 3.

63 Ibid., p. 4.

64 Ibid., p. 5f.

> is why these words—heroes, saints, martyrs—have a "democratic" smell driving the persecutor mad, why the zeal with which he seeks to annihilate their memory touches a draconic threshold.[65]

The Condurache-edited volumes were extensively cited in an article published by Professor Gabriel Andreescu, who joined the attacks against Florian, including personal family allegations for which he was forced to apologize when threatened with a lawsuit.[66] Andreescu, among the first to embrace the "symmetry," that is, the Double Genocide argument in Romania and for this (and other) reasons to oppose Ordinance 31/2002,[67] also honored the author of these lines with a few paragraphs, in which he reproached me with lack of compassion for the Iron Guard victims.[68]

But Andreescu was neither the most prominent nor the most influential among "mainstream" intellectuals to express misgivings or outright opposition vis-à-vis the amended law. The list is too long to reproduce in

---

65 Ibid., p. 8.

66 Nonetheless, Andreescu republished the same article soon after, replacing the original attacks *ad personae* with others, seeking to demonstrate that under the Communist regime, Florian, "who determines the policy of the Elie Wiesel Institute, promoted under the former regime Lenin's ideas, nourished the Nicolae Ceaușescu cult, and was an active supporter of communist ideology." The citations were an obvious effort to discredit the institute through "guilt by association." In fact, very few social science or history authors had a chance to see their work published if they declined to introduce quotes such as those mentioned by Andreescu. See his "Etica, politica memoriei şi 'legea anti-legionară,'" *Contemporanul* 4 (2016): 21–22. By the same (unjustified) token, I could associate Andreescu with the promotion of the Codreanu cult. Back in 2011, I stopped collaborating with *Contemporanul* following the publication by its editor-in-chief, writer Nicolae Breban, of excerpts from a book exalting the leader of the Legion. For details, see: "Doamnei Aura Christi, redactor-șef, 'Contemporanul. Ideea Europeană,'" *Acum* (July 15, 2011): http://acum.tv/articol/34873/.

67 Andreescu, Gabriel (2002). Necesitatea amendării Ordonanţei de urgenţă nr. 31 privind organizaţiile şi simbolurile cu caracter fascist, rasist sau xenofob, *Revista română de drepturile omului* 23: 8–19.

68 Andreescu, Gabriel (2015). Temele "legii antilegionare" din perspectiva eticii memoriei, *Noua revistă a drepturilor omului* 4: www.revistadrepturileomului.ro/propunere.html. I found it amusing to be charged with lack of compassion by the author of a volume titled *I hated Ceaușescu*—compassion being probably one of the opposites of hate (Andreescu, Gabriel (2009). *L-am urât pe Ceaușescu*. Iași). So much for Mr. Andreescu's "ethics," to which, however, one should add that such criticism is never included in his production destined for foreign consumption.

full, but two names deserve mention in particular—although (metaphorically speaking) oceans divide the quality of their product: Andrei Pleșu on one hand and Oana Stănciulescu on the other.

Radu Preda might have been the first to claim that the new law was discriminatory, calling it "pro-Communist," since it ignored crimes committed by the Communist regime,[69] but the most influential voice to insist on this aspect belonged to aesthetician, philosopher, and former minister of culture and of foreign affairs Andrei Pleșu. Though Pleșu and Andreescu are known personal adversaries, they were on the same "wavelength" vis-à-vis the amended legislation. In the best spirit of Double Genocide and of Holocaust obfuscation, Pleșu called for "symmetry" in addressing legally the two totalitarian legacies and claimed the tribunals that had sentenced wartime Romanian intellectuals had been under Communist influence.[70] Starting with the initial reactions to the amendent published by *Permanențe* (see above), this was one of the leitmotive that bridged between radical right, conservative, and even some liberal critics of Law 217/2015. As in other former Communist countries, there is a predominant sentiment in Romania that the trauma of Communist rule is neglected by the West, which imposed on the new post-Communist regimes a memory that is not its own. Sometimes (Andreescu's, but not Pleșu's case) the implication is that this imposition is instrumentalized by the Jews. In the preface of a book published in 2014 jointly with philosopher Gabriel Liiceanu [71] and conservative author Horia Roman

---

69 Fati, Sabina (2015). Interviu cu Directorul ICCMER: Legea Antilegionară Este Procomunistă, *România liberă* (August 23).

70 See the articles of Andrei Pleșu on August 3, 2015, September 7, 2015, February 1, 2016, in *Adevărul* and on February 18, 2016, in *Dilema veche* ("Memorie înjumătățită"). For an excellent response, see: Ioanid, Radu (2016). Aproximațiile păgubitoare ale domnului Andrei Pleșu, *Adevărul* (February 5).

71 The director of the publishing house "Humanitas," Gabriel Liiceanu was the first to indulge into comparative trivialization of the Holocaust and has become the main conservative promoter of the Double Genocide theory in his country. See: Liiceanu, Gabriel (2002). *Ușa interzisă*. Bucharest, p. 256f., and the repeated statements in the collection of interviews in Liiceanu, Gabriel (ed.) (2012). *Estul naivităților noastre. 27 interviuri 1990–2011*. Bucharest, p. 77, pp. 83–103, p. 133f., p. 164. On Liiceanu, see: Shafir 2002, p. 70f.; Shafir, Michael (2000). The Man They Love to Hate: Norman Manea's Snail House Between Holocaust and Gulag, *East European Jewish Affairs* 30(1): 60–81, here p. 74f.; Shafir, Michael (2010). Strange Bedfellows: Digging Under Post-Communist "Polished Polishness," *Holocaust. Studii și cercetări* 1(3): 157–185, here

Patapievici,[72] the authors wrote that European reunification has been pursued "exclusively through the westernization" of the East. This, however, had imposed on the region a "new iron curtain." Unlike the former curtain, the new one is "no longer dividing Europe in line with a geographic axe running—as the old one did—from Szeczin to Trieste, but runs through the soul of every European, dividing his memory and dissociating his sensibility." Those who lived behind the former iron curtain, they write, "have other memories, are *marked by other traumas*, remember differently and are otherwise wounded in their soul than [are] people in the former West." Post-Communist Westernization has meant the transformation of its memory (the allusion to the Holocaust is clear) "into a common memory." Yet, "[t]he other memory, the memory of communism and of the totalitarian trauma that did not last a decade but half a century, is still not common."[73]

Oana Stănciulescu is altogether another cup of tea. A rather inglorious journalist, she is editor-in-chief of *Express Magazin*, one of Romania's numerous weeklies without readership whose survival remains a mystery. She is also a TV journalist. Having worked for the private TV channel Antena 3 from where she was fired, she switched to another TV channel, Realitatea TV. Participating in a talkshow titled "Power Games" anchored by Realitatea TV general director Rareș Bogdan, she reapeated the Double Genocide argument that reproached Law 217 of not forbidding in parallel Communist propaganda. She displayed on the screen a few publications authored by interwar publications with Iron Guard sympathies, claiming that the new law aimed at cleansing them out of Romania's history. She also spoke at length and with admiration of Radu Gyr. Furthermore, Stănciulescu displayed an appalling lack of familiarity (or maybe ill will) with the background of the amended legislation; no one, she claimed, has ever denied the Holocaust in Romania. Her aggressive tone was completed by the anchor with readouts of an

---

pp. 175–177; Laignel-Lavastine, Alexandra (2004). Fascism and Communism in Romania: The Comparative Stakes and Uses, in Rousso, Henry (ed.). *Stalinism and Nazism. History and Memory Compared*. Lincoln/London, pp. 194–217, here p. 178f.

72 On Patapievici, see: Shafir, Michael (2013). Reconciliation at the Wrong End, in Blomqvist, Anders E. B. (ed.). *Hungary and Romania Beyond National Narratives. Comparisons and Entanglements*. Oxford, pp. 691–709, here pp. 696–701.

73 Pleșu, Andrei et al. (2014). *O Idee care Sucește Mințile*. Bucharest, p. 7f.; emphasis by the author.

article by Pleșu, who reiterated the obviously distorted argument according to which the *literary* and *philosophical* production of interwar authors with Iron Guard sympathies would be taken out of circulation; this would, he wrote, be tantamount with deleting from the world cultural patrimony the works of Ezra Pound, Louis-Ferdinand Céline, and Martin Heidegger.[74]

On her blog, Stănciulescu gave vent without any restriction to her views. She posted a message received from one of her readers, commenting that she entirely identifies with it. Among other things, the reader said: "when in Majadahonda, I am proud [of] Moța and Marin." The two were prominent Iron Guardists killed at Majadahonda while fighting on Franco's side. At other times, he went on, "I am Nae Ionescu and suffer for the white race." An ideologist of the Guard (though apparently never a registered member), Ionescu is famous for his ethnocratic views. Finally, the message went on to say, "I am Ion and Ică Antonescu, caught between Moscow and Berlin." Ică (Mihai) Antonescu was the marshal's deputy, executed together with him in 1946. Congratulating the author of the message, Stănciulescu wrote: "I feel the same. Maybe there are more like ourselves."[75] On one occasion, she publicly stated that the promoters of the law intended to take out of public space figures that were her "moral guide marks."[76] In January 2016, Stănciulescu participated alongside leaders of the Legionary Ogoranu Foundation in a symposium dedicated to the memory of a prominent Iron Guard leader, Gogu Puiu, who committed suicide while in prison.[77] One could hardly find a better example of "heroization" utilized for the purpose of competitive martyrdom and Holocaust obfuscation. This partly explains why Octav Bjorza, president of the Association of Former Political Prisoners in Romania (AFDPR), called Stănciulescu "our adoptive daughter."[78]

---

74 See the precedent of Romanian Writers' Union president Nicolae Manolescu, who made the same claim in 1997, coming out against voices objecting to the publication in Romania of a translation of a negationist book (Shafir 2000, p. 71). The Realitatea TV program is available on: www.dailymotion.com/video/x30csfg.

75 http://oanastanciulescu.ro/index.php/2015/08/13/mihai-boeru-sunt/.

76 https://www.youtube.com/watch?v=-dHBKk_j09M.

77 "Simpozion memorial Gogu Puiu și rezistența anticomunistă din Dobrogea": https://www.facebook.com/events/215691255438908/.

78 "Mesaj pentru Oana Stănciulescu: Ești fiica noastră adoptivă," *Știri sociale* (March 21, 2016): http://stirisociale.ro/mesaj-pentru-oana-stanciulescu-esti-fiica-noastra-adoptiva.

Stănciulescu as well as other intellectuals with similar sentiments bitterly attacked INSHREW director Alexandru Florian—with good reason, from their perspective. Florian and his institute had been the driving force behind the initiative to amend Law 107/2006. Once that purpose achieved, he was adamant on insisting on its application in public space. He demanded the names of streets or squares named in honor of those sentenced by Peoples' Tribunals in the late 1940s for war crimes be changed and statues erected in their honor be demolished. He also insisted that honorary citizenships bestowed on them be annulled. This turned him into the target of a hate campaign, including death threats. One of these quests (the case of exiled writer Vintilă Horia, who is on record for having been an admirer of Adolf Hitler) turned out to be particularly bitter, for Horia had achieved some notoriety in exile.[79] The campaign became even bitterer after the locality of Horia's birthplace (Segarcea) acquiesced in withdrawing the honorary citizenship it had bestowed on him.

However, as long as the Romanian cultural and historical establishment remains packed with overt and covert admirers of the Iron Guard, and as long as the judiciary writ large either ignores the current legislation or interprets it distortedly, the capabilities of INSHREW remain constrained. One example should suffice: in 2014, Florian received a reply from the Prosecutor General's Office in regard to his protests regarding the toleration of neo-Fascist groups in Romania. As in many other instances, Romanian prosecutors said they decided not to launch procedure against one of the several revived Legionary movement organizations, which was openly displaying the Iron Guard insignia on the building of its seat in Bucharest (see above). The prosecutors specified that the decision was partly based on the testimony of Șerban Suru, the organizations' leader, who said the Iron Guard emblem was not an infringement of the law prohibiting the display of fascist symbols, as it merely symbolized opposition to Soviet expansion. The second ground on which the prosecution refused to heed the complaint, however, was the opinion of one of the Academy's vice chairmen, who said historians are divided over

79 See: *Adevărul* (January 20, 2016); *Rost Online* (January 20, 2016); *Adevărul* (February 6, 2016); *Adevărul* (February 8, 2016). For responses, see: Ioanid 2016; *e-leonardo* (February 5, 2016); *Adevărul* (February 8, 2016); *Argumente și fapte* (February 28, 2016); *Observator cultural* (March 4, 2016); Climescu 2016.

identifying the Iron Guard as a fascist organization. The prosecutor did not venture the name of this person, but he is more than likely to have been Dan Berindei, the only historian occupying that position (see above).[80]

The 2015 change does not appear to have moved things further—at least not for now. When INSHREW again addressed the Prosecutor General's Office on the Iron Guard display of insignia and on provocative Nazi salutes made right in front of the INSHREW seat by leader Șerban Suru and posted on his organization's webpage, the response was that legislation does not apply retroactively and the offense might have been committed before Law 217/2016 went into force. A similar response was received concerning the case of outright Holocaust denier Vasile Zărnescu.[81] An opus by Zărnescu was launched at the "respectable" Mihai Eminescu bookshop in Central Bucharest in April 2016, but the volume had been on sale for more than one year. It is by no means different from those authored in the West by the likes of David Irving, Arthur Butz, or Robert Faurisson.[82] The author is a retired cadre of the Romanian Information Service (SRI), with the rank of colonel.[83] So far, the only instance when Prosecutor General's Office initiated the prosecution of offenders of the legislation prohibiting fascist-like manifestations was in 2014, and this was against members of the Hungarian minority exalting Hungarian irredentism.[84] This can hardly be accidental.

There is, consequently, little ground for optimism. Indeed, shortly after Stănciulescu's display of solidarity with, and admiration for, the interwar extreme right, she was nominated by the PNL for a position of member on the Administrative Council of Romanian TV. And while the appointment triggered a letter of protest addressed to the party's leaders and signed by prominent intellectuals, it also triggered a counterresponse by

---

80 I owe this information to Alexandru Florian.

81 Ibid.

82 Zărnescu, Vasile I. (2015). *Holocaustul. Gogorița diabolică. Extorcarea de "bani de Holocaust."* Bucharest. On earlier Romanian outright deniers, see: Shafir, Michael (2003). *Ex Occidente Obscuritas*: The Diffusion of Holocaust Denial from West to East, *Studia Hebraica* 3: 23–82.

83 Iacob, Bogdan Tiberiu (2016). Scandal de proporții: SRI are dispensa să nege Holocaustul?, *inPolitics.ro* (April 8): http://inpolitics.ro/scandal-de-proportii-sri-are-dispensa-sa-nege-holocaustul_18433163.html.

84 www.mpublic.ro/presa/2015/c_02_12_2015.htm.

her supporters.[85] What is more frightening, Stănciulescu's colleagues from Realitatea TV called the signatories of the former letter "traitors" in the service of the KGB, the Mossad, and the Freemasons. One was also back at the Nazi and Iron-Guard "zoologic" vocabulary that depicted adversaries as repulsive creatures—"worms." One of these, journalist Octavian Hoandră, said he could well understand Jewish support for the new law, but not support coming from ethnic Romanians.[86] In other words, not only the Judeo-bolshevism legend was back, but so was the Iron Guardist image of the "Yiddized" (*Jidovit*) being more dangerous than the Jew. The station's main shareholder, Cosmin Gușă, announced on the same program that he would never let Stănciulescu's critics set foot in the studio again.[87]

The new Administrative Council including Stănciulescu was validated by parliament on March 22, 2016, with the overwhelming majority of 312 votes in favor and 21 against. FCER president, Deputy Aurel Vainer, explained why Sănciulescu's positions on the Iron Guard disqualified her for that post and Markó Belá, former chairman of the Hungarian Democratic Union of Romania, announced his formation would boycott the vote in view of eulogies having been uttered in parliament for the Legionary movement for the first time in the post-Communist period. This referred to the position of Cristina Anghel, a senator representing the Conservative Party, who, among other things, reiterated the hoax about the Legionary movement's exoneration in Nürnberg; she also used the occasion to launch an attack on the Hungarian minority. Justifying the PNL proposal of Stănciulescu for the Administrative Council, PNL deputy chairman Puiu Hașotti misleadingly said Stănciulescu had not been defending the Iron Guard and had only referred to cultural figures with sympathies for it, who should not be eliminated from the country's national patrimony. To exemplify, he said that Radu Gyr had been not just the author of the Legionary anthem but also of other patriotic verse, from

---

85 *Observator cultural* (March 17, 2016); Andreescu, Crișan (2016). Oana Stănciulescu, scrisoare deschisă de susținere a jurnalistei în CA al TVR: www.dcnews.ro/oana-stanciulescu-scrisoare-deschisa-de-sus-inere-a-jurnalistei-in-ca-al-tvr_500490.html.

86 See the editorial by Ovidiu Șimonca in *Observator Cultural* (March 23, 2016).

87 Realitatea TV: *Jocuri de Putere* (March 17, 2016): https://www.youtube.com/watch?v=XFD8K1WNeSg.

which he recited. But the quoted verse had been authored by someone else—long forgotten nationalist poet Mircea Rădulescu.[88]

Following two failed designations of its candidate for the post of Bucharest mayor in the local elections due to be held on June 5, the PNL announced on June 13 it has designated Marian Munteanu as its candidate for the post.[89] The two PNL co-chairpersons, Alina Gorghiu and Vasile Blaga, told the media that Munteanu would be joining the party and that the designation was an illustration of PNL's quest to represent "civil society." Blaga added that he was "unaware of any dubious spot in Munteanu's past." Obviously, for the PNL leadership being founder of the first post-Communist Legionary party was not a "dubious spot." Instead, emphasis was placed on Munteanu's leadership of the anti-Communist protest in Bucharest's University Square following Ion Iliescu's election as Romania's first post-Communist president, which ended in his brutal beating by the miners called on the capital by the president. There was an obvious trace of "competitive martyrology" in this as well.

Initially, pundits and politicians who reacted critically to the designation tended to refer in passing or not at all to the candidate's Legionary past. This was another illustration of the dominance of the Double Genocide approach, albeit an indirect one. A notable exception was Bucharest University professor Ioan Stanomir, who instantly pointed out to the ethnocratic character of Munteanu's unchanged positions. [90] Instead,

---

88 *Romania TV.net* (March 22, 2016): www.romaniatv.net/plenul-parlamentului-valideaza-astazi-noul-ca-al-srtv_281837.html. The parliamentary debate on: https://www.youtube.com/watch?v=mkDoW7EqH78; Totok, William (2016). Aufstieg des Legionarismus zur parlamentarischen Leitkultur, *Halbjahresschrift-online* (March 2016): http://halbjahresschrift.blogspot.ro/2015/11/nachrichten-stiri-news.html. The Alliance of Liberals and Democrats (ALDE) published the next day a strong-worded communiqué denouncing the vote in parliament. See: *Agerpres* [official Romanian news agency] (March 23, 2016): www.agerpres.ro/comunicate/2016/03/22/comunicatdepresadanielbarbualde.

89 *Evenimentul zilei* (April 13, 2016).

90 Stanomir noted that by embracing him, the PNL "identifies with the ideological line organically leading from Legionarism to Nicolae Ceaușescu's National Stalinism and to the National tribalism of the Romanian Cradle and Corneliu Vadim Tudor." The "common denominator" of these, Stanomir wrote, "is the appeal to autochthonism, to autarchic isolation, and to ethnic messianism." According to Stanomir, "Marian Munteanu is the contemporary image of this hybrid, but no less toxic, formula." Stanomir, Ioan (2016). Marian Munteanu—etnocrația ca proiect politic, *contributors.ro*

they took distance due to Munteanu's alliance with former SRI director Virgil Măgureanu ahead of the 2000 elections.[91]

But ignoring Munteanu's activity in the early 1990s quickly ended. On April 14, several NGOs demanded from the PNL to withdraw support from Munteanu, pointing out that he "had and continues to have sympathies for a current of fascist orientation, from which he never distanced himself." It was further stated that Munteanu "is promoting a discourse entrenched in Orthodox-fundamentalist values, incompatible with democratic and even constitutional values."[92]

The Group for Social Dialogue began on April 15 gathering signatures for a protest letter addressed to the PNL. Among other things, the letter stated that the PNL was free to designate as candidate for the mayor's office whomever it pleased, but it must be aware of the fact that Munteanu's designation compromises liberal values with which he has nothing in common:

> The leap Marian Munteanu makes today from presidential candidate (in 2000) proposed by an alliance including Virgil Măgureanu's National Romanian Party to being the National Liberal Party's candidate for the General Mayoralty is just as stupefying as that made from the values of University Square to those of the Movement for Romania [which were] impregnated with ideologies that ravaged 20th century Europe.[93]

Specifying that as a governmental institution the INSHREW must stay away from interfering in elections, its Director General Alexandru Florian reacted only when Munteanu said on April 13 on the Antena 3 private TV channel in response to a question that Law 217/2015 was "anti-Semitic"

(April 13): www.contributors.ro/reactie-rapida/marian-munteanu-etnocratia-ca-proiect-politic/?cfcc.

91 The National Party led by Măgureanu announced the designation of Munteanu as presidential candidate of an alliance of which it was member, but in the end Munteanu did not run for the position.

92 *HotNews* (April 14, 2016): www.hotnews.ro/stiri-alegeri_locale_2016_bucuresti-20936014-institutul-pentru-politici-publice-alte-ong-uri-cer-pnl-retraga-marian-munteanu-are-simpatii-pentru-curente-orientare-fascista.htm. The list of signatories also included the following NGOs: Romanian Academic Society; Filia Center; Romani Criss; Communitarian Development Agency "Together"; Accept; Euroregional Center for Public Initiative; European Center for the Rights of Children with Disabilities.

93 *Revista 22* (April 15, 2016).

because it generated anti-Semitism.[94] The argument, of course, was as old as anti-Semitism itself, blaming Jews for its existence—in fact, an oblique justification for it.

FCER president Vainer's reaction to the designation was this time more cautious than what one might have expected or wished. He said he was "somewhat worried," but "for now we place question marks, to avoid utilizing exclamation marks." It was, however, "hard to believe" the choice was the best possible one, in view of the fact that "the movement to which he belonged in the past was very nationalist-oriented." Nonetheless, Munteanu "might respond and show that he has changed."[95] He did respond, and we shall presently show how. Finally, MCA director Marco Katz asked Munteanu to clarify his present position vis-à-vis the Legionary movement, Law 217/2015, and "the atrocities committed by the Antonescu regime." According to "information we received, in the 1990s you have led a pro-Legionary, pro Zelea Codreanu party, called Movement for Romania," said Katz in a letter addressed to Munteanu and published by the negationist and anti-Semitic *Rost Online.*

In his response to Katz, Munteanu claimed the MpR (Mişcarea pentru România) has never been an Iron-Guardist party, a "label" allegedly attached to it by the then ruling National Salvation Front in order to discredit it and hide its own Communist roots. The MpR ideology, he claimed, had been democratic and inspired by what he dubbed the "conservative-popular" ideology of Nicolae Iorga's National Democratic Party and by French and British conservative parties: "Despite an intoxication mechanically assimilated, the Movement for Romania was no neo-Legionary organization. In my vision, the Legionary movement is a historic phenomenon that emerged in Romania in a muddy context specific to the disorderly unrest preceding wars and is non-repeatable."[96] He also

---

94 "Declarația Institutului 'Elie Wiesel' în privința candidaturii domnului Marian Munteanu la funcția de Primar al Capitalei": www.inshr-ew.ro/ro/presa/comunicate-de-presa/288-declaratia-institutului-elie-wiesel-in-privinta-candidaturii-domnului-marian-munteanu-la-functia-de-primar-al-capitalei.html.

95 Udrea, Andreea (2016). Candidatul PNL la Capitală, pus la zid de ONG-uri și Elie Wiesel, *Evenimentul zilei* (April 15, 2016).

96 Marincu, Tudor (2016). Marian Munteanu răspunde acuzațiilor din ultimele zile, *Rost Online* (April 16): www.rostonline.ro/2016/04/marian-munteanu-raspunde-acuzatiilor-din-ultimele-zile/.

wrote that he is ready to send Katz the MpR's party statutes to demonstrate his points. But it is precisely those statutes that demonstrate the opposite, as I have proved in several articles written at that time. Sadly (or ironically), the title of one of these tracts was "Marginalization or Mainstream? The Extreme Right in post-Communist Romania." Looking back, I wish this prophecy had failed.[97]

Acknowledging that he had participated at meetings with veterans of the Legion, Munteanu claims that this was due only to show respect for those incarcerated in Communist prisons and that he was later attacked by them precisely because he would not identify with their ideology. His memory must have suitably failed him. Yes, the Timișoara-based wing of the Iron Guard that was linked to Codreanu's successor, Horia Sima, and published *Gazeta de vest* had indeed criticized him, but the MpR publication *Mișcarea* openly and repeatedly hailed Codreanu, to which the rivals concurred. He also "forgets" to mention that a Codreanu photo embellished his office.[98] He no less conveniently omits to mention his open letter to the former members of the Legion. In that letter, the MpR leader wrote that different times call for different strategies, but added: "we are all streams in one and the same river."[99]

He also writes in the letter to Katz: "I never was and will never be an anti-Semite. I am not, and will never be, a xenophobe. I am solidary with the suffering of the Jewish people hit by the holocaust [*sic!*] provoked by Nazism, just as the suffering of Romanians marks me and other peoples hit by Bolshevik terror." Leaving the Double Genocide premise aside, one

---

97 Shafir, Michael (1992). The Movement for Romania: A Party of "Radical Return," *RFE/RL Research Report* 29, pp. 16–21; Shafir, Michael (1994). The Romanian Extreme Right in the Post-Communist Period, *Sfera politicii* 15 and 16–17, pp. 4–6 and p. 16, p. 16f.; Shafir, Michael (1994). The Inheritors: The Romanian Radical Right After 1989, *East European Jewish Affairs* 24(1): 70–89; Shafir, Michael (1999). The Mind of Romania's Radical Right, in Ramet, Sabrina P. (ed.). *The Radical Right in Post-Communist East and Central Europe*. University Park, pp. 213–222; Shafir, Michael (2000). Marginalization or Mainstream? The Extreme Right in post-Communist Romania, in Hainsworth, Paul (ed.). *The Politics of the Extreme Right. From the Margins to the Mainstream*. London/New York, pp. 247–267.

98 Totok, William and Elena-Irina Macovei (2016). *Între mit şi bagatelizare. Despre reconsiderarea critică a trecutului, Ion Gavrilă Ogoranu şi rezistenţa armată anticomunistă din România*. Fragment published in: *Halbjahresschrift-online* (April 18): http://halbjahresschrift.blogspot.ro/2015/11/nachrichten-stiri-news.html.

99 *Mișcarea*, no. 1 (March 1992).

wonders how is Munteanu then explaining the repeated publication in *Mișcarea* of negationist articles translated from other languages.[100] Or his own statement, according to which Jews had invented a high number of Holocaust victims in order to "obtain illicit moneys from Romanian people through disinformation and manipulation of public opinion, with the complicity of treacherous elements who infiltrated the Romanian institutional structures."[101]

The rest of the letter merely repeats the claims already found in *Permanențe* and many other publications concerning Law 217/2015. Unlike the Western part of Europe, where "those who had instigated to crimes, those who took decisions and ordered executions were identified and their deeds were punished and criminalized," Romania's case is different. The coming to power of "the Bolsheviks" right after the war "superposed and toxically interfered with the natural process of sentencing deciders guilty of crimes and abuses." That natural process was replaced by one aiming at "cleansing a whole political and cultural class" out of pursuit of "power interests." According to Munteanu, "a great many number of people and cultural productions were labeled [by the regime] '*fascists*' '*legionary*' or more vaguely '*reactionary element*' despite having nothing in common with events or decisions of criminal nature." Such "unjustified trials and the traumas of affected families left deep sensibilities among those affected, inclusive of a background of vulnerabilities." The time that has hence passed "is too short and the mixed emotions stirred by such still living traumas have not yet settled." Hence, "hastening this kind of emotions might produce negative social effects, undesired by either of us." This, Munteanu concluded, "determined me to evaluate Law 217/2015 as being a Trojan Horse in some of its aspects," one that "serves the interests of groups or directions contrary to those entertained by yourself and me, namely the building of a stable and powerful society around values and fundamental democratic benchmarks."[102] In short, this was a considerably more sophisticated formulation of the same "Jews generate anti-Semitism" claim, and at the same time a veiled warning.

---

100 For example, *Mișcarea*, no. 5, (March 1–15, 1995).

101 Cited in: *The Jerusalem Post* (April 18, 2016).

102 Marincu 2016.

In an interview with the Mediafax independent news agency on April 17, Munteanu was asked whether or not he considered that Codreanu had been a criminal. He answered that "Romanian justice has said 'no,'" referring to the trial in which Codreanu was acquitted by a panel of sympathetic judges for killing Iași prefect Constantin Manciu in 1924. Pressed by the interviewer to speak in his own name rather than "Romanian justice," all Munteanu was able to come up with was: "I do not know, I have long been waiting from historians, from the justice system, to clarify that." The interviewer confronted him with a citation from his own earlier writings where he had said: "The historic experience of the Legionary Movement enriches the national Romanian patrimony, presenting it with a valuable model for the purity of its spiritual message, the firmness of its political discourse, the performance of its organizing techniques and above all its elevated capacity of national and Christian experience." Did he maintain that claim? Obviously embarrassed, Munteanu once again provided a typical "competitive martyrdom" reply: "Only inasmuch as it refers to the sacrifice of those imprisoned, who were fighting against Bolshevik occupation."[103]

The PNL's reaction was similar, only a lot less sophisticated. Defying all evidence, in an "Open Letter" addressed to those contesting Munteanu's candidacy, the liberals said the accusation concerning "the alleged proximity of Mr. Marian Munteanu to the extreme right was nothing but a myth" originally launched by former President Iliescu. Unlike the days of 1990, however, nowadays the accusations stem from

> organizations and people who apparently consider they have a monopoly over the idea of civil society. [...] As long as Mr. Munteanu is accused without proof of entertaining political beliefs that do not represent him in actual fact, the PNL appreciates such accusations as being part of a propagandist political discourse often encountered in the politicking game.

There were speculations in the media that Munteanu's designation as mayoral candidate was due to alleged orders received by the PNL from the presidential palace. Veteran journalist Ion Cristoiu, who specializes in conspiration theories, was only one of the theory's proponents (Cristoiu, who is an admirer of Codreanu's Legion, reproached Munteanu of

103 *Mediafax* (April 18, 2016).

not being a genuine exponent of its values!).[104] These speculations largely ceased following a presidential administration press release stating that President Johannis had "neither proposed, nor backed, nor imposed this candidacy on the PNL leadership" and was "consequently in no way involved in this proposal." The decision to opt for Munteanu, the administration concluded, "strictly belongs to the PNL leadership, reflecting internal [party] evaluations."[105] Indeed, PNL deputy chairman and former defense minister Teodor Atanasiu assumed the responsibility for having first contacted Munteanu with the proposal, although he claimed he had done so in the name of some ten PNL leaders backing the idea.[106]

The Gorghiu–Blaga PNL leadership's decision to promote Munteanu at the head of the party's Bucharest local elections campaign eventually began to be questioned and challenged from within the party's own ranks. One might have expected former PNL chairman Crin Antonescu, as initiator of Law 217, to take the pole position in this quest. Not only did Antonescu fail to do so, but he called criticism directed at the decision "agitation with hysterical accents." One could, according to the former chairman, "say anything about him, but not that he is an uninteresting person," and his role in the 1990 University Square protests "triggers in me positive emotions."[107]

The first dissenting voice unexpectedly came from former culture minister Alexandru Paleologu, who bluntly stated that he was not going to vote for Munteanu.[108] Petre Roman, nowadays a PNL member (he was NSF premier in the tumultuous days of 1990), revealed that in an article published in April 1994 in *Mişcarea*, Munteanu had called Liberal Premier I.G. Duca (shot by an Iron Guard squad on December 31, 1933) an "assassin." Duca had outlawed the Iron Guard. The PNL leadership, Roman said, had called for proof that Munteanu had Legionary sympathies. What better proof than this article, he asked. The revelation

104 Cristoiu, Ion (2016). Marian Munteanu-un pîrţ al lui Klaus Iohannis pe care liderii PNL l-au votat fără să-şi ducă mîna la nas, *Evenimentul zilei* (April 14).

105 Vintilă, Carmen (2016). Prima reacţie a lui Klaus Iohannis cu privire la candidatura lui Marian Munteanu. Preşedintele se delimitează de decizia PNL, *Evenimentul zilei* (April 15).

106 Zachmann, Sebastian (2016). Sforarul PNL. Portretul lui Teodor Atanasiu, omul care l-a reinventat pe Marian Munteanu, *Adevărul* (April 15).

107 *Ziare.com* (April 19, 2016).

108 Interviu—Paleologu despre conducerea PNL, *Mediafax* (April 14, 2016).

prompted historian and journalist Ion M. Ioniță to publish an appeal to PNL honorary chairman Mircea Ionescu-Quintus titled "Mr. Quintus, do not endorse Romania's return to the 1930s!" The nonagenarian honorary chairman (the only one to have abstained in the vote for Munteanu's designation) found himself in an awkward position, for Duca had been a friend of his family and his assassination prompted his own decision to join the party.[109]

Even worse for the PNL leadership was the announcement made by two Bucharest administrative sector candidates (eventually joined by a third) that their own electoral campaign would be conducted separately from that of Munteanu's. Ovidiu Raețchi, the party's sector 5 candidate, said:

> I have heard him [Munteanu] saying he did not know whether Zelea Codreanu had been a criminal or not. [...] I myself am certain he was one. I have also seen things written [by him] about the importance and the positive elements of the Legionary Movement. I believe [...] it was a terrorist movement that killed three premiers.[110]

A real danger of a split seemed now to be looming over the PNL. Under these circumstances, on April 20 the leadership of the PNL announced it was "withdrawing" Munteanu's candidacy, replacing it with that of Bucharest PNL chairman Cătălin Predoiu. Although Gorghiu tried to claim the decision for Munteanu had not been a mistake, she hardly sounded convincing; the more so as Predoiu, a former justice minister who aspires to the premiership, had refused to run on the eve of Munteanu's selection. The attempt was made to present the decision as consensual, but Munteanu admitted he had in fact *consented* to withdraw. The planned gracious exit turned out to be rather tumultuous, with Munteanu threatening to sue those who had allegedly tarnished his image. Ionescu-Quintus' attempt to embellish the outcome ("We have lost a mayor and won an

---

109 Mihalache, Mădălina (2016). Petre Roman: Munteanu a scris în 1994 că I.G. Duca a fost "asasin." Conducerea PNL să spună dacă se dezice de istoria sa, *Adevărul* (April 17); Ioniță, Ion M. (2016). Domnule Quintus, nu girați întoarcerea României în anii '30!, *Adevărul* (April 18).

110 *Hotweek.ro* (April 19, 2016): www.hotweek.ro/scandal-in-pnl-doi-candidati-ai-pnl-la-primariile-de-sector-se-leapada-de-marian-munteanu/; *știripesurse.ro* (April 20, 2016): www.stiripesurse.ro/inca-un-candidat-pnl-de-sector-se-delimiteaza-de-munteanu_991516.html.

honorary member of the PNL")[111] did not last more than a couple of days. On April 23, Munteanu announced he intends to set up a new political formation, with the purpose of changing the government. The executive, he said, must put the country "on a new path" where Romanians "would not be ashamed of being Romanians." The government, he added, must "respect our values, our identity."[112] In turn, Predoiu announced the PNL has eliminated Munteanu from its list of Bucharest municipal councilor candidates, where originally he occupied the first spot.[113]

What prompted the PNL leadership to rally behind Stănciulescu and then Munteanu is yet unclear. One possibility is that with the 2017 general elections approaching, the party feared Crin Antonescu's "sin" would be sanctioned by the nationalist segment of the electorate. Atanasiu, in a talk show on Antena 3 on April 14, mentioned as explanation the hope to enlist the nationalist electorate of the PRM, left leaderless after the death of Vadim Tudor. But the PNL traditional electorate (upper middle class; successful businesspeople) and that of the PRM (losers of the transition; pseudo-intellectuals of the former regime and former secret police) are in many ways mutually exclusive. An additional possibility is that the PNL hopes to sail the populist-nationalist winds blowing in other Eastern European countries (but also in Western Europe), such as Hungary, Poland, Croatia, and Slovakia.[114] In any case, in the PNL the unofficial narrative had once more prevailed over its official version. That a significant segment of civil society proved capable of rejecting that discourse is the good news.

111 *Evenimentul zilei* (April 20, 2016).

112 *Ziare.com* (April 23, 2016): www.ziare.com/marian-munteanu/stiri-marian-munteanu/dupa-primarie-munteanu-vrea-la-guvernare-lucrez-la-o-noua-constructie-politica-1418534. He formally launched the new party, called "Our Alliance-Romania," on August 10, 2016.

113 Romanian TV (April 25, 2016): www.romaniatv.net/catalin-predoiu-marian-munteanu-nu-mai-este-pe-lista-pnl-ciprian-ciucu-va-fi-primul-pe-lista-pentru-consiliul-general_288743.html.

114 See: *Adevărul* (April 13, 2016); *Spiegel Online* (April 26, 2016).

Simon Geissbühler

What We Now Know about Romania and the Holocaust—and Why It Matters

Introduction

While there are still major research gaps to be closed, events and contexts to be interpreted, and debates to be conducted about Romania and the Holocaust, the main basic facts about this dark chapter of Romanian history are well known and uncontested among serious historians.[1] But these facts have not yet entirely reached the mainstream of Holocaust studies nor has there been a comprehensive scholarly discussion on what their significance is for the understanding of the Holocaust in general.[2] Sometimes one has the impression that if the Holocaust perpetrated by Romanians and in Romania and in those territories controlled by Romania during the Second World War is taken note of at all, what happened in Northern Bukovina, Bessarabia, and Transnistria is seen as an aberrant or obscure element of the history and historiography of the Holocaust,[3] or a mere footnote, but not as an integral part of it.

Public knowledge in Romania about the Holocaust is thin, too. Romanian public opinion about Romania's role in the Second World War and in the Holocaust is still shaped by superficial knowledge and conscious suppression. The Holocaust is largely forgotten, or to use an expression by Paul Ricoeur, there is a strong will of "wanting-not-to-know."[4] For the majority of Romanians the Holocaust is not a phenomenon that

1 This contribution is partly based on my speech at Yad Vashem on October 29, 2015, and on my presentation at the EHRI Summer School in Amsterdam on July 10, 2014, as well as on my article Тринадцять тез про Голокост на підконтрольних Румунії територіях у липні 1941 року (13 Theses on the Holocaust in Romanian-Controlled Territories in July 1941) in *Holocaust and Modernity* 12(1): 87–104.

2 Altmann, Ilja (2008). *Opfer des Hasses. Der Holocaust in der UdSSR 1941–1945.* Gleichen/Zürich, p. 256f.

3 Kaplan, Robert D. (2016). The Antonescu Paradox, *Foreign Policy* (February 5): "an important, if relatively obscure, chapter in the overall story [of the Holocaust]."

4 Ricoeur, Paul (2006). *Memory, History, Forgetting.* Chicago/London, p. 448f.

has any relevance to them and to present-day Romania. According to a poll commissioned by the Elie Wiesel Institute in Bucharest in 2015, 62% of the respondents said that they have very little or little interest in the Holocaust. More importantly, not even a third of the respondents believe that the Holocaust also happened in Romania.[5] Among the meager 28% who state that the Holocaust also took place in Romania, only 19% say that the Antonescu government was responsible for what had happened, and 69% see Germany as the main culprit of the Holocaust in their country.

This data reveals a huge gap between public knowledge about the Holocaust and scholarly research. While the majority of the Romanian population now seems to accept grudgingly, as Ana Bărbulescu notes, "that something bad happened to the Romanian Jews during the war,"[6] only a small minority acknowledges who the perpetrators were: the Romanians themselves. The dissemination of information about the Holocaust in Romanian schools and universities is also fragmentary even though progress has been made in the last few years.[7]

In the following, I outline some of the main insights I believe can be gained from research into the Holocaust perpetrated by Romanians and in Romanian-controlled territories. Some of these insights and lessons learnt are derived from international research controversies, and they are intended to provide starting points for further research and especially debate. A few of these insights are rather general and might rightfully be considered common knowledge by historians. Such insights are addressed to a broader interested public. Other insights, however, are new and indeed are directed to the scholarly community which, as I stated above, has yet to fully acknowledge what the Holocaust in Romania means and why it matters.

---

5 INSHR-EW (ed.) (2015). *Sondaj de opinie privind Holocaustul din România și percepția relațiilor interetnice*. Bucharest.

6 Bărbulescu, Ana (2015). Discovering the Holocaust in Our Past: Competing Memories in Post-Communist Romanian Textbooks, *Holocaust Studies. A Journal of Culture and History* 21(3): 139–156, here p. 151.

7 Bărbulescu, Ana et al. (2013). The Holocaust as Reflected in Communist and Post-Communist Romanian Textbooks, *Intercultural Education* 24(1/2): 41–60.

Ten insights

Non-German perpetrators played an important role in the Holocaust

The Holocaust was a German plan, and the key architects and enablers of the *Endlösung* and the perpetrators were mostly German. But Daniel Goldhagen's reductionist thesis according to which only the Germans had the will and developed the initiative to implement the mass killing of Jews has long been proven wrong.[8] As Omer Bartov says, the Holocaust "was an international project."[9] The naming of perpetrators of other nationalities is certainly not intended to relativize Germany's responsibility. However, it is a fact that Romania was responsible for the death of over 300,000 Jews on territories its armies conquered and it controlled. Romania conducted a war of destruction on Germany's side and its own war against the Jews.[10] As Mihai Chioveanu writes, the Romanians "followed their own path, developed and later implemented their own project, in most respects independently from the Nazi one."[11] No other state—obviously besides Germany—carried out the Holocaust as independently and on the same scale as Romania.[12]

The German-centered approach, which dominated Holocaust studies for decades, was and is understandable, considering the principal role Germany and German perpetrators played. However, a comprehensive analysis of the Holocaust must also take into account the actions as well as the often considerable scope of action of non-German perpetrators in general and of Romania in particular. Indeed, the role of non-German perpetrators and the interaction between German and non-German perpetrators has received much more scholarly attention in the last few

---

8 Goldhagen, Jonah (1996). *Hitler's Willing Executioners: Ordinary Germans and the Holocaust.* New York.

9 Bartov, Omer (2008). Eastern Europe as the Site of Genocide, *The Journal of Modern History* 80(3): 557–593, here p. 560.

10 Förster, Jürgen (2005): Hitlers Verbündete gegen die Sowjetunion 1941 und der Judenmord, in Hartmann, Christian et al. (eds.). *Verbrechen der Wehrmacht. Bilanz einer Debatte.* München, pp. 91–97, here p. 96; Kaplan 2016.

11 Chioveanu, Mihai (2012).The Dynamics of Mass Murder. Grasping the Twisted Decision-Making Process behind the Romanian Holocaust, *Sfera Politicii* 2(168): 25–36.

12 Clark, Roland (2012). New Models, New Questions: Historiographical Approaches to the Romanian Holocaust, *European Review of History* 19(2): 303–320, here p. 303f.

years.[13] However, more research is needed, especially on the Romanian case.

The argument put forward by Holocaust relativists that Romania was simply following German orders and had no options for action is verifiably wrong. The fact that Romania's decision to reject German demands later in the war to send the Jews of the Old Kingdom to Auschwitz was determined by the rapidly worsening fortunes of war in the east and certainly not by a change of heart on the part of Antonescu and the Romanian regime[14] proves that Romania had a choice. Its choice at the beginning of the war was to kill as many Jews as possible and to ethnically cleanse Northern Bukovina, Bessarabia, and Transnistria and to establish and administer a dense network of ghettos and camps in Transnistria. Henry Eaton has correctly emphasized that Romania "was conducting [its] own genocidal operation."[15]

The Holocaust is more than Auschwitz

The Holocaust was the mass murder of six million Jews—men, women, and children—by the Nazis and other perpetrators during the Second World War with intent to destroy, in whole or in part, the Jews. Auschwitz is and should be an important symbol for the Holocaust. But the reduction of the systematic annihilation of the Jews to Auschwitz is problematic. Approximately half of all Jewish victims were not gassed or killed in a German *Konzentrationslager* or *Vernichtungslager*, but shot, tortured, beaten, or starved to death mostly in the east of Europe.[16] By somehow and probably often unintentionally reducing the Holocaust to Auschwitz,

---

13 Grabowski, Jan (2013). *Hunt for the Jews, Betrayal and Murder in German-Occupied Poland*. Bloomington/Indianapolis; David-Fox, Michael et al. (eds.) (2014). *The Holocaust in the East. Local Perpetrators and Soviet Responses*. Pittsburgh; Beiträge zur Geschichte des Nationalsozialismus 19 (2005). *Kooperation und Verbrechen. Formen der "Kollaboration" im östlichen Europa 1939–1945*. Göttingen.

14 Glass, Hildrun (2014). *Deutschland und die Verfolgung der Juden im rumänischen Machtbereich 1940–1944*. München.

15 Eaton, Henry (2013). *The Origins and Onset of the Romanian Holocaust*. Detroit, p. x.

16 Heer, Hannes (1999). *Tote Zonen. Die deutsche Wehrmacht an der Ostfront*. Hamburg; Manoschek, Walter (2008). "Wo der Partisan ist, ist der Jude, und wo der Jude ist, ist der Partisan." Die Wehrmacht und die Shoah, in Paul, Gerhard (ed.). *Die Täter der Shoah. Fanatische Nationalsozialisten oder ganz normale Deutsche?* Göttingen, pp. 167–185.

the actual scale of the evil done is reduced too. If the Holocaust is Auschwitz, then, as Timothy Snyder points out,[17] the mass murder of hundreds of thousands of Jews in the east—the "Holocaust by bullets"[18]—"can be excluded from history and commemoration."

This is not a theoretical discussion but a very real danger as opinion polls in Romania clearly show. The poll cited above, which was published by the Elie Wiesel Institute in Bucharest in May 2015, shows that 59% of the Romanian population associate the Holocaust with the German concentration camps and 46% with the gas chambers, but only 20% with Transnistria and 14% with pogroms.[19] As mentioned above, only 28% of the respondents say that the Holocaust also took place in Romania. Of these 28%, 69% believe that Germany was primarily responsible for the Holocaust in Romania; only 19% see the main responsibility with the Antonescu government.

Some Romanian revisionists argue to this day that there was no Holocaust in Romania because there were no extermination camps in Romania and because no Jews from the Old Kingdom were sent to Auschwitz. Some Romanian historians also feel compelled to underline that "no train carrying Jews has left Romania for Poland."[20] Others emphasize that the Holocaust perpetrated by Romania was "incomplete."[21] Both arguments are off the mark. They do not make the more than 300,000 Jews killed by Romanians and in territories controlled by Romania disappear.

In February 2013, a former university professor reasoned in a presentation at the prestigious Romanian Academy, and was even met with applause by the audience, that the "Holocaust in Romania is a huge lie. The Holocaust happened in Germany and Hungary, since only from

17 Snyder, Timothy (2015). *Black Earth. The Holocaust as History and Warning*. London, p. 208.

18 Desbois, Patrick (2009). *The Holocaust by Bullets: A Priest's Journey to Uncover the Truth Behind the Murder of 1.5 Million Jews*. New York.

19 INSHR-EW 2015.

20 Giurescu, Dinu C. (2000). *Romania in the Second World War (1939–1945)*. Boulder/New York, p. 212.

21 Iancu, Carol (2010). *Alexandre Safran et la Shoah inachevée en Roumanie. Recueil de documents (1940–1944)*. Bucharest.

these countries Jews were sent to Auschwitz."[22] Such claims, that because no Jews from the Old Kingdom were sent to Auschwitz the Holocaust did not happen in Romania, are at the least selective and a falsification of history. At worst, they are nothing else but outright Holocaust denial.

The symbolic centrality of Auschwitz to the Holocaust should not be challenged. However, the Holocaust was much more than Auschwitz.[23] As Timothy Snyder points out, there are malicious attempts to deceive as well as widespread "misunderstandings regarding the sites and methods" of the Holocaust.[24] It is crucial to broaden the perception of the Holocaust in the public mind to include the hundreds of thousands of Jews shot over pits in the east, killed in mass shootings, beaten, tortured or starved to death, also by Romanian soldiers and gendarmes and by their Romanian, Ukrainian, and other neighbors.

A dynamic cumulative radicalization led to the Holocaust

The Holocaust "did not arrive in Romania like a meteorite from outer space."[25] It was dependent not only on situational factors but also on "long-term cultural and psychological preparation."[26] There was no inevitable straight line from the anti-Jewish measures and violence of the interwar period to the mass murder of Jews in Northern Bukovina and Bessarabia in the summer of 1941. But there was a process of what Ian Kershaw has called in the German context a "dynamic cumulative radicalization"[27] in interwar Romania which could no longer be stopped after the massacre in Iaşi in late June 1941, and there was indeed nobody in the political and military leadership at that time who even contemplated stopping the escalation. The mass murder of Jews in the first few days of the

---

22 Cited in: *The Times of Israel* (March 7, 2013): www.timesofisrael.com/romanian-historian-publicly-denies-holocaust/ (accessed on January 23, 2016).

23 Benz, Wolfgang (2008). *Der Holocaust*. München.

24 Snyder, Timothy (2010). *Bloodlands. Europe Between Hitler and Stalin*. London, p. xiii.

25 International Commission on the Holocaust in Romania (ed.) (2005). *Final Report*. Iași, p. 55.

26 Kallis, Aristotle (2007). "Licence" and Genocide in the East: Reflections on Localised Eliminationist Violence during the First Stages of "Operation Barbarossa" (1941), *Studies in Ethnicity and Nationalism* 7(3): 6–23, here p. 8.

27 Kershaw, Ian (1994). *Der NS-Staat. Geschichtsinterpretationen und Kontroversen im Überblick*. Reinbek bei Hamburg, p. 157. The same argument is put forward by Eaton 2013.

war in Romanian-occupied territories was a continuation of the anti-Jewish policies of persecution[28]—but now in the radicalized context of the war of destruction.

Romania was one of the victors of the First World War, and it expanded massively. The new Greater Romania included all important ethnic Romanian settlements. But Greater Romania also became a strongly multiethnic state. Its Jewish population alone increased to 800,000. The representatives of the Romanian central state, however, saw Greater Romania as a homogenous, ethnic Romanian state. They were unprepared to deal with strong ethnic minorities. Instead of furthering peaceful coexistence, they pursued an aggressive and repressive policy of forced Romanization.[29]

Romanian anti-Semitism, which had traditional and often religious roots, but was also economically and increasingly racially motivated, radicalized throughout the interwar period.[30] Like German anti-Semitism, the Romanian strain was also driven by envy, the fear of failure, and the greed of the Romanian majority vis-à-vis the Jews.[31] Most of all, the Jews were the ideal scapegoat for the failures of the Romanian state, which gradually lost control over wide sectors of society. Especially after the "national disgrace" of summer 1940 when Romania was forced to cede Northern Bukovina and Bessarabia to the Soviet Union within a few days, the (of course, untenable) thesis of Judeo-Bolshevism, according to which all Jews were Communists and had plotted against Romania, served as proof that the Jews had to be eliminated.

---

28 Ancel, Jean (2011). *The History of the Holocaust in Romania*. Lincoln/Jerusalem, p. 216.

29 Hausleitner, Mariana (2001). *Die Rumänisierung der Bukowina. Die Durchsetzung des nationalstaatlichen Anspruchs Grossrumäniens 1918–1944*. München.

30 Pană, Georgeta (2010). Ortodoxia românească şi atitudinea sa de faţă de evrei, *Holocaust. Studii şi cercertări* 3: 113–132; Brustein, William and Amy Ronnkvist (2002). The roots of anti-Semitism: Romania before the Holocaust, *Journal of Genocide Research* 4(2): 211–235; Brustein, William I. and Ryan D. King (2004). Anti-Semitism as a Response to Perceived Jewish Power: The Cases of Bulgaria and Romania before the Holocaust, *Social Forces* 83(2): 691–708; Butaru, Lucian T. (2010). *Rasism românesc. Componenta rasială a discursului antisemit din România până la Al Doilea Război Mondial*. Cluj-Napoca.

31 For this argument, see: Aly, Götz (2012). *Warum die Deutschen? Warum die Juden? Gleichheit, Neid und Rassenhass 1800–1933*. Frankfurt am Main.

Violence against Jews was never the exception but the rule in interwar Romania. The perpetrators were frequently members of the Iron Guard and students although these two groups often overlapped. They did not act in a political and social vacuum, neither did they represent marginal splinter groups but counted on the more or less explicit support of the security forces, wide sections of society, and partly on the political leadership of the country. The Romanian state massively toughened anti-Semitic legislation throughout the 1930s. The increasingly aggressive and widespread anti-Semitism—one should point to the bloody pogroms in the summer of 1940 and at the end of January 1941 in Bucharest[32]—was a precondition for the war of destruction in the east and the mass murder of Jews in Northern Bukovina, Bessarabia, and Transnistria.

The massacre in Iaşi at the end of June 1941 represented a paradigm shift in both qualitative and quantitative terms. Approximately 13,000 Jews, men, women and children, were killed in Romania and mainly by Romanians.[33] The mass murder of Jews in the Romanian town of Iaşi was an important and—in the perception of the Romanian political and military leadership—successful test. Iaşi was by no means an isolated event but marked the starting point of the Holocaust in Romania and in Romanian-controlled territories in the east.[34]

The Holocaust in Romania was neither a coincidence nor did it happen out of the blue. It was not an unintended by-product of the war against the Soviet Union. The mass killing of defenseless Jewish men, women, and children in Northern Bukovina, Bessarabia, and Transnistria, the deportations, and the camps and ghettos in Transnistria were the results of a constant and accelerating radicalization.

---

32 Ancel 2011, pp. 71–88, 149–164; Ioanid, Radu (2000). *The Holocaust in Romania: The Destruction of Jews and Gypsies under the Antonescu Regime, 1940–1944*. Chicago, pp. 38–43, pp. 52–60.

33 Florian, Radu (1997). The Jassy Massacre of June 29–30, 1941: An Early Act of Genocide Against the Jews, in Braham, Randolph L. (ed.). *The Destruction of Romanian and Hungarian Jews during the Antonescu Era*. Boulder/New York, pp. 63–85; Voicu, George (ed.) (2006). *Pogromul de la Iași (28–30 iunie 1941) – prologul Holocaustului din România*. Iași.

34 Eaton 2013.

The mass murder of Jews was a pre-defined goal of the war in the east and was often improvised or steered from below

The objectives of the Romanian participation in the war in the east were by no means restricted to the "liberation" of Northern Bukovina and Bessarabia. They included what Ion Antonescu had again and again referred to as the "annihilation of the Bolshevist enemy"[35] as well as the comprehensive "cleansing" and "homogenization" of these territories (and of Transnistria).[36] Why would the Romanians have had to shoot thousands of defenseless Jews, to plunder and rape in order to recapture the two "lost" provinces? The mass murder of Jews was neither a by-product of the war nor collateral damage but an integral part and predefined goal of the Eastern Campaign.

But the mass murder of Jews did not solely depend on the wish of a dictator or the signature of a bureaucrat. Such a narrow intentionalist interpretation of events clearly falls short. The Holocaust was not defined and steered exclusively from above. Important impetus came from below, killing techniques and rationalizations for killing were invented and refined in the field by German[37] as well as Romanian commanders. Jean Ancel has underlined the "lack of foresight" and "the improvisation and extraordinary brutality" of the Romanian perpetrators.[38] The Holocaust in the east was often chaotic and improvised, especially in the Romanian case. Simple soldiers, gendarmes, and neighbors killed Jews, and they did it because they wanted to.

The improvised character of the Holocaust in Romanian-controlled territories can also be shown by the incoherent and polycratic administra-

---

35 "Ferngespräch mit Armeechef," in Bundesarchiv Freiburg, RH/20/11 (490), Kriegstagebuch Nr. 1, Chefsache (11. Armee).

36 Solonari, Vladimir (2009). *Purifying the Nation: Population Exchange and Ethnic Cleansing in Nazi-Allied Romania*. Baltimore; Achim, Viorel (2009). Die Deportation der Juden nach Transnistrien im Kontext der Bevölkerungspolitik der Antonescu-Regierung, in Benz, Wolfgang and Brigitte Mihok (eds.). *Holocaust an der Peripherie*. Berlin, pp. 151–160, here p. 154.

37 Snyder 2015, p. 148; see also Mallmann, Klaus-Michael (2008). "Mensch, ich feiere heut' den tausendsten Genickschuss." Die Sicherheitspolizei und die Shoah in Westgalizien, in Paul, Gerhard (ed.). *Die Täter der Shoah. Fanatische Nationalsozialisten oder ganz normale Deutsche?* Göttingen, pp. 109–136.

38 Ancel, Jean (1988). The Romanian Way of Solving the "Jewish Problem" in Bessarabia and Bukovina, June–July 1941, *Yad Vashem Studies* 19: 187–232, here p. 220.

tion of Transnistria in general and of the camps and ghettos there in particular.[39] Paul Shapiro made the same point in his study on the Chișinău ghetto: specific guidelines and orders were largely absent, directives "sometimes mutually contradictory."[40] The leadership, lower-level officials and collaborators in the Romanian as well as the local administrative structures, which were often intertwined, had considerable room for manoeuver to develop their own strategies to deal with the deported and local Jews in the camps and ghettos. This also opened the doors to massive corruption.

The lesson to be learnt is that the planning of genocide on the one hand and improvisation in its implementation on the other are not two mutually exclusive categories. In reality, they often overlap. The Romanian case shows this clearly. Underlining the importance of improvisation and of genocidal steering from below does not mean that the political and military leadership was weak. Quite to the contrary, because the leadership was strong or perceived to be strong, the perpetrators in the field felt shielded and were sure to fulfill their superiors' wishes even though these wishes were often not even explicitly stated.

Local pogroms in Romanian-controlled territories in the summer of 1941 were widespread

The topic of local perpetrators during the first phase of the Holocaust in the east became a focus of research especially after Jan Tomasz Gross' book on the Polish town of Jedwabne (see the contributions of Kai Struve and of Witold Mędykowski in this volume).[41] Even earlier, other authors had pointed out that a wave of pogroms took place in the borderlands on the eve of or during Operation Barbarossa—that is to say, before the *Einsatzgruppen* deployed.

In many places the Jews' neighbors themselves exploited the power vacuum between the departure of one government and the arrival of the next to initiate pogroms. Omer Bartov has spoken fittingly of communal

39 Baum, Herwig (2011). *Varianten des Terrors. Ein Vergleich zwischen der deutschen und rumänischen Besatzungsverwaltung in der Sowjetunion 1941–1944*. Berlin, passim, p. 101ff., p. 135ff.

40 Shapiro, Paul A. (2015). *The Kishinev Ghetto 1941–1942. A Documentary History of the Holocaust in Romania's Contested Borderlands*. Tuscaloosa, p. 18.

41 Gross, Jan T. (2002). *Neighbors. The Destruction of the Jewish Community in Jedwabne, Poland*. New York.

genocide and Aristotle Kallis of "localized eliminationist violence."[42] More recent studies by authors such as Sara Bender, John-Paul Himka, Wendy Lower, Alexander Prusin, or Witold Mędykowski have shed light on actions of locals in the summer of 1941 in what is now western Ukraine.[43] Kai Struve's monumental monograph published in 2015 on the summer of 1941 in western Ukraine is the most comprehensive oeuvre on the subject too.[44]

The pogroms initiated and implemented by local perpetrators immediately before, during, and directly after the start of Operation Barbarossa were by no means limited to Poland, Lithuania, or Galicia. Such pogroms were widespread in Northern Bukovina and Bessarabia, too. In many villages, *shtetlekh* and small towns in these regions, parts of the local population used the vacuum created by the retreat of the Soviets and the arrival of Romanian troops to instigate pogroms. Jeffrey S. Kopstein and Jason Wittenberg appropriately talk about a wave of "intimate violence" that swept over Eastern Europe in July 1941.[45]

Such pogroms took place in Stăneştii de Jos, Banila on the Cheremosh River, Milijeve, Nepolokivtsi, Kyseliv, and Sadagura—to name just

42 Bartov 2008; Kallis 2007.

43 Bender, Sara (2013). Not Only in Jedwabne: Accounts of the Annihilation of the Jewish *Shtetlach* in North-eastern Poland in the Summer of 1941, *Holocaust Studies. A Journal of Culture and History* 19(1): 1–38; Himka, John-Paul (2011). The Lviv Pogrom of 1941: The Germans, Ukrainian Nationalists, and the Carnival Crowd, *Canadian Slavonic Papers* LIII(2-4): 209–243; Lower, Wendy (2011). Pogroms, Mob Violence and Genocide in Western Ukraine, Summer 1941: Varied Histories, Explanations and Comparisons, *Journal of Genocide Research* 13(3): 217–246; Prusin, Alexander V. (2013). A "Zone of Violence." The Anti-Jewish Pogroms in Eastern Galicia in 1914–1915 and 1941, in Bartov, Omer and Eric D. Weitz (eds.). *Shatterzone of Empires: Coexistence and Violence in the German, Habsburg, Russian, and Ottoman Borderlands*. Bloomington/Indianapolis, S. 362–377; Mędykowski, Witold (2012). *W cieniu gigantów. Pogromy 1941 r. w byłej sowieckiej strefie okupacyjnej*. Warsaw.

44 Struve, Kai (2015). *Deutsche Herrschaft, ukrainischer Nationalismus, antijüdische Gewalt. Der Sommer 1941 in der Westukraine*. Berlin.

45 Kopstein, Jeffrey S. and Jason Wittenberg (not dated). *Intimate Violence: Anti-Jewish Pogroms in the Shadow of the Holocaust* (Draft Introductory Book Chapter Version 1.0).

a few examples.[46] In rural Northern Bukovina, the perpetrators were often, though by no means always, ethnic Ukrainians, in Bessarabia often ethnic Romanians.[47] But there are still very few systematic examinations of such local pogroms in Romanian-controlled areas based on the testimonies of survivors that seek to determine how and under what conditions local perpetrators plundered or murdered their Jewish neighbors. What is also missing are comparative studies looking at local dynamics in different parts of Eastern Europe.

Open to debate is, furthermore, the question of whether these local pogroms were "spontaneous" or initiated or aided from the outside. On the one hand, the Romanian secret service did indeed issue instructions to create a hostile environment for the Jews. A written plan—following up on oral orders given on July 8, 1941—was presented to the mobile section of the General Headquarters close to the frontlines on July 11, 1941.[48] However, this plan covered only central and southern Bessarabia. Furthermore, the first wave of pogroms in Northern Bukovina and the northern part of Bessarabia was already abating when this plan was issued to the commanders in the field. On the other hand, there is some evidence that Ukrainian nationalist groups, especially the Organization of Ukrainian Nationalists (OUN), instigated several pogroms in Northern Bukovina (see Alti Rodal's contribution in this volume).[49]

Diana Dumitru has argued that we "will probably not be able to find a definitive answer" to the question of whether the pogroms were

46 Geissbühler, Simon (2014). "He spoke Yiddish like a Jew": Neighbors' Contribution to the Mass Killing of Jews in Northern Bukovina and Bessarabia, July 1941, *Holocaust and Genocide Studies* 28(3): 430–449.

47 Solonari, Vladimir (2007). Patterns of Violence: Local Population and the Mass Murder of Jews in Bessarabia and Northern Bukovina, July–August 1941, *Kritika: Explorations in Russian and Eurasian History* 8(4): 749–787.

48 Instructions for the Propaganda units; Instructions for the Services of propaganda and counter-propaganda in the Army, USHMM (United States Holocaust Memorial Museum), RG-25.003 (Selected Records from the Romanian Ministry of Defense, 1940–1945), reel 11.

49 Fostii, Ivan [Фостій, Іван] (2000). Діяльність ОУН на Буковині у 1940–1941 pp., *З архівів ВУЧК-ГПУ-НКВД-КГБ* 2/4 (13/15). I thank Alti Rodal for pointing this article to me and for providing the English translation.

"caused by Romanian [or Ukrainian] provocateurs" or were "spontaneous."[50] In fact, it is unnecessary to make the distinction: many local pogroms and massacres in the summer of 1941 in Northern Bukovina and in Bessarabia were driven by the locals and more or less "spontaneous," but that does not exclude the possibility that some were incited and facilitated by outside actors. What is also a fact is that these local pogroms were by no means isolated events, but covered wide areas in Northern Bukovina and in Bessarabia.

The Holocaust in the east was not modern but bloody handiwork

The Holocaust is often presented as a modern, industrial, and structured process of mass killing in gas chambers. This view is only partially correct. The Holocaust in the east in the summer of 1941 in general and in the Romanian-controlled territories in particular was mostly perpetrated by acts of pure savagery. These massacres represent the "distinctly unmodern side of the Holocaust."[51]

Local perpetrators often shot their Jewish victims, but as they did not always have guns at their disposal, they sometimes used hammers, axes, hacks, or other agricultural tools to kill Jews or they simply beat them to death. In Valea lui Vlad in the south of Bălţi, local peasants killed Jews with sticks and scythes.[52] In Briceni, Romanian soldiers tied the feet of the local rabbi to a horse's saddle with a rope and let the horse gallop through the town dragging the rabbi to his death.[53] According to the survivor Chana Wiesenfeld, local Ukrainian perpetrators cut off the head of a pregnant Jewish woman close to Stăneştii.[54] In Nepolocăuţi, local peasants attacked the Jews with pitchforks.[55]

The soldiers usually shot their victims (Holocaust by bullets).[56] They were, therefore, directly involved in the mass murder. They had to pull

---

50 Dumitru, Diana (2011). Attitudes towards Jews in Odessa: From Soviet Rule through Romanian Occupation, 1921–1944, *Cahiers du Monde russe* 52(1): 133–162, here p. 150.

51 Wistrich, Robert S. (2003). *Hitler and the Holocaust*. New York, p. 224.

52 Carp, Matatias (2000 [1946]). *Holocaust in Romania. Facts and Documents* (*Cartea Neagră*) (edited by Andrew L. Simon). Safety Harbor, p. 171.

53 Visual History Archive (VHA), Eti Talis (33952).

54 VHA, Chana Wiesenfeld (15665).

55 Solonari 2007, p. 766f.

56 Desbois 2009.

the trigger and they saw the victims—men, women, and children—in front of them. Many mass shootings of Jews by Romanian units were unorganized and random. In Novoselitsa, for example, almost 900 Jews were killed by Romanian soldiers "in the streets and homes of the town."[57] In Zguritsa, Romanian soldiers are said to have used Jews as targets for shooting practice.[58] Close to Tăura Veche, a group of Romanian soldiers executed approximately 50 fleeing Jews on the roadside.[59]

In fact, the Germans regularly complained about the "inefficient way" in which the Romanians killed Jews.[60] They complained about the "complete disorganization" (*völlige Desorganisation*)[61] of the Romanians, the plunder and rape. In the *Ereignismeldung Nr. 67* of the *Einsatzgruppe* dated August 29, 1941, for example, the Germans heavily criticized the Romanian army: "Behavior of the Romanians: in general, no village [...] has not been looted, robbed, ruined, and defiled."[62]

Looking at the Holocaust exclusively through the prism of Auschwitz (mis)leads one into interpreting the Shoah as a modern and industrial assembly-line mass murder. But as we see from the above, there is more to the Holocaust than Auschwitz. When we look at the Holocaust perpetrated over the pits, in the villages and small towns, and in the ghettos and camps in the east, we understand that there was nothing modern about these mass killings; they were simply bloody handiwork.

The motives of the perpetrators were complex, and, yes, anti-Semitism was a key factor

The motives and scope of action of the perpetrators were complex and cannot be generalized. It is clear, however, that ideological and political as well as economic motives are crucial to explaining the violence

---

57 Ioanid 2000, p. 102f.

58 *Jewish Virtual Library*: www.jewishvirtuallibrary.org: *Zguritsa*: www.jewishvirtuallibrary.org/jsource/judaica/ejud_0002_0021_0_21521.html (accessed on January 23, 2016).

59 Carp 2000 (1946), p. 171.

60 Ancel 2011, p. 230; Shapiro 2015, p. 8.

61 "Ereignismeldung UdSSR Nr. 39 v. 31.7.1941," in Mallmann, Klaus-Michael et al. (eds.) (2011). *Die "Ereignismeldungen UdSSR" 1941. Dokumente der Einsatzgruppen in der Sowjetunion*. Darmstadt, p. 211.

62 "Ereignismeldung UdSSR Nr. 67 v. 29.8.1941," in Mallmann et al. 2011, p. 378: "Verhalten der Rumänen: Insgesamt [gibt es] kein Dorf, wo nicht geplündert, geraubt, zerstört und geschändet wurde" (translated to English by the author).

against defenseless Jews. Anti-Semitism and a widespread and strong belief among ordinary Romanians, who for years had been indoctrinated and subjected to the propaganda that all the Jews were Communists and responsible for the downfall of Greater Romania, certainly played a role in facilitating the mass killings of Jews.

Timothy Snyder writes in *Black Earth* that "age-old anti-Semitism cannot explain why pogroms began precisely in summer 1941."[63] Yes, it does, and Snyder himself partially gives the answer: state structures no longer existed by July 2, 1941, when Romanian troops invaded Northern Bukovina and Bessarabia, and anti-Semitic violence literally exploded. No one stopped or wanted to stop the perpetrators. Mass murder was possible only after the Soviet order had collapsed and the perpetrators in the field—the army, the gendarmerie, and the locals—had gained access to the defenseless Jewish population. There was a close relationship between prewar and wartime anti-Semitism,[64] the war itself and the extermination of the Jews.

In a new meticulous study on local perpetrators in Romanian-controlled territories in southern Ukraine, Vladimir Solonari shows that anti-Semitism was a crucial motivating factor. The locals who killed Jews were "often ideologically motivated, crusading, and vengeful murderers."[65] The deeply rooted anti-Semitic and nationalistic attitudes, combined with the largely risk-free opportunity to enrich themselves by plundering Jewish property, were the most important factors driving many perpetrators' desire to initiate or participate in pogroms and soldiers' readiness to shoot Jews. Few seem to have hesitated. Almost nobody opposed them. To create the impression that the locals as well as the soldiers got embroiled somewhat unwillingly in the Holocaust and that most of them stood by looking at what happened in disgust is false. In fact, the Jews also in Northern Bukovina and in Bessarabia were confronted by the stark "reality of pervasive betrayal."[66]

---

63 Snyder 2015, p. 150.

64 Grabowski, Jan (2015). Review: Timothy Snyder, Black Earth: The Holocaust as History and Warning, *Zagłada Żydów. Studia i Materiały* 11: 726–733.

65 Solonari, Vladimir (2014). Hating Soviets—Killing Jews. How Antisemitic Were Local Perpetrators in Southern Ukraine, 1941–42?, *Kritika. Explorations in Russian and Eurasian History* 15(3): 505–533, here p. 533.

66 Bartov, Omer (2016). How Not to Write a History of the Holocaust, *The Chronicle of Higher Education* (March 6).

The Holocaust allowed locals, soldiers, as well as the Romanian government to expropriate Jewish property and dispossess the Jews on a massive scale.[67] The seizure and plunder of Jewish possessions all over Europe, and especially in the east, was an "additional and extremely important factor."[68] Dora Nadler reports that the family's Romanian neighbors immediately took over their house in Râşcani and even put on their clothes when the Nadler family fled the town.[69] The flight aborted and the family came back to Râşcani to be confronted with the theft of their belongings. In Ciudei, the plunder was massive: "The windows were gone! The doors were gone! The bricks were missing."[70] In Czernowitz, Romanians immediately took possession of the empty apartments of deported Jews.[71]

Many Ukrainian local perpetrators, furthermore, hoped that the German invasion would ultimately lead to Ukrainian independence (see Kai Struve's contribution in this volume).[72] They believed that the Jews, as well as the Poles, were in their way to realizing this dream. In Northern Bukovina, the situation was more complicated than in western Ukraine as the Romanians played the key role in the conquest and the occupation of the region. The Ukrainians in Northern Bukovina mistrusted the Romanians, who were generally seen as enemies, but they anyway hoped that they could, with German help, become a part of a new Ukrainian state, which, of course, never materialized as the German leadership had very different plans. In Lujeni, close to Czernowitz, for example, marauding bands of Ukrainian farmers plundered Jewish property and killed Jews shouting "Heil, Hitler! Now we will have a free Ukraine!"[73]

---

67 Shapiro 2015, p. 1, p. 16f.

68 Arad, Yitzhak (2001). Plunder of Jewish Property in the Nazi-Occupied Areas of the Soviet Union, *Yad Vashem Studies* 29: 109–148, here p. 113.

69 VHA, Dora Nadler (19012).

70 Eisig, Moses (1998). *Yizkor Book for the Martyrs of Ciudin*: www.jewishgen.org/yizkor/Chudyn/chu001.html (accessed on February 28, 2016).

71 Grossman, Wassili and Ilja Ehrenburg (eds.) (1995). *Das Schwarzbuch. Der Genozid an den sowjetischen Juden* (edited by Arno Lustiger on the basis of the 1945 manuscript and the proofs of 1946–47). Reinbek bei Hamburg, here p. 153.

72 Struve 2015; Rossoliński-Liebe, Grzegorz (2014). *Stepan Bandera. The Life and Afterlife of a Ukrainian Nationalist. Fascism, Genocide, and Cult*. Stuttgart, pp. 241–289.

73 Yad Vashem, O.3, Sara Gruenberg, File 1744, Item 3739705.

Some ethnic Ukrainians and Romanians in the region hated the Jews because they saw them as the main agents and beneficiaries of the Soviet occupation[74]—which was, of course, not true. The topos of Judeo-Bolshevism was influential and instrumentalized by the German as well as the Romanian propaganda.[75] Serge Moscovici reports in his memoirs that the equating of Jews with Communists could be read and heard everywhere in Romania in the late 1930s and early 1940s.[76] In fact, invented stories of Jewish brutality against Romanians in Northern Bukovina and in Bessarabia in the summer of 1940 and during the one-year Soviet occupation became, as Mariana Hausleitner shows in her contribution to this volume, a leitmotiv endlessly repeated by Romanian propaganda[77] as well as by Ion Antonescu and other Romanian political and military leaders.[78] Even today, this rationale for the mass murder of Jews by Romanians is put forward by Romanian revisionists and neo-Fascists.

There were orders from the political and military leadership to ethnically cleanse the occupied territories and put in concrete form what was already well known to the soldiers when they crossed the Romanian-Soviet border: the Jews were to be liquidated. It could be argued that within the context of a dynamic cumulative radicalization and once the Romanian armed forces had access to the defenseless Jewish population, these orders would not even have been necessary for the implementation of the Holocaust in Romanian-controlled territories in the east.

Doubtlessly, there was group pressure but Romanian soldiers were not forced to kill Jews. Like their German counterparts,[79] Romanian soldiers were not punished if they did not want to participate in shootings of Jews. It is also plausible to claim that local perpetrators killed their Jewish neighbors simply because they wanted to. Many Romanian and local

74 Struve 2015; Solonari 2007, p. 771.
75 Solonari 2014.
76 Moscovici, Serge (1997). *Chronique des années égarées*. Paris, p. 216.
77 Achim 2009, p. 152.
78 Shapiro 2015, p. 11.
79 Snyder 2015, p. 190.

perpetrators acted extremely brutally, as testimonies from survivors indicate. The rape of Jewish women and girls by Romanian soldiers was widespread.[80]

Underlining the importance of anti-Semitism and of anti-Semitic propaganda does not render situational factors irrelevant. In fact, these two elements go hand in hand. Anti-Semitic violence broke out in the summer of 1941 because the war situation and the power vacuum lowered or completely removed the barriers to such behavior. With the "suspension of those hindrances that keep violence (however desirable) at bay" and the "promise of impunity and reward,"[81] the perpetrators—locals, mixed groups, and military and police units—initiated mass killings of Jews—with the explicit approval of the military and political leadership.

The Holocaust in the east was often a public event

After the war, a myth developed among the general public in Germany that claimed ordinary people did not know and did not hear about the mass killings of Jews. This myth is nonsense as more recent studies, for example, by Frank Bajohr and Dieter Pohl as well as Peter Longerich convincingly show.[82] The same myth was constructed and handed down in Romania and in the territories in the east that Romania conquered in the Second World War and are now part of Ukraine and the Republic of Moldova.

But this myth is nonsense in the Romanian case, too. In most circumstances, the local non-Jewish population in Northern Bukovina and in Bessarabia saw first-hand what happened to their Jewish neighbors. The local population knew very well what was going on and who the perpetrators and the collaborators were. Jews were taken from their houses,

---

80 Podolsky, Anatoly (2010). The Tragic Fate of Ukrainian Jewish Women under Nazi Occupation, 1941–1944, in Hedgepeth, Sonja M. and Rochelle G. Saidel (eds.). *Sexual Violence against Jewish Women during the Holocaust*. Waltham, pp. 94–107; Geissbühler, Simon (2013). The Rape of Jewish Women and Girls during the First Phase of the Romanian Offensive in the East, July 1941: A Research Agenda and Preliminary Findings, *Holocaust Studies. A Journal of Culture and History* 19(1): 59–80.

81 Kallis 2007: 8.

82 Bajohr, Frank and Dieter Pohl (2008). *Massenmord und schlechtes Gewissen. Die deutsche Bevölkerung, die NS-Führung und der Holocaust*. Frankfurt am Main; Longerich, Peter (2007). *"Davon haben wir nichts gewusst!" Die Deutschen und die Judenverfolgung 1933–1945*. München.

beaten, tortured, and killed. As Jan Tomasz Gross writes, "[The locals] knew right away, and they knew pretty much everything there was to know."[83] But there was no noteworthy opposition or resistance against the mass murder of Jews either from the population in the capital or from the local population in Bessarabia, Northern Bukovina, and Transnistria.[84]

In Edineţi, for example, hundreds of Jews were brought to the Jewish cemetery on the outskirts of the town and executed there. The locals surely saw and heard what happened. In Climăuţi, around 400 Jews from the village and the surroundings were also shot in fields close to the village's center. In Costești, villagers helped to round up the Jews and led them through the village to the fields where they were shot by Romanian soldiers.[85]

It was not very difficult to get relatively precise information already in July/August 1941 in Bucharest about the Holocaust in the east. There is ample evidence that interested observers in Bucharest knew what was going on.[86] In a short article published on August 5, 1941, the Jewish Telegraphic Agency (JTA) estimated that "[approximately] 10,000 civilian Jews have been executed in Rumania since the outbreak of the Russo-German war on the allegation that they were pro-Russian."[87]

On August 21, 1941, Mihail Sebastian noted in his diary his impressions of a discussion with a cavalry lieutenant returning from a tour on the frontlines in the east: "He explained many things about the extermination of the Jews on both sides of the Dniester. Dozens, hundreds, thousands of Jews shot. He, a simple lieutenant, could have killed at command or single-handedly as many Jews he had wanted to."[88] Already on July 18, 1941, Sebastian wrote that he had heard that the Romanian

83 Gross, Jan T. (2007). *Fear. Anti-Semitism in Poland after Auschwitz*. New York, p. 170.

84 Solonari 2007, p. 787.

85 Geissbühler, Simon (2013). *Blutiger Juli. Rumäniens Vernichtungskrieg und der vergessene Massenmord an den Juden 1941*. Paderborn, pp. 72–74, p. 76, p. 63.

86 Iancu, Carol (2007). *Alexandre Safran. Une vie de combat, un faisceau de lumière*. Montpellier, p. 114f.

87 *JTA Jewish News Archive*: report dated August 5, 1941: http://archive.jta.org (accessed on January 31, 2016);

88 Sebastian, Mihail (2005). *"Voller Entsetzen, aber nicht verzweifelt." Tagebücher 1935–44*. Berlin, p. 532.

army had orders to shoot all Jews in Northern Bukovina and in Bessarabia. On July 16, 1941, he had seen a picture in the *Ordinea* newspaper depicting a long row of miserable-looking women and small children, their clothes in shreds, but not one single man among them. The subtitle of the picture said that these were Judeo-Communists captured by the Romanian army who would now pay for their misdeeds.[89]

The Holocaust in the east was no secret. Villagers, bystanders, and local perpetrators as well as soldiers all saw what happened or directly participated in it. They talked about it and the news spread. Information was readily available for those who wanted to know.

Survivors' testimonies are a key source

As Omer Bartov, Waitman Wade Beorn, and others have argued, researchers should no longer ignore the testimonies of survivors.[90] In fact, writing the history of the Holocaust without taking into account the perspective of the victims is one-sided and will yield a distorted and incomplete picture of the multifaceted and complex reality of the Holocaust. Obviously, the perpetrators had little interest to document their crimes in detail. Often, as Henry Eaton shows in his contribution to this volume, statements of the perpetrators were flat-out lies. Frequently documents incriminating perpetrators were falsified or destroyed later on. In many cases, survivors' testimonies therefore represent the only evidentiary material on the topic.

The case of Romania underlines that there is a wealth of untapped information such as taped testimonies in the University of Southern California Shoah Foundation Institute (Visual History Archives), written reports in Yad Vashem's Record Group O.3, the oral history collection at the USHMM, Jewish memory (yizkor) books, and memoirs of Holocaust survivors to be utilized more systematically in the future. Some contributions in this volume attest to the fact that much can be learned about the

---

89 Ibid., p. 512.

90 Bartov 2008, p. 583; Bartov (2011). Wartime Lies and Other Testimonies: Jewish-Christian Relations in Buczacz, 1939–1944, *East European Politics and Society* 24(3): 486–511; Beorn, Waitman Wade (2014). *Marching into Darkness. The Wehrmacht and the Holocaust in Belarus*. Cambridge/London, pp. 22–24.

Holocaust by consulting and carefully crosschecking on survivors' testimonies. Obviously, we must read these testimonies critically and in the light of whatever other evidence may be available.

The Holocaust in Romanian-controlled territories is largely "forgotten" and still marginalized in the public discourse

The exposure of the general public in Romania and in many other countries of Central and Eastern Europe to the Holocaust and knowledge about the history of it has been and continues to be minimal. Under the Communist regimes acknowledgment of the Holocaust was all but impossible. The Shoah was a taboo for almost 50 years. Romania was no exception to that rule.[91] Having been a close ally of Nazi Germany and having implemented the mass murder of Jews and of Gypsies autonomously, Romania under Communist rule felt an even more acute urge to draw a veil of silence over its inglorious past.[92]

The breakup of the Soviet bloc and the end of the Ceaușescu regime did not lead to a comprehensive and meticulous reassessment of Romanian history. Quite to the contrary, in the 1990s, mainstream Romanian historiography sought to create the basis for a new national self-esteem. The Antonescu cult reemerged. The ghosts of the past—Fascist as well as Communist—and especially questions about Romania's collaboration with Nazi Germany and its involvement in the Holocaust in the east were left undisturbed. Fascism was presented as an alien, German concept and Romania as a victim "innocent of any wrongdoing or crime."[93] Throughout the 1990s, high-ranking government officials regularly denied that Romania had anything to do with the Holocaust. In fact, this "recurring cycle of official denial was not broken until 2003–04."[94]

Even today, the revisionists, who try to minimize or trivialize Romanian crimes during the Second World War in general and Romania's responsibility for the Holocaust in Northern Bukovina, Bessarabia, and Transnistria in particular, are still influential in Romania (see Michael

91 Cioflâncă, Adrian (2004). A "Grammar of Exculpation" in Communist Historiography: Distortion of the History of the Holocaust Under Ceausescu, *Romanian Journal of Political Science* 4(2): 29–46.

92 Weber, Petru (2004). The Public Memory of the Holocaust in Postwar Romania, *Studia Hebraica* 4: 341–348.

93 Cioflâncă 2004: 36.

94 Shapiro 2015, p. 91.

Shafir's contribution in this volume).[95] Against this backdrop, it is not surprising that in 2012 a young senator from the Socialist Party said on a TV show that only twenty-four Jews were killed by Germans in Iași at the end of June 1941.[96] If a young politician with a law degree does not know better—or does not want to know better—what can be expected of the general public?

Another thorny issue is the role of the Romanian army and of "simple" Romanian soldiers in the Holocaust.[97] Lucian Nastasă correctly observed that the "Odessa massacre and similar crimes, which the so-called 'heroic Romanian army' committed in World War II, are still essentially a taboo in society—also among historians."[98] The myth that the Romanian military led a "just" or "preventive" war of liberation in the summer of 1941 is still pervasive in Romania. Indeed, it is not a paradox,[99] but a historical fact that the "liberation" and "reintegration" of Northern Bukovina and Bessarabia went hand in hand with the ethnic cleansing of these territories and the annihilation of tens of thousands of Jews. Furthermore, the Romanian army did not stop once it had recuperated these areas, but marched on eastward committing—like the German army—innumerable war crimes on its bloody way.

Holocaust memory in Romania as well as in those areas controlled by Romania during the Second World War which are now part of Ukraine and the Republic of Moldova is fragile, fragmented, and often guided by a semi-passive, semi-active attitude of wanting-not-to-know. To claim, as has been done by Marek Kucia, that Holocaust "memory has developed

---

95 Shafir, Michael (2014). Unacademic Academics: Holocaust Deniers and Trivializers in Post-Communist Romania, *Nationalities Papers* 42(6): 942–964; Geissbühler, Simon (2012). Staring at the Past with Eyes Wide Shut: Holocaust Revisionism and Negationism in Romania, *Israel Journal of Foreign Affairs* VI(3): 127–135.

96 Segal, Sahar and Elisheva Goldberg (2012). Where Did Romania's Holocaust Go?, *The Daily Beast* (August 8).

97 For an overview of the results of the fierce controversy and the scholarly research about the crimes of the Wehrmacht, see: Hartmann, Christian et al. (eds.). *Verbrechen der Wehrmacht. Bilanz einer Debatte*. München 2005.

98 Cited in: Verseck, Keno (2012). Romania's Forgotten Holocaust: Filmmaker Confronts Leaders Over Silence, *Spiegel Online International*: www.spiegel.de/international/europe/filmmaker-confronts-leaders-over-forgotten-holocaust-in-romania-a-867058.html (accessed on May 29, 2016).

99 Florian, Alexandru (2015). Prefață, in Geissbühler, Simon (2015). *Iulie însângerat. România și Holocaustul din vara lui 1941*. Bucharest, pp. 5–7.

immensely [...] particularly in Eastern Europe"[100] over the last two decades is an undue and naively optimistic generalization at best and a dangerous denial of the empirical evidence at worst.

A big gap exists between public knowledge about the Holocaust and scholarly research. Large parts of the Romanian population as well as people now living in those places where atrocities were perpetrated by Romanians do not want to know. Most traces of Jewish life before the Holocaust and of the Holocaust itself have been neglected or even erased.[101] Jewish cemeteries in Northern Bukovina, southwestern Ukraine, and the Republic of Moldova are often in a state of neglect. Very few synagogues still exist, and most have long since been destroyed or converted for other purposes. Mass graves are difficult to locate and most often not even recorded on maps. There are only very few and no new Jewish or Holocaust museums in these regions. Omer Bartov's writings about Galicia could just as well apply to Northern Bukovina, Bessarabia, and Transnistria and, to a lesser degree, to parts of Romania as well: "When one travels deeper into [these regions], one discovers [...] remarkable neglect, suppression, and even destruction of all signs of the land's multiethnic past and that past's tragic end in a campaign of mass murder."[102] There are some positive countertrends, however, but it is too early to speak about a strong wind of change when it comes to Holocaust memory in present-day Romania.

Wanting-not-to-know has much to do with a conscious decision to remain unaware. Humans often dismiss unpleasant and painful facts: the will not to know follows the will of self-delusion.[103] On the other hand, remembrance is, as Yosef Hayim Yerushalmi has underlined, also a question of justice.[104] The current and future Romanian generations are not guilty of the crimes committed by their forefathers. But they have a special responsibility to want-to-know.

---

100 Kucia, Marek (2016). The Europeanization of the Holocaust Memory and Eastern Europe, *East European Politics and Societies and Cultures* 30(1): 97–119, p. 115.

101 Bartov, Omer (2007). *Erased. Vanishing Traces of Jewish Galicia in Present-Day Ukraine*. Princeton/Oxford.

102 Bartov 2007, p. 40.

103 Sofsky, Wolfgang (2016). Glauben, Leugnen, Hoffen, *Neue Zürcher Zeitung* (February 13), p. 43.

104 Yerushalmi, Yosef Hayim (1996). *Zakhor. Jewish History and Jewish Memory*. Seattle/London, p. 117.

As I have underlined in the introduction to this volume, one does find signs of a change in mentality. Romania's presidency of the International Holocaust Remembrance Alliance (IHRA) 2016–17 is one such encouraging sign. Furthermore, more young historians—including Romanians—are now doing research on Romania and the Holocaust. Different organizations, research groups, and individuals are working on specific aspects of Romania and the Holocaust. In July 2016, the parliament of the Republic of Moldova "adopted" the 2004 Final Report on the Holocaust in Romania, thus recognizing the crimes committed in Bessarabia by the Romanian authorities.[105] But it would be fatuous and naive to believe that such a profound transformation could take place rapidly and without the opposition of certain political and societal forces.

Remembrance and the will to deal with the past should not or not primarily be imposed from outside or from above. But researchers—both Romanian and international—can and are contributing to change by exposing again and again the historical facts as we can reconstruct them on the basis of the sources.

Conclusion

The Holocaust is one of the best-researched events of the 20th century. Scholarly publications on this subject fill entire libraries. To brush aside the cumulative research of seven decades and to deny the Holocaust in general and Romania's complicity in the Shoah in particular is only comparable to someone who earnestly claims that the earth is flat. This being said, there are still major gaps in our knowledge about the Holocaust. The Holocaust perpetrated by Romanians and by locals in Northern Bukovina, Bessarabia, and Transnistria is one of the less developed fields of research. The Holocaust in Romanian-controlled territories in general and the first phase of the mass murder of Jews in Northern Bukovina and in Bessarabia in the summer of 1941 in particular are topics that warrant

---

105 "Parlamentul de la Chișinău și-a asumat Raportul Wiesel despre participarea României la Holocaust," *Radio Europa Liberă* (July 22, 2016); e-mail by Michael Shafir to the author on July 24, 2016. This step is positive, however, it will take much (more) effort for the Republic of Moldova to broadly and effectively deal with its past, especially the local Holocaust perpetrators and collaborators.

more scholarly attention. Furthermore, with the passage of time since the Holocaust, new interpretations inevitably emerge.[106]

The main objective of the ten insights presented above is to stimulate debate. Each of these ten insights could and should be taken as starting points for additional research. What we now know about Romania and the Holocaust and what further research will bring to the surface probably won't force us to fundamentally rewrite the history of the Holocaust. Obviously, however, history is never written once and for all but is being constantly rewritten and reinterpreted as we view the past from the perspective of the present.[107] What we can learn from the history of Romania and the Holocaust matters because it complements, sharpens, and broadens our understanding of the origins and the background, the contexts, the perpetrators, collaborators and bystanders, the victims, and the aftermath of the Holocaust in general.

Perpetrators and collaborators from nations other than Germany played an important role in the Holocaust, also those from Romania, Germany's most important ally in the Eastern Campaign, which occupied Northern Bukovina, Bessarabia, and Transnistria. Most Romanian perpetrators were soldiers and gendarmes, but locally instigated pogroms in Romanian-controlled territories were widespread too.

The Holocaust was not a coincidental event; a dynamic cumulative radicalization led to it, as the Romanian case clearly shows. The motives of the perpetrators were complex, but anti-Semitism was a key factor. This anti-Semitism among the perpetrators plainly burst into the open when the barriers to violence and ultimately genocide, especially state structures, came down in the context of the war of destruction—as Timothy Snyder has pointed out the obvious or unsurprising.[108] While the "purification" of Romania and of the reconquered territories in the east,[109] which meant the elimination of the Jews by whatever means, was a predefined goal of the war in the east, the Holocaust was often improvised and steered from below.

The Holocaust was much more than Auschwitz. The reduction of the Holocaust to Auschwitz is not only inaccurate historically; it also plays

106 Bartov 2016.

107 Ibid.

108 Snyder 2015, p. 234; Bartov 2016; Grabowski 2015.

109 Solonari 2009.

into the hands of Holocaust relativists or trivializers in Eastern Europe. Around half of the victims were not gassed or otherwise killed in a German *Vernichtungslager*, but annihilated in the east in the Holocaust by bullets and by bloody handiwork. Mistaken reductionism also blocks one's view of the fact that the Holocaust was only partially an industrial and rationalized endeavor. It further disguises the fact that the Holocaust did not happen exclusively in some isolated zones, namely in concentration and death camps, but in or on the outskirts of towns and villages all over Eastern Europe.

Contributors

Diana Dumitru is an Associate Professor of History at Ion Creangă State Pedagogical University of Moldova. Her first book on Great Britain's role in the union of the Romanian Principalities was published in 2010, and her second book, *The State, Antisemitism and the Collaboration in the Holocaust: The Borderlands of Romania and the Soviet Union*, was published by Cambridge University Press in 2016. Her articles have been published in *Holocaust and Genocide Studies, Cahiers du monde russe*, and *Yad Vashem Studies*, among others. Her *World Politics* article "Constructing Interethnic Conflict and Cooperation: Why Some People Harmed Jews and Others Helped Them during the Holocaust in Romania" received the 2012 Mary Parker Follett Award for the best article or chapter published in the field of politics and history.

Henry L. Eaton is Emeritus Professor of History at the University of North Texas. He received his Ph.D. in history at the University of Illinois. He taught Russian history, the Holocaust, and a course on Great Books. In 2013, he has published *The Origins and Onset of the Romanian Holocaust* (Wayne State University Press). In 1990–91, he was a Fulbright Scholar in Iași, Romania.

Tuvia Friling is a Professor and a Senior Researcher at the Ben-Gurion Research Institute at the Ben-Gurion University of the Negev. Friling was the head of the Ben-Gurion Institute (1993–2001) and the State Archivist of Israel (2001–4). Among his publications are *Arrow in the Dark: David Ben-Gurion, the Yishuv Leadership and Rescue Attempts during the Holocaust* (2005), *A Story of a Capo in Auschwitz. History, Memory and Politics* (2014), *Critique du post-sionisme: Réponses aux "nouveaux historiens" israéliens* (editor, 2004), and *Ambitious Moves. Cooperation between Revisionist Zionists and Anti-Nazi Germans in Attempt to Defeat the Third Reich* (2015).

Simon Geissbühler is a historian, political scientist (Dr.rer.soc.), and diplomat. He has published extensively on Romania and the Holocaust and on Jewish heritage in Eastern Europe. Among his books are *Blutiger Juli. Rumäniens Vernichtungskrieg und der vergessene Massenmord an den Juden 1941* (2013) and *Once Upon a Time Never Comes Again. The Traces of the Shtetl in Southern Podolia (Ukraine)* (2014). He has published articles in scholarly journals such as *Holocaust and Genocide Studies*, *Holocaust Studies*, and *Israel Journal of Foreign Affairs*.

Mariana Hausleitner is Lecturer (Dr.) and currently running a project on the resettlements from the Bukovina in 1940. Her books include *Die Rumänisierung der Bukowina. Die Durchsetzung des nationalstaatlichen Anspruchs Großrumäniens 1918–1944* (2001), *Deutsche und Juden in Bessarabien 1814–1941. Zur Minderheiterpolitik Russlands und Großrumäniens* (2006), and *Die Donauschwaben 1868–1948. Ihre Rolle im rumänischen und serbischen Banat* (2014).

Witold Mędykowski, Ph.D., was born in Lublin and is a historian and political scientist. He graduated from the University of Life Sciences in Lublin, the Tel Aviv University (Jewish and general history), and the Hebrew University of Jerusalem (contemporary Jewry). He received his Ph.D. in political science at the Institute of Political Studies in 2010, Polish Academy of Sciences, and another Ph.D. in contemporary Jewry at the Hebrew University of Jerusalem in 2014. He works as a senior specialist at the Yad Vashem Archives. He is a former fellow of the foundation "Remembrance, Responsibility and Future" (*Erinnerung, Verantwortung und Zukunft*). His research interests are the Polish Jewish relations, the Holocaust, the Second World War, ethnic conflicts, economic questions, political science, and archival science.

Alti Rodal is a historian, writer, former professor of Jewish history, and former official and advisor to the government of Canada. She holds degrees from McGill and Oxford universities and is the author of a number of publications on aspects of Jewish history. She served as Director of Historical Research for the Canadian government's Commission of Inquiry on Nazi War Criminals (1985–6). She is one of the founders and serves as Co-Director of the Ukrainian Jewish Encounter, a privately funded multinational organization whose goal it is to promote mutual, empathetic understanding between Ukrainians and Jews in all countries where these peoples and their descendants live.

Sarah Rosen, Ph.D., Hebrew University of Jerusalem (2013), has been working at Yad Vashem since 2005 as an interviewer of Holocaust survivors. She has published several articles on the life of Jews during the Holocaust in Northern Transnistria, including "Surviving in the Murafa Ghetto: A Case Study of One Ghetto on Transnistria" in *Holocaust Studies* (2010). She was a lecturer at the Gordon College of Education, Haifa.

Michael Shafir is Professor Emeritus at the Institute for Doctoral Studies, School of International Relations and Strategic Studies, Babeș-Bolyai University, Cluj-Napoca, Romania. Shafir received his Ph.D. in political science from the Hebrew University of Jerusalem in 1981. He taught political science at the University of Tel Aviv and was Chair of International Relations at the Faculty of European Studies, Babeș-Bolyai University, until 2012. He was Director of Foreign News at Kol Israel, Deputy Director of Radio Free Europe's Audience and Public Opinion Research, as well as chief of the Romanian Research Unit at Radio Free Europe Research Institute in Munich. Between 1995 and 2005, Shafir lived in Prague, his last position being that of European Affairs Coordinator at Radio Free Europe/Radio Liberty. He is the author of several books and of over 350 articles on Communist and post-Communist affairs in scholarly journals and edited volumes.

Kai Struve is a Research Fellow at the Institute of History at Martin Luther University Halle-Wittenberg. He received his Ph.D. in history at the Free University of Berlin in 2002, and he completed his habilitation at Halle in 2014. Among his publications are *Deutsche Herrschaft, ukrainischer Nationalismus, antijüdische Gewalt. Der Sommer 1941 in der Westukraine* (2015), and *Shared History—Divided Memory. Jews and Others in Soviet-Occupied Poland, 1939–1941* (2007, co-edited with Elazar Barkan and Elizabeth A. Cole).

Gali Tibon is the founder and CEO of the Institute for Excellence in the Humanities and the head of the educational board of the Lochamei Hagetaot ghetto fighters' museum. In 2014–15, she was a Postdoctoral Fellow, Sawyer Seminar Postdoctoral Fellowship, at Carnegie Mellon University, Department of History. Her Ph.D. dissertation *The Jewish Leadership of the South Bukovina Communities in the Ghettos in the Mogilev Region in Transnistria and Its Dealings with the Romanian Regime (1941–1944)* was completed at Tel Aviv University. She has published an annotated edition of a diary from the Shargorod ghetto in Transnistria. Tibon is a former award-winning high-school principal.

ibidem-Verlag / *ibidem* Press
Melchiorstr. 15
70439 Stuttgart
Germany

ibidem@ibidem.eu
ibidem.eu